# The Definitive Betty Boop™

The Classic Comic Strip Collection

# THE DEFINITIVE BETTY BOOP™

ISBN: 9781848567078

Published by Titan Comics
A division of Titan Publishing Group Ltd.
144 Southwark St.
London
SE1 0UP



First Titan edition: September 2015



A CIP Catalogue record for this title is available from the British Library

10 9 8 7 6 5 4 3 2 1

Printed in China

Strip Publishing History
**Out of the Inkwell (Sunday Strip)** - November 25, 1934 – December 15, 1934
**The Original Boop-Boop-A-Doop Girl** (Sunday Strip) - August 5, 1934 – October 12, 1934
**Betty Boop** (Sunday Strip) - November 25, 1934 – November 27, 1937
**Betty Boop** (Daily Strip) - July 23, 1934 – March 18, 1935



**Picture Credits:**
Thad Komorowski (www.whataboutthad.com)
Heritage Auction Site
Fleischer Studios

www.bettyboop.com www.bettyboopstore.com

This book is a work of fiction. Characters may have views and use language which some of today's readers may find offensive. The Publisher and copyright holder in no way endorse character depiction, the views expressed or language used.

**Much of the comic strip source material used by Titan Comics in this edition is exceedingly rare. As such, we hope that readers can appreciate that the quality of reproduction achievable can vary.**

With grateful thanks to Scott Marilyn, Poppy Thornton, Susan Liberator of the Cartoon Library and Museum, Ohio State University, David Leach, Steve Saffel, Oz Browne, Bobbie West, Jerry Beck, Glenn Mott and Rinaldo Traini.

The Definitive Betty Boop Collection is the most complete collection of Betty Boop so far published – however it's not a complete collection and we need your help to make that a reality. If you have tear sheets of any of the missing Sunday or daily newspaper strips from the 1930s then please don't hesitate to get in touch, we'd love to hear from you!
Email us at: readerfeedback@titanemail.com or write to us at the above address.

# The Definitive Betty Boop™

## The Classic Comic Strip Collection

MAX FLEISCHER

# About our granddad,

# Max Fleischer...

Everyone in our family called him Popmax, or 'Pops' for short. As grandkids we had no idea that this unassuming, patient, and loving person – our granddad – was also an important pioneer in the history of film who created some of the most popular cartoons of the day, was head of a major animation studio, held over 20 innovative patents related to motion pictures, and created the Rotoscope which changed the course of animation history. Though best remembered for his cartoons that continue to entertain audiences worldwide, he also foresaw the educational value of film to explain complicated new ideas like 'evolution,' and 'relativity' to the general public. That complex person was the gentle grandfather we called "Pops."

Pops claimed his career as an artist began when, standing in his crib, he scrawled pencil drawings on the wallpaper. But it wasn't until 1900 that he started his first real job. At the age of seventeen, he rode his bike across the Brooklyn Bridge to apply for a job in the art department of the *Brooklyn Daily Eagle*. He was so determined to work there that he offered to pay them $2 a week if they would take him on. Intrigued, they instead offered him $2 a week to run errands for them! Within a year his small cartoons on political and social commentary appeared in the pages of the *Eagle*. By 1903, his artwork extended to multi-panel comic strips where the joke isn't contained in just one frame, but rather *in a sequence of frames*. That's starting to sound like an animated film!

His work at the *Eagle* was just the beginning of an amazing career. He would go on to become an animator, writer, inventor, director, producer, and ultimately the head of Fleischer Studios. In spite of his great success he remained unpretentious. He was always 'Pops' to family. And at work, even when Fleischer Studios grew to over 700 employees, EVERYONE there called him by his first name, 'Max.'

One of the great stories about Pops, which became family lore, was that he was always being made fun of at the studio because at lunch he usually spilled some food on his shirt. One day he decided to show them. He invited a large group of his co-workers to lunch and swore that he would get through the entire meal without a spill. Pops ordered a steak. When it arrived, he made a big show of cutting off a piece and, with a great flourish, lifted the fork to his mouth. What he hadn't noticed, however, was that the piece of meat was still connected to the steak by a tiny strand and, as he lifted the fork to his mouth, the entire steak came flying off the plate and landed firmly in the center of his chest!

Pops was equally amazing at home where his many 'works-in-progress' would cover the dining room table, a table that was never used for eating. Most of his inventions were related to film, but his wide-ranging other projects included educational toys for children, a mail order animation school, Detergent Pellets, and even a perpetual clock!

But of all the things he ever created, Betty Boop remains the most beloved and famous. In 1930 Betty was just a sexy new-comer, the first fully female animated character in film history. She would go on to appear in over 100 films and become the Fleischer studio's biggest star!

So that was Pops, the quiet, unassuming gentle guy who changed animation history and created one of the flashiest, most enduring cartoon characters of all time.

***Mark Fleischer and Virginia Mahoney, two of Pops' grandkids.***

MAX FLEISCHER—

# MADE OF PEN AND INK, SHE CAN WIN YOU WITH A WINK

**BY BRIAN WALKER**

Betty Boop is the foremost leading lady in the history of animation. She is unique in that she is not defined by her relationship to a male character, like Minnie Mouse or Olive Oyl. Although many potential suitors romanced her over the years, she never tied the knot. Betty Boop continues to captivate admirers around the world as a resolutely independent woman.

Betty made her first appearance on August 9, 1930 in the Fleischer Studios Talkartoon, *Dizzy Dishes*. Designed to provide a love interest for the series' canine star Bimbo, Betty has a brief cameo as a cabaret singer and looks like a French poodle with puffy cheeks, protruding teeth and droopy ears. Over the course of the next ten films, her appearance gradually changed into the wide-eyed, pouty-mouthed, spit-curled ingénue with the skimpy flapper dress that movie audiences adored.

Although many animators contributed to this graphic evolution, Grim Natwick is the one most often credited with establishing her definitive look. Natwick was a classically trained artist who was adept at rendering the human form. He turned the dog ears into hoop earings, shrank her poodle nose to a button-size, and gave her a curvaceous female figure. In addition to Natwick, Shamus Culhane and Al Eugster were Betty Boop "specialists" who contributed to her ever-changing appearance in these early films. Her full name appeared on the opening credits of *Minding the Baby* (September 26, 1931) and her canine features were gone by *Any Rags* (January 2, 1932).

Betty's voice, inspired by the performances of popular singer Helen Kane, was provided by Margie Hines, Kate Wright, Bonnie Poe and Annabel Little, until Max Fleischer hired Mae Questel in 1931. Questel's chirpy singsong vocals, which had an unmistakable New York accent, became synonymous with the character from that point onward.

The phrase "boop-oop-a-doop" was popularized by Kane in the song, "I Wanna Be Loved By You," which she performed in Oscar Hammerstein's 1928 show *Good Boy*. It was typical of the "scat" singing style used by jazz vocalists of the era, in which nonsensical syllables mimicked the sounds of musical instruments. The origins of this technique have been traced back to West African percussive singing, as well as early Delta blues and New Orleans jazz. Gene Greene, Al Jolson, Gene Rodemich and Cliff Edwards

were among the many artists who experimented with similar vocal improvisations in the teens and twenties. Louis Armstrong's 1926 recording, *Heebie Jeebies*, was one of the first definitive scat songs. Cab Calloway, who came to be known as "The Hi De Ho Man," injected humor into his performances with lyrics like, "When you feel like shoutin', advertise it just this way: skeep-beep de bop-bop beep bop bo-dope skeetle-at-de-op-de-day!" from *The Scat Song* (1932). Calloway appeared in three Betty Boop cartoons during the early 1930s, both as a live-action bandleader and an animated dancing walrus.

A week after Betty made her first appearance in *Dizzy Dishes*, another female character with a similar name was also making her debut. On August 16, 1930, newspaper editors around the country received an elegantly printed announcement from Mr. and Mrs. J. Bolling Bumstead informing them of the engagement of their son, Dagwood Bumstead, to Miss Blondie Boopadoop. Three days later, a letter arrived from the Bumstead's lawyer, Dudley L. Cartwright, which stated in no uncertain terms that the announcement was "a pure fabrication of fancy, if not a malicious attempt on the part of this Miss Blondie Boopadoop."

These mailings, which were followed by handwritten notes, a telegram and a suitcase of paper doll clothing, were sent by King Features Syndicate to promote a new comic strip, which made its debut on September 8, 1930. Chic Young's *Blondie* struggled to sign up clients initially and didn't take off until the millionaire's son and the ditzy flapper finally married, in defiance of Dagwood's parents, on February 17, 1933.

After her debut, Betty appeared in different roles and eventually became the star of the Talkartoons. On August 12, 1932, she launched her own series, beginning with the film, *Stopping the Show*. Over the course of the next seven years, 90 Betty Boop cartoons were produced until the last, *Rhythm on the Reservation*, was released on July 7, 1939.

***Opposite:*** Willard Bowsky's model sheet for Betty, circa 1934.

***Above:*** Bimbo sees Betty for the first time. From: Dizzy Dishes (1930)

***Left:*** Betty, Bimbo promo art.

Born in Vienna in 1883 and raised in Brooklyn, Max Fleischer was an artist and a tinkerer. His first important invention was the Rotoscope, a device that projected live action film, frame-by-frame, on a light-table enabling animators to capture realistic motion by tracing the sequential images. He produced three films between 1914 and 1916 to demonstrate the Rotoscope and was hired by animation pioneer John R. Bray in 1918 to create the Out of the Inkwell series. Max filmed his brother Dave performing in a clown costume and used the Rotoscope to animate the studio's first star, eventually named Koko the Clown.

Max and his brothers Dave and Lou started their own studio in 1921 and during the decade released 62 Out of the Inkwell cartoons starring Koko and 56 Inkwell Imps films with Koko and Fitz the Dog. They also created the innovative Song Car-Tunes series in 1924, in which audiences were invited to sing along with a ball that bounced in sync with song lyrics printed on a revolving title card. Max also developed the "rotograph" which combined live-action footage with cel overlays, devised a special "3-D Process" that used dioramas to add depth and perspective to his cartoons and pioneered many advancements in sound technology.

In 1929 the Fleischers launched two sound series, Talkartoons and Screen Songs. The following year, a new star was born when Bimbo the dog debuted in the Talkartoon *Hot Dog*. Although his appearance changed drastically from one film to the next, Bimbo remained a cartoon canine even when cast as Betty Boop's boyfriend.

Between 1929 and 1932, the Fleischers released 42 Talkartoons, which starred Bimbo, Betty Boop, and Koko the Clown. The Screen Songs series continued until 1938 and featured live performances by many popular musicians of the era, including Rudy Vallee, Ethel Merman, and the Mills Brothers.

Dave Fleischer often told his artists, "If it can be done in real life, it isn't animation." The Fleischer cartoons had a surreal quality as inanimate objects of all types, including lamps, furniture, automobiles and buildings, morphed into characters with moving lips and eyes that bounced along to the beat of the music.

In October 1930, there were 90 people on the staff of the Fleischer Studios. Ted Sears, a veteran animator, served as "scenario editor." In 1931, Bill Turner took over as head of the new Story Department but had little experience as a writer. Al

***Opposite top:*** The staff of Fleischer Studios circa 1931, showing, among others, Betty Boop animators Willard Bowsky (second row, sixth from left), J. H. Culhane (third row, eighth from left) and Grim Natwick (third row, ninth from left). Max Fleischer can be seen middle of the top row. ***Opposite bottom:*** Cab Calloway and Orchestra as seen in the Betty Boop short, *Minnie the Moocher*.
***Above:*** Two pieces of promo art created to promote sales of the Betty Boop shorts to cinemas.

Eugster claimed that stories were "sort of worked on as we went along...Dave [Fleischer] would make the rounds almost every day and suggest gags." Dave wanted every scene jammed with funny business. Three head animators, Willard Bowsky, Seymour Kneitel, and Al Eugster, supervised production and were, in effect, the directors of the studio's films. Betty starred in fairy tale adaptations, atmospheric mystery dramas and rollicking adventure yarns, but most of the Fleischer cartoons were little more than sequences of sight gags with musical accompaniment.

Some of the most remarkable Betty Boop films, like *Bimbo's Initiation* (1931), *Minnie the Moocher* (1932) and *Snow White* (1933), have a dark, dreamlike quality that was described by animation historian Leonard Maltin as "cartoon noire." With jazz soundtracks, spooky backgrounds, and bizarre images, these films are now regarded as classic cartoons of the early sound era. In 1996, The National Film Registry designated *Snow White*, which co-starred Cab Calloway, for historic preservation.

The Fleischer Studios were located at 1600 Broadway in New York City and their cartoons captured the urban environment where the animators lived and worked. They drew gritty street scenes populated with disheveled immigrants and created an atmosphere that was distinct from the sunny, country barnyard look that typified the Walt Disney Studio cartoons, which were produced in southern California. The Fleischer artists were also familiar with the jazz music coming out of Harlem in the 1920s and 1930s and popular bandleaders like Cab Calloway and Louis Armstrong made guest appearances in a number of the Betty Boop cartoons.

In 1932, singer Helen Kane filed a $250,000 lawsuit against the Fleischers and their distributor, Paramount, for appropriating her persona and performance style. There was some legitimacy to her claim, since she had worked for Paramount on stage, records and film as the "boop-oop-a-doop girl" in the late 1920s. Kane lost the suit in 1934 when it was revealed that other female stars had pioneered her style of singing, most notably Esther Jones, who had performed as "Baby Ester" at Harlem's Cotton Club and on film years before Kane started doing her signature act.

"It just happened that [Kane] was popular with that boop-oop-a-doop before us," Dave Fleischer claimed. "But it was a song. And anybody could use a song if he got permission, and we did that. But we called the character Betty Boop, and that was not a boop-oop-a-doop."

The Betty Boop cartoons were filled with sexual innuendo. Her curvaceous body was frequently silhouetted in front of strategically placed light sources and her skimpy dress was often blown up by gusts of wind. In *Betty Boop's Bamboo Isle* (1932), she appeared topless, her breasts barely covered by a Hawaiian lea.

***Above:*** An advertising promotional sheet showcasing a variety of Betty Boop themed merchandising from the 1930s.
***Opposite:*** Popeye, Betty and Olive Oyl admire the newly built Fleischer Studios in Miami, Florida when the animation studio moved there in 1938.

In the 1932 film *Boop-Oop-a-Doop*, a lecherous circus ringmaster threatened to fire Betty if she didn't submit to his sexual advances. Betty pleaded; "Don't take my boop-oop-a-doop away," until Koko came to her rescue.

The Motion Picture Production Code was adopted in 1930 but was not actively enforced until 1934, when the lascivious antics of Mae West provided the impetus for a concerted crackdown. The Hays Office, as it came to be known, set strict moral standards for American studio productions and had a major effect on Betty Boop's personality and appearance. She was forced to clean up her act by wearing a longer and less revealing dress, she abandoned her trademark hoop earrings and garter and stopped winking suggestively and wiggling her hips in the opening credits of her films.

Secondary characters started to steal the show. A bland boyfriend, Freddie, made his debut in *She Wronged Him Right* (1934) and Betty adopted a cute puppy, Pudgy, in *Betty Boop's Little Pal* (1934). In *Betty and Grampy* (1935) she teamed up with a bald-headed, white-bearded crackpot who ingeniously solved her domestic problems. Famous comic strip characters, including Carl Anderson's Henry, Jimmy Swinnerton's Little Jimmy and Otto Soglow's Little King, made guest appearances.

In 1933, the Fleischer Studios initiated negotiations with King Features Syndicate to release a comic strip adaptation of Betty Boop's film adventures. When they couldn't come to terms, Helen Kane suggested that they do a comic strip based on her life story. King signed a short-term contract with Kane and *The Original Boop-Boop-A-Doop Girl*, initially drawn by Ving Fuller, appeared briefly as a Sunday page in the *New York Mirror* from August 5 to October 21, 1934.

Around the same time, King signed a contract with the Fleischers to release a Sunday page version of their long-running Out of the Inkwell series. There was not much interest in this offering after it debuted on November 25, 1934 and it only lasted a few episodes until December 15, 1934.

King finally came to an agreement with the Fleischers to do a Betty Boop daily comic strip, which was drawn by Bud Counihan with assistance from some of the Fleischer Studio animators and released on July 23, 1934. Counihan started his career as a sports cartoonist in Norwich, Connecticut, before joining the *New York World* in 1915. Among his many short-lived comic strip creations were *Little Napoleon* (1923) and *Pinhead Dooley* (1928). The daily *Betty Boop* strip lasted until March 30, 1935. A Sunday page version, also done by Counihan, ran from November 25, 1934 to November 28, 1937.

*The Betty Boop Fables* radio show, which featured the voices of both Mae Questel and Bonnie Poe, was broadcast for 15 minutes every Tuesday night at 7:30 PM on the NBC Network from November 15, 1932 to January 27, 1933. During the peak years of her popularity, hundreds of licensed products bearing Betty's image hit the marketplace, including books, games, clothing, handkerchiefs, playing cards, tea sets, dolls, watches, toys, candy, and soap.

By 1939, Betty had lost most of her sex appeal and the Fleischers ended the series. But Betty's career was far from over. In 1955, the Betty Boop cartoons were acquired by a syndication company and shown regularly on TV stations across the country. In the 1960s and 70s, college students unearthed old 16mm prints of black-and-white Betty Boop cartoons to show at campus film festivals. In the 1980s, two animated specials were produced, *The Romance of Betty Boop* (1985) and *The Betty Boop Mystery* (1989). Betty also made a cameo appearance in the 1988 feature film, *Who Framed Roger Rabbit?*

In 1984, King Features teamed Betty up with another animation icon, Felix the Cat, in a comic strip produced by four of *Beetle Bailey* creator Mort Walker's sons, Greg, Brian, Morgan, and Neal. *Betty Boop and Felix*, later renamed *Betty Boop and Friends,* appeared in about one hundred newspapers at its peak and lasted until 1988.

A new generation rediscovered the magic of the boop-oop-a-doop girl when an eight-volume set, *Betty Boop: The Definitive Collection*, was released on home video in 1996. The VHS tape and Laserdisc editions included all surviving Fleischer Studio cartoons starring Betty, as well as a biographical introduction hosted by Max's son Richard.

The Betty Boop franchise grew into a global marketing phenomenon during the latter half of the 20th Century. There are now more than 200 licensees in the U.S. and nearly twice as many internationally that produce products bearing Betty's likeness in every category ranging from designer fashions to toddler toys. Betty has appeared in promotions for Lancôme, Benetton, Adidas, MasterCard, Coca Cola, NASCAR, Harley Davidson, and Universal Theme Parks. King Features Syndicate and the Fleischer Studios are partners in this multi-million dollar licensing empire.

In 1996, Betty Boop became the first cartoon character to be profiled on A&E's *Biography* series and in 2002, *TV Guide* rated Betty number 17 in the list of the "50 Greatest Cartoon Characters of All Time." Simon Cowell's Syco Entertaiment and Animal Logic, the company that did the animation for *The Lego Movie*, are currently developing a "music-driven hybrid animated comedy" feature film set for release in 2016.

Even after 85 years, Betty Boop's star power is still shining brightly.

# OUT OF THE INKWELL

## KOKO THE KLOWN

-BY-
MAX FLEISCHER

The ***Out of the Inkwell*** animated series, which ran from 1918 – 1929, combined live action footage of Max Fleischer with both Koko the Clown and his dog Fitz. In 1931, Betty Boop would become the star of the Fleischer Studios ***Talkartoons*** series, with Koko relegated to the role of a backup character. However in 1935, it was ***Out of the Inkwell*** that became the first Fleischer Studios property to be syndicated by Hearst's King Features Syndicate and turned into a comic strip. Unfortunately the subsequent silent cartoon strip featuring just Koko the Clown (and notably neither of his two animated buddies) failed to interest enough newspapers and was discontinued after only four weeks. Although Koko's early demise was disappointing, the foray had proved there was a potential for a Fleischer newspaper comic strip and led ultimately to Betty Boop taking up the mantle.

DRAW
INK

OUT OF THE INKWELL
INK
"KOKO"
THE KLOWN
BY~ MAX FLEISCHER
INK
INK
INK
INK
INK
INK
E-EK!
EEE-EK!
INK
INK
E-EEK
11-25

OUT OF THE INKWELL
INK
"KOKO"
THE KLOWN
BY
MAX FLEISCHER
E-EEK-
INK
E-EEK-
INK
EE-E-EEK-
INK
INK
GR-R-R-R-R-R
INK
INK
© 1934, King Features Syndicate, Inc.; Great Britain rights reserved
INK
12·1

OUT OF THE INKWELL
DRAWING INK
"KOKO"
THE KLOWN
BY
MAX FLEISCHER
?
CANDY
KOKO MATCHES
ERASER FOR INK
ERASER FOR INK
CANDY
ERASER
CANDY
DRAWING INK
© 1934, King Features Syndicate Inc., Great Britain rights reserved
12-8
ERASER FOR INK
DRAWING INK

OUT OF THE INKWELL
INK
KOKO
THE KLOWN
-BY-
MAX FLEISCHER
R-RIP
WAM!
12-15

# The Original BOOP-BOOP-A-DOOP GIRL

In 1933, ***Betty Boop*** comic strip negotiations between Hearst's King Features Syndicate and Fleischer Studios had stalled over money. Actress Helen Kane, who had provided the original voice for Betty Boop, saw an opportunity and approached King Features, suggesting that a strip based on her portrayal of Betty Boop could work just as well as the real thing – and King Features agreed. The strip was launched on August 5, 1934 and appeared only in the tabloid ***New York Sunday Mirror***. It lasted 11 weeks until October 12, 1934 when Fleischer Studios agreed terms with the syndicate and ***Helen Kane's The Original Boop-Boop-A-Doop Girl*** was dropped and replaced by ***Betty Boop***.

# By Helen Kane

MAJOR OPUS
VING FULLER

THE ORIGINAL
BOOP-BOOP-A-DOOP-GIRL
BY
HELEN KANE
TO STAGE ENTRANCE
THEATRE
SIGN MY AUTOGRAPH BOOK- MISS KANE?
I TINK YOURE TH' CUTEST MOST WHIMSIKIL GOIL IN TH' WOILD!
WHIM I?
TANKS FER TH' OTTYGRAFF MISS KANE!
HEE-E-HEE- YOU'RE WELCOME!
LATER
OH!
OH!
SOMETHING'S PHONEY ABOUT THIS--- HELEN NEVER SIGNS ANY $560 CHECKS WITH-OUT FIRST SEEING HER MANAGER --- I'LL CALL UP THE BANK!
HELEN DID YOU SIGN THIS?
OH! THAT-- YES-- I REMEMBER THAT-- I AUTOGRAPHED IT FOR A GREAT BIG HE MAN!
COULDN'T YOU SEE IT WAS A BLANK CHECK YOU WERE PUTTING YOUR SIGNATURE TO?
DEARIE- HOW COULD I HELP IT- EVERY-BODY WAS HANDING ME PAPERS TO AUTOGRAPH-
A-LING
A-LING
HELLO-THIS IS INSPECTOR DIXON-- WE'VE GOT YOUR MAN---YOU BETTER COME DOWN HERE WITH MISS KANE TO IDENTIFY HIM!
HELLO THERE!
YES THAT'S THE MAN! THAT'S THE MAN-
OKAY THAT'S ALL!
YER FACE IS FAMILIAR-- BUT I CAN'T SEEM TO REMEMBER THE NAME!
I'M AWFULLY SORRY- ARE YOU MAD AT ME?
OH- NO-O- MISS KANE I STILL WORSHIP YOUR OTTYGRAFF!
C'MON HELEN!
WELL-- HERE'S ONE THAT WON'T GET YOU IN DUTCH!
Boop-Boop-a-Doop-

LUCKY BUCKS
PLAY MONEY
2
LUCKY BUCKS
PLAY MONEY
2
LUCKY BUCKS
PLAY MONEY
2

MAJOR OPUS
by VING FULLER
THE ORIGINAL BOOP-BOOP-A-DOOP GIRL BY HELEN KANE
RING 'ROUND THE ROSIE POCKET FULL O' POSIES
OO-O- I HOPE THOSE KIDS'LL LET ME JOIN THEM--- I HAVEN'T PLAYED THOSE GAMES IN YEARS!
LONDON BRIDGE IS FALLING DOWN FALLING DOWN FALLING DOWN
SCAT!
THAT'S MISTER GUZZLE -- HE WON'T LET US PLAY AROUND HERE!
OH - HE WONT EH?
DEE YO DEE DEE DEE DO
YOU-
MY WINE!
NOW YOU HOLD YOUR THUMB OVER IT -- WHILE I GET YOU A STOPPER!
BOOP -BOOP-A- DOOP
SALE TO-DAY
VING FULLER
LUCKY $ BUCKS
PLAY MONEY
2 BUCK
LUCKY $ BUCKS
PLAY MONEY
2 BUCK
LUCKY $ BUCKS
PLAY MONEY
2 BUCK

THE ORIGINAL
BOOP-BOOP-A-DOOP GIRL
BY HELEN KANE
I'M HUNGWY!
AH! HA!-- I KNEW YOU'D SAY IT!
LUMS INN
EXCELLENT FOOD
CHOICE WINES
-SO I WAS ALL PREPARED-- NO CLASSY RESTAURANTS TO-DAY-- JUST A NICE LIL' PICNIC ALL BY OUR-SELVES!
WHAT!!! ME SIT DOWN WITH THOSE ANTS? NOTHING DOIN'--- BESIDES I LIKE MUSIC WITH MY MEALS!
I BROUGHT MUSIC TOO!
SKIN FLINT!
OH WELL- I GIVE UP-- I'M SO HUNGWY- I COULD BEAT A HOLLYWOOD EXTRA IN A PIE EATING CONTEST!
WAYDAMINNIT BOOPIE- LET'S HAVE A LIL' DANCE FIRST!
BUT I'M HUNGWY!
C'MON---ONLY PEOPLE WITH-OUT BRAINS EAT ALL THE TIME!
SNIFF
SNIFF
9-2
BOOP BOOP-A-DOOP--
VING FULLER
LUCKY BUCKS
PLAY MONEY
2
LUCKY BUCKS
PLAY MONEY
2
LUCKY BUCKS
PLAY MONEY
2

THE ORIGINAL
BOOP-BOOP-A-DOOP GIRL
BY HELEN KANE
WE'RE IN THE MONEY
$ 67,000—$87,000
$ 90,000—$ 91,000-
$ 92,000—$ 98,000-
$ 99,000
EEK-
HOW DID YOU GET IN HERE?
$ 100,000- I'LL TAKE IT WITH OUT TH' COUNTIN' C'MON PUT 'EM UP-
DON'T CHANGE THE SUBJECT HOW DID YOU GET IN HERE?
OUTCH- IS SHE DUMB!
TEE-HEE-HEE- TAKE IT ALL--- IT'S NOT REAL- IT'S STAGE MONEY.
WELL I'LL BE----
TH' JOKE'S ON ME -- ALL Y'GOT IS STAGE-MONEY LIKE ALL THE ACTORS-HAW-HAW-HAW- SAY- YOU'RE KIND O'CUTE-- HOW'D YA LIKE TO JOIN MY ACT? H-M-M---SUCH NIMBLE LOOKIN' FINGERS--
ALL MY LIFE I'VE WANTED TO WIN MY WAY THROUGH THE HEART OF A BAD BAD MANS---
OH NO YOU WON'T--NOT WITH THIS RED DRESS---- Y'KNOW WOT HAPPENED TO THAT GUY IN CHICAGO WHEN A DAME IN A RED DRESS WON HER WAY THRU HIS HEART!
DON'T WORRY YOU SILLY SILLY MANS- I'LL THROW AWAY EVERY RED DRESS I'VE GOT- JUS' B'CAUSE I LOVES -O-O-O-
YOU WAIT HERE WHILE I CHANGE-- WHAT COLOR SHALL I PUT ON HONEY?
LET'S SEE--- WOT'S MY FAVORITE COLOR?----- OH-YES- BLUE THAT'S IT BLUE-
YES HURRY COME UP THE BACK WAY!
LUCKY BUCKS PLAY MONEY 2
LUCKY BUCKS PLAY MONEY 2
LUCKY BUCKS PLAY MONEY 2

THE ORIGINAL
BOOP-BOOP-A-DOOP GIRL
BY Helen Kane
MAYOR'S COMMITTEE
CONEY ISLAND BOOSTERS
MISS KANE! AS CHAIRMAN OF THE BATHING BEAUTY JUDGES, WILL YOU HONOR US BY ENTERING THE CONTEST!
O.K. BOYS
SWELL LOOKER
AND WHAT FORM
THE BEST GAL WON!
MISS KANE WOULD YOU LIKE A WRIST WATCH WITH 18 JEWELS FOR FIRST PRIZE.
PRIZE COMMITTEE
NO THANKS— I HAVE A WATCH. JUST GIVE ME THE 18 JEWELS
NOW THAT YOU ARE QUEEN HOW ABOUT A DIP IN THE OCEAN
GOODIE
LIFE GUARD
?
BANG!
BEACH CENSOR
LIFE GUARD
MISS KANE WILL YOU MAKE A STATEMENT TO THE PRESS WHY YOU SLAPPED THE BEACH CENSOR
SURE! HE WANTED TO CHECK MY SUIT—AND NOBODY IS GOING TO MAKE A NUDIST OF ME!
BOOP-BOOP-A-DOOP
LUCKY BUCKS
PLAY MONEY
2
LUCKY BUCKS
PLAY MONEY
2
LUCKY BUCKS
PLAY MONEY
2

THE ORIGINAL
BOOP-BOOP-A-DOOP GIRL
BY Helen Kane
STAGE DOOR
GOOD EVENING, MISS KANE MR LASTFOGEL WOULD LIKE TO SEE YOU!
O.K TELL HIM TO COME TO MY DRESSING ROOM, PLEASE.
OVERTURE
LOOKS LIKE 'NOTHER BAD HOUSE, MIS HELEN.
SWEENEY AND COOK
HELEN MRS ASTORBILT WOULD LIKE YOU TO SING AT HER SOCIETY AFFAIR AFTER THE SHOW TONIGHT!
WOULD I WORK WITH A BAND?
THEATRE
GOSH! NO, THE POLICE WOULD INSIST THAT YOU WEAR MORE THAN THAT!
AND BY THE WAY ABE. REMIND ME TO GIVE IN MY TWO WEEK NOTICE.
MISS KANE ON STAGE
NO SMOKING
DON'T SAMPLE
JOE LAURIE TRAINED SEALS
ACT 3
BUT HELEN! YOU CAN'T QUIT YOU HAVE A RUN OF THE PLAY CONTRACT. WHAT'S WRONG?
I DON'T LIKE THE LINES.
FOR THE LOVE OF MIKE! WHAT LINES DO YOU OBJECT TO?
THE THIN LINES AT THE BOX OFFICE!
BOOP BOOP A-DOOP
LUCKY BUCKS PLAY MONEY 2
LUCKY BUCKS PLAY MONEY 2
LUCKY BUCKS PLAY MONEY 2

THE ORIGINAL
BOOP-BOOP-A-DOOP GIRL
BY Helen Kane
ALL PRINCIPALS ON THE STAGE!
TAKE IT UP, JOE!
TELL THOSE KIDS TO KEEP QUIET!
GIRLS! QUIET!
CHORUS DRESSING ROOM
NO SM
ACT 3
THEATRE
THEATRE BOOP BOOP A DOOP COMPAN
ALL THE PRODUCER ASKS IS A RUN FOR HIS MONEY.
YOU TOLD ME THE MAN WHO BACKED THIS SHOW WAS WELL OFF.
HE WAS, BUT HE DIDN'T KNOW IT!
THE MANAGER HASN'T ANYTHING ON THE GIRL WHO POSES NUDE!
MR. RANDAZZEL, IN THE SECOND ACT YOU ARE SUPPOSED TO PICK MISS KANE, UP IN YOUR ARMS
BUT, MR KEYSER, MY CONTRACT DISTINCTLY SAYS, THAT I AM NOT ALLOWED TO RAISE KANE!
MR LASTFOGEL! I HAVE BEEN INSULTED BY WISE CRACKS AND I INSIST, MY CONTRACT BE BROKEN—
AND WHAT'S MORE! I WANT BENNY BEMISCH TO BREAK THE CONTRACT FOR ME.
BUT HELEN! IS MR. BEMISCH A GOOD LAWYER?
I SHOULD SAY HE IS— HE SAT UP ALL LAST EVENING TRYING TO BREAK A GIRL'S WILL!
BOOP-BOOP-A-DOOP
LUCKY BUCKS PLAY MONEY
LUCKY BUCKS PLAY MONEY
LUCKY BUCKS PLAY MONEY

THE ORIGINAL
BOOP-BOOP-A-DOOP GIRL
BY Helen Kane
STAGE DOOR
CALL BOARD
DR. JOS. YATES
WHO IS THE YOUNG MAN OUTSIDE WITH THE BIG BLACK EYE?
OH! JUST A JOHN WHO WAS STRUCK BY THE BEAUTY OF THE SHOW!
GIRLS, BE CAREFUL OF THOSE COSTUMES
MY DEAH! TO SUCCEED IN THIS BUSINESS I FOUND OUT THAT A GIRL SOMETIMES HAS TO GO WITHOUT THINGS!
OVERTURE
NO WONDER SHE IS A GREAT COMEDIENNE. SHE ALWAYS HAS HER WITS ABOUT HER!
MISS KANE A WOMAN REPORTER FROM THE DAILY BLAH-BLAH WOULD LIKE TO INTERVIEW YOU!
O.K. ABE SEND HER IN.
OH! MISS KANE, I SAW YOUR SHOW AND YOU WERE DIVINE AND I WOULD LIKE TO GET A STORY FOR MY PAPER!
PERHAPS YOU WOULD LIKE TO TELL OUR READERS JUST WHAT STEPS LED TO YOUR FAME!
BABY STARES!
BOOP-BOOP-A-DOOP
LUCKY BUCKS PLAY MONEY 2
LUCKY BUCKS PLAY MONEY 2
LUCKY BUCKS PLAY MONEY 2

THE ORIGINAL
BOOP-BOOP-A-DOOP GIRL
BY Helen Kane
HELLO GIRLS
HELLO HELEN
HELEN SURE INTENDS TO KEEP HER YOUTH!
YES! I NOTICED SHE DIDN'T INTRODUCE HIM!
STAGE DOOR
WELL! HE'S NO BARGAIN! HE TOOK HER OUT LAST NIGHT AND ONLY SPENT 8 DOLLARS.
SHOW CLOSES SAT NITE
REWARD
I GUESS THAT WAS ALL SHE HAD!
SH! THERE'S HELEN TALKIN TO THE COMIC.
FIRE
CHORUS DRESSING ROOM
HELLO HELEN! SURE IS TOO BAD THE SHOW IS FOLDING UP SATURDAY NIGHT
O.K. BY ME! I JUST TURNED DOWN A JOB IN THE FOLLIES ON ACCOUNT OF THE RED TAPE.
WHY, DID THEY ASK A LOT OF QUESTIONS?
NO! I MEAN THE LITTLE PIECE OF RED TAPE THEY WANTED ME TO WEAR AS A COSTUME!
GEE! SOME OF THOSE PRODUCERS HAVE A NERVE TO EXPECT A GIRL TO GO AROUND WITH SO LITTLE ON AND NOT BE EMBARRASSED
OH! I DON'T KNOW I GUESS GIRLS WERE BORN THAT WAY!
WELL! I GUESS YOU CAN NEVER TELL ABOUT WOMEN
EVEN IF YOU COULD, YOU SHOULDN'T
BOOP-BOOP-A-DOOP
2 LUCKY BUCKS PLAY MONEY 2
2 LUCKY BUCKS PLAY MONEY 2
2 LUCKY BUCKS PLAY MONEY 2

THE ORIGINAL
BOOP-BOOP-A-DOOP GIRL
BY Helen Kane
GEE! IT SURE IS GREAT TO BE ABLE TO LIE IN BED NOW THAT THE SHOW HAS CLOSED.
OPHELIA
OPHELIA! YOU HAVE BEEN VERY NEGLECTFUL IN DUSTING. LOOK I CAN WRITE MY NAME ON THIS TABLE!
Helen
GOSH! MISS KANE, AIN'T IT GREAT TO HAVE AN EDUCATION!
Helen
I HAD TO DISCHARGE MY MAID AND I WOULD LIKE TO INSERT AN AD. FOR AN EXPERIENCED LADY'S MAID WHO SPEAKS FRENCH AND WHO CAN FURNISH THE BEST OF REFERENCES.
NEXT DAY
YOUNG LADY, YOU LOOK AS IF YOU WOULD DO!
DO YOU SPEAK FRENCH?
NO MADAM!
WELL! YOU HAVE A WRITTEN REFERENCE FROM YOUR LAST EMPLOYER?
NO MADAM!
WELL! AT LEAST YOU HAVE BEEN A MAID BEFORE?
NO MADAM!
THEN WHY DID YOU ANSWER THE ADVERTISEMENT IN THE MORNING PAPER?
I JUST CAME TO TELL YOU I COULDN'T TAKE THE JOB!
10-21-34
LUCKY BUCKS PLAY MONEY
LUCKY BUCKS PLAY MONEY
LUCKY BUCKS PLAY MONEY

THE ORIGINAL
BOOP-BOOP-A-DOOP GIRL
BY Helen Kane
I CAME IN ANSWER TO YOUR ADVERTISEMENT FOR A LADY'S MAID!
OH! YES, STEP INSIDE PLEASE!
OF COURSE YOU HAVE A REFERENCE FROM YOUR LAST EMPLOYER!
YES MADAM!
THIS IS VERY GOOD WHEN CAN YOU START?
TOMORROW MORNING
AS YOU KNOW, I WORK IN THE THEATRE AND YOUR POSITION WILL ENTAIL SOME NIGHT DUTIES!
PARLEZ VOUS FRANCAIS?
HUH!
I SAID DO YOU SPEAK FRENCH?
OH SURE!
SI SI SENORITA!
WHY THAT'S NOT FRENCH, THAT'S SPANISH!
CAN YOU IMAGINE THAT! I DIDN'T KNOW I COULD SPEAK SPANISH!
BOOP-BOOP-A-DOOP!
10-28
LUCKY BUCKS PLAY MONEY
LUCKY BUCKS PLAY MONEY
LUCKY BUCKS PLAY MONEY

THEY SAY THAT I CAN FILL GARBO'S SHOES!
BETTY BOOP TO-DAY

# BETTY BOOP

## THE SUNDAY STRIPS

November 25, 1934 – August 21, 1937

TO WAKE UP IN THE MORNING!
SLEEPER" WHEN THE CHECKS ARE DOWN - AFTER YOU SEE THE MORNING PAPERS
-BY-
Registered U S Patent Office
IS SHE BLONDE OR BRUNETTE?
OH! DARK GLASSES!
WOW! YOU'RE TELLIN' ME!

BETTY BOOP
BY MAX FLEISCHER
I SEE YOU'RE SHOOTING THE FIRE SCENE BEFORE MY NEXT SHOTS?
YES, BETTY— THEN YOU COME IN FOR THE BIG RESCUE SCENE!
WHO'S THE STAR OF THIS PICTURE— THE FIRE OR ME?
NOW DON'T GET TEMPERAMENTAL— THIS SPECTACULAR CONFLAGRATION WILL MAKE THE PICTURE AND ADD TO YOUR REP!
FIRE SCENE SET III
I DON'T WANT ANY HITCH IN THIS BIG FIRE SHOT— GET THE TORCHES AND GASOLINE READY AND BE IN YOUR PLACES!
GASOLINE
AT LAST THIS STUPENDOUS SET IS READY FOR THE BIG FIRE — IT WILL BE MY MASTERPIECE, BETTY!
I'M SCARED OF FIRES— I'LL BE WAITING ON SET "FOUR"!
OKAY! APPLY THE TORCHES— CAMERA!!!
E-EEK HELP!
IT'S BETTY!
QUICK! BETTY'S IN TROUBLE!
OW! A $75,000 SET BURNED DOWN AND NOBODY HERE TO PHOTOGRAPH IT!!!
WHAT IS IT BETTY?
O-O-O!! A MOUSE!
SET 4
RUINED!
DON'T WORRY, BETTY— WE'VE GOT HIM!
OH! ISN'T HE CUTE?
EEK
E-EEK
© 1934, King Features Syndicate, Inc. Great Britain rights reserved
11-25

BETTY BOOP
BY MAX FLEISCHER
YES, BETTY - WE'RE STARRING YOU IN A BIG COSTUME PICTURE NEXT!
O-OH! WONDERFUL! THAT'S ALWAYS BEEN MY GOAL!
I MUST LOOK MY BEST - THIS IS A CHANCE OF A LIFETIME - I'LL "OUT-GARBO" GARBO!
THAT'S WHAT I SAID, MADAME - I'LL NEED YOUR WHOLE STAFF!
YOU SAY YOU'RE STARTING ME OFF WITH YOUR MASSEUSES?
YES, MISS BOOP - THIS WAY, PLEASE!
SO YOU'RE GOING TO STAR IN WHEN KNIGHTS WERE BOLD?
YES, IT'S A MEDIEVAL PICTURE - IT'LL GIVE ME A SWELL CHANCE TO WEAR BEAUTIFUL COSTUMES!
NOW DO YOUR BEST, GIRLS - I MUST LOOK BEAUTIFUL!
OH, BOY! WON'T I LOOK STUNNING?
THAT'S PUTTING IT MILDLY, MISS BOOP!
HM-M! USE A BRIGHT VERMILLION TINT - THE PICTURE IS GOING TO BE IN COLOR!
OH! MISS BOOP, YOU'LL BE JUST RAVISHING!
WELL, HOW DO I LOOK, VON SCRIPT?
GORGEOUS! EXQUISITE! I'LL HAVE YOUR COSTUME SENT RIGHT IN!
PUT MISS BOOP INTO HER COSTUME - WE'RE SHOOTING SOME CLOSE-UPS RIGHT AWAY!
I'M AFRAID WE'LL NEED MORE HELP, SIR!
SURPRISE! PERFECT! NOW REGISTER CHAGRIN - WONDERFUL! MARVELOUS!
12-2

BETTY BOOP
BY MAX FLEISCHER
HO-HUM-M! THAT REMINDS ME- I'VE GOT TO REPORT EARLY THIS MORNING!
BR-R-R R-RING R-R
I MUSTN'T BE LATE EITHER-IT'S A VERY IMPORTANT SCENE!
ONE TWO THREE
OH-OH! AND TIME MARCHES ON!
I COULD QUALIFY AS A LIGHTNING CHANGE ARTIST AFTER THIS!
WHAT! NO APPETITE THIS MORNING, MA'AM?
FAR FROM IT, MAGGIE-BUT I ONLY HAVE TIME FOR A CUP O' COFFEE!
NOT A COP ON THE ROAD- NOW I'LL FIND OUT IF THAT SALESMAN LIED ABOUT WHAT THIS CAR COULD DO!
OW! A BLOW-OUT AT A TIME LIKE THIS!
BANG
THERE WOULDN'T BE A CAR IN SIGHT- I'LL JUST HAVE TO RUN FOR IT!
PHEW! AT LAST!! I JUST HAVE TIME TO GET INTO MY COSTUME AND---
BETTY BOOP
OH, DEAR! I'M ALL IN BUT I MADE IT RIGHT ON TIME- HO-HUM-M---
BUT EVERYTHING IS READY FOR SHOOTING THE SCENE!
SH-H-! ACCORDING TO HER CONTRACT SHE CANNOT BE DISTURBED WHILE SLEEPING!
SNORE
BETTY BOOP
SNORE
SNORE

 12-9

BETTY BOOP
BY MAX FLEISCHER
HO-HUM-M! OW! THESE EARLY MORNING SHOTS - AND I'M LATE AS USUAL!
I HOPE THERE'S GAS IN THE CAR AND THE TRAFFIC COPS ARE IN GOOD HUMOR!
YES AND THE LIGHTS, CAMERAS, MIKE, PROPS 'N'EVERYTHIN' ARE READY AND NO BETTY!
'PHONE HER AGAIN - SEND A MESSENGER - SEND TEN - GET HER HERE!
HO-HUM-M! 'MORNING, VON!
AH! HERE AT LAST - WELL, IT'S BETTER LATE THAN NEVER!
BUT I'M SO TIRED I WISH YOU'D POSTPONE THAT SHOT TILL TOMORROW!
CAN'T DO IT, BETTY - WHY, IT'S JUST AN EASY SCENE!
SEE, IT'S A BEDROOM SCENE - NOW ALL YOU DO IS ACT ASLEEP!
OBOY! ACT IT!
HURRY, GET INTO YOUR PAJAMA COSTUME! QUICK! EVERYTHING IS WAITING!
I'LL BE FASTER THAN THAT!
NOW WE WANT THIS SHOT AS NATURAL, REAL-LOOKIN' AS POSSIBLE. BETTY - IT'S VERY IMPORTANT!
MY! DOESN'T IT LOOK COMFY?
GET IT, BETTY? YOUR S'POSED TO BE SOUND ASLEEP - OKAY, LIGHTS - CAMERA!
© 1934, King Features Syndicate, Inc., Great Britain rights reserved
CUT! MARVELOUS ACTING, BETTY - SO NATURAL, SO REALISTIC - IT'S THE BEST I'VE SEEN!
SCENE #5
12-15
IT OUGHT TO BE - SHE'S REALLY SOUND ASLEEP!
BZZZ
BZ-Z

BETTY BOOP
BY MAX FLEISCHER
AND THE OTHER NEIGHBORHOOD LISTS WILL BE HERE ANY MOMENT--
VERY GOOD, POOLES- NOW GET THE BUS COMPANY ON THE 'PHONE!
HURRY- TAKE THESE LISTS OF ADDRESSES AND GIVE ONE TO EACH OF THE BUS-DRIVERS- THEY HAVE THEIR ORDERS!
YES, MISS BOOP, THEY'RE WAITING AT THE MAIN GATE!
THAT'S A SWELL IDEA, BETTY!
-AND YOU'RE TO BE THE SANTA CLAUS- WE'RE GOING TO CELEBRATE CHRISTMAS RIGHT THIS YEAR!
VON SCRIPT DIRECTOR
TOY DEPARTMENT? MISS BOOP, TALKING- YES, I WANT THAT ORDER DELIVERED AT THE STUDIO RIGHT AWAY!
THE TREE HAS ARRIVED, MISS BETTY- ALSO THE DECORATIONS!
FINE! THE TOYS WILL BE HERE SOON- HAVE THEM PLACED AROUND THE TREE!
CHRISTMAS COLORED BALLS
THEY'RE ALL AT THE GATE AND OBOY, WHAT A MOB OF THEM!
WELL LET THEM IN- EVERYTHING IS READY!
I LOOK MORE LIKE SANTA THAN THE OLD BOY HIMSELF!
GREETINGS, MY DEAR KIDDIES!
YOO-HOO! RIGHT THIS WAY BOYS AND GIRLS!
HELLO, SANTY CLAUS!
OH! THERE'S BETTY BOOP!
WHAT A PARTY- LOOK AT THOSE HAPPY FACES!
DON'T RUSH-STAND IN LINE, SANTA HAS TOYS FOR ALL- NOW ONE AT A TIME, MY DEARS!
© 1934, King Features Syndicate, Inc., Great Britain rights reserved
12-22
MERRY CHRISTMAS TO ALL!

BETTY BOOP
BY MAX FLEISCHER
YES, BETTY, WE'RE GOING TO STAR YOU IN "PEG O' MY HEART" NEXT!
OH! I THINK I'LL LIKE THAT!
I THOUGHT YOU WOULD-YOU KNOW THERE'S A DOG PART IN IT, TOO?
YES, I KNOW - AND I'M JUST WILD ABOUT DOGS
NOW HERE'S A LIST OF ALL THE PET SHOPS - I WANT YOU TO SELECT THE CUTEST LIL' POOCH IN TOWN FOR THE PART!
TAKE THIS LIST, POOLES - YOU'LL HAVE TO DRIVE ME TO EACH ONE OF THEM!
AS Y'SAY, MISS!
OH! THE LITTLE DARLINGS!
PET SH
WE HAVE MORE IN THE NEXT ROOM, MISS!
I DON'T WANT TO MISS ANY - IT'S A VERY IMPORTANT DOG PART!
NOW, THERE'S ONLY ONE MORE STORE ON THE LIST, POOLES!
I NEVER THOUGHT THERE WERE SO MANY IN THE WORLD, MISS!
AND AIN'T THAT LIL' SCOTTIE CUTE? - AND THE LIL' BOSTON AND-
OH! I THINK THEY'RE ALL JUST TOO CUTE FOR WORDS!
FOR SALE
-BUT I SAID TO SELECT ONE - NOT ONE HUNDRED!
I KNOW, BUT YOU'LL HAVE TO WRITE A DOG SHOW SCENE INTO THE SCRIPT-
THEY'RE ALL SO CUTE I JUST COULDN'T PICK OUT THE CUTEST!
© 1934, King Features Syndicate, Inc., Great Britain rights reserved
12-29

BETTY BOOP
BY MAX FLEISCHER
YES, BETTY, THIS NEXT PICTURE IS A "WESTERN"- YOU HAVE A SWELL PART!
HM-M! I'M TO PLAY A DANCE HALL GAL, HUH?
NOW IN THIS FIRST SHOT YOU RACE TO THE ARMY POST ON HORSE-BACK---
ON HORSE-BACK?
THAT SEEMS SILLY-WHY NOT CHANGE IT TO A CAR?
THIS SCENE IS S'POSED TO BE IN THE NINETIES -THERE WASN'T ANY CARS THEN!
ALL SET, CHIEF!
SEE? ALL YOU HAVE TO DO IS FOLLOW THE TRAIL-THE CAMERAS ARE ALL PLACED--
THAT'S IT BETTY, GET HIM GALLOPIN'- CAMERA!
FASTER, BETTY- REMEMBER YOU'RE S'POSED TO BE RIDING TO THE POST FOR HELP--
LATER
OKAY, BETTY- STOP HIM, CUT!
W-WHOA! WHOA!
OH, MY! I'M GLAD THAT "PAUL REVERE" STUFF IS OVER- PHEW!
YOU DID FINE, BETTY- NOW WE'LL SHOOT THE INTERIOR SCENES!
--AND YOU SIT DOWN- REGISTERIN' EXHAUSTION AND---
SIT DOWN?
BUT, BETTY, THIS SCENE CALLS FOR YOU TO SIT DOWN-
I'M SORRY, VON-
1-5
BUT YOU'LL HAVE TO CHANGE IT TO STANDING UP!

BETTY BOOP
BY MAX FLEISCHER
BUT I'M SURE PARAGRAPH #417 OF YOUR CONTRACT FORBIDS PROPOSALS - ENGAGEMENTS AND--
I'LL SOON FIND OUT- I'M CALLING IN MY LAWYERS!
OH, YEAH? THEN I'LL CALL IN MINE, TOO!
GO AHEAD - AND IT'S ONLY FAIR THAT WE ALLOW "PRINCE OKEY DOKEY" TO BRING ALONG HIS LEGAL ADVISERS!
GREETINGS, MY DEAR BETTY- HAVING CONTRACT TROUBLE AGAIN?
YES, BOYS- PRINCE OKEY DOKEY WANTS TO PROPOSE AND "VON" HERE SAYS HE CAN'T!
BETTY, MEET MY LAWYERS! STEP INTO THE CONFERENCE ROOM, GENTS!
HOWDY, MISS BOOP!
HM-M! WHERE'S THE BODY?
YOU MAY CALL THE MEETING TO ORDER- MY LAWYERS ARE HERE!
I DIDN'T KNOW "BINGER'S MIDGETS" WERE IN TOWN!
CUTE! AREN'T THEY?
LET THE LAWYERS SETTLE IT!
I MUST GO IN AND HELP PRESENT MY CASE - I WILL SEE YOU ANON, BETTY!
HO-HUM! SOUNDS LIKE A RIOT!
@!!! ?? TWO HOURS AND NO DECISION YET!
SPEAK! HAVE YOU REACHED A VERDICT YET?
PHEW! YES, AFTER MUCH DEBATE AND DELIBERATION - THE VERDICT WAS UNANIMOUS!
YES, SIR - WE DECIDED THERE WAS NOTHING IN THE CONTRACT TO STOP THE PRINCE FROM PROPOSING!
OH, GOODY!
OH! PRINCE OKEY DOKEY-- HOORAY! YOU CAN PROPOSE NOW!
GIVE HIM AIR GANG-WAY!
HM-M! AND HE WON!
MAKE WAY! FOR THE PRINCE!
© 1935, King Features Syndicate, Inc., Great Britain rights reserved.
1-12

BETTY BOOP
BY MAX FLEISCHER
YOU SAY PRINCE OKEY DOKEY IS STILL IN THE STUDIO HOSPITAL?
YES, HE WAS PRETTY WELL BUSTED UP AT THAT CONFERENCE!
OH, I MUST VISIT THE POOR BOY!
DON'T DO THAT - HE'LL PROPOSE AND THE ARGUMENT WILL START ALL OVER AGAIN!
DON'T BE SILLY - THE DOCTOR WON'T LET HIM TALK IN HIS CONDITION!
SAYS YOU - NOBODY CAN STOP THAT BABY FROM PROPOSING!
PRINCE OKEY DOKEY'S ROOM, PLEASE!
SH-H-H!! - BE VERY QUIET - THIS WAY, MISS BOOP!
96 97 98 99 - ER -
SPRAINED WRIST - DISLOCATED SHOULDER - - WRENCHED KNEE - HIGH FEVER - - LOW PRESSURE - - WELL DONE GENERALLY ABSOLUTE QUIET - NO EXCITEMENT - -
CHART
OW!
BAM
HERE AT YOUR DAINTY FEET, MISS BETTY, I - - -
B-BUT, DOCTOR -
OW!
BAM
WAM
ABSOLUTE QUIET
PRINCE - REMEMBER YOUR CONDITION!
LET ME AT HIM!
GANGWAY! GANGWAY!
YOO-HOO! PRINCEY - DON'T BE LIKE THAT!
YOUR HIGHNESS - CALM YOURSELF!
YOU OLD "BUILDER-UPPER" - NO WONDER YOU WOULDN'T LET ME TALK!
HELP! HALP! 'ELP! 'LP!
1-19

BETTY BOOP
BY
MAX FLEISCHER
OBOY! THIS'LL BE THE LAST SHOT AND THE PICTURE IS FINISHED!
IT'S GREAT TO KNOW IT'S ALL BUT COMPLETED, I'LL SAY!
AND WITHOUT A MISHAP OR HOLD UP OF ANY KIND - IT'S A RECORD!
KNOCK WOOD!
OKAY, BETTY? CAMERA!
MIKE
COUGH COUGH
WHAT THE - CUT!!
I TELL YOU - IT WAS ONLY SOME DUST THAT GOT IN MY THROAT!
HEY! MEN! GET SOME ASPIRIN AND GET SOME -
QUICK, A HOT BOTTLE AND SOME COUGH SYRUP AND -
HURRY WITH THOSE COUGH REMEDIES!
COMIN' UP - CHIEF!
DRUGS - PRESC
STUDIO DRUG STORE
WE GOT ALL THEY HAD!
BUT LISTEN - I NEVER FELT BETTER IN MY LIFE AND -
NOW TAKE SOME MORE OF THIS BETTY -
SEE IF SHE HAS A FEVER!
THIS HOT WATER BOTTLE WILL MAKE IT WORK FASTER!
JUST ONE MORE DOSE OF THIS OLD REMEDY - IT'S A SURE CURE!
-AND SPRAY HER THROAT-
NOW PUT SOME DROPS UP HER NOSE!
NOW GARGLE THIS, BETTY!
LET HER INHALE SOME MORE OF THAT VAPOR!
LET'S SEE - IS THERE ANYTHING ELSE WE CAN GIVE HER?
OW! SHE SEEMS TO BE GETTING WORSE!
CALL A DOCTOR, QUICK - WE MUST GET HER WELL TO FINISH THIS EXPENSIVE PICTURE!
TELL US THE WORST, DOC!
THERE'S NOTHING THE MATTER WITH HER BUT AN UPSET SYSTEM --
BETTY BOOP
IT WAS CAUSED BY FORCING HER TO TAKE SUCH A MIXTURE OF COUGH REMEDIES - SHE'LL HAVE TO TAKE A LONG REST!
BETTY BOOP
1-26

BETTY BOOP
—BY—
MAX FLEISCHER
CUT! THAT WAS SWELL ACTING, BETTY-NOW GET READY FOR THE CRYING SCENE!
CRYING SCENE ?
NOW THIS BED ROOM SEQUENCE IS THE BIG SCENE OF THE PICTURE! GET IT? YOU'RE DESPONDENT-BROKEN-HEARTED! SEE? ALL YOU DO IS CRY-OKAY? CAMERA!!
?
CRY! GOOD GRIEF-CAN'T YOU CRY?
-ER-I'M AFRAID I CAN'T!
IT'S NO USE I JUST CAN'T CRY-I FEEL TOO HAPPY!
HEY! HUGO! GET THAT SOB VIOLINIST HERE, PRONTO! WE MUST GET BETTY INTO A CRYING MOOD!
NO, I DON'T FEEL A BIT LIKE CRYING BUT I'D LOVE TO WALTZ TO THAT LOVELY MUSIC-DA-DA-TEE-TUM--
YOU WOULD! I'LL HAVE TO TRY SOME SAD STORIES ON YOU!
-SNIFF-AND THERE WAS P-POOR LIL' NELL OUT IN THE COLD-FREEZING, STARVING, DYING AND---
HO-HUM-M!
LITTLE NELL
WAKE UP! THIS SAD STORY IS TO HELP YOU TO CRY-NOT SLEEP!
SORRY! HO-HUM! BUT THOSE BEDTIME STORIES ALWAYS MAKE ME SLEEPY!
THINK! THINK! DID YOU EVER LOSE A LIL' PET YOU LOVED DEARLY OR -----
NO, REALLY NOTHING SAD EVER DID HAPPEN IN MY LIFE THAT I CAN REMEMBER!
THERE'S NO WAY TO MAKE YOU CRY. I'LL HAVE TO USE A DOUBLE -YOU'RE HOPELESS-THERE'S MORE EMOTION IN AN OLD RUBBER BOOT!
SNIFF-SNIFF! YOU OLD MEANY!
? ? ?
BOO-HOO-THAT LAST CRACK WAS UNCALLED FOR-BOO-HOO-O-O
2-3
QUICK! GET THE CAMERAS SET-HOOK UP THE SOUND TRACK-EVERYTHING'S OKEY DOKEY!
BOO-HOO-O-O-O-
© 1935, King Features Syndicate, Inc., Great Britain rights reserved.

BETTY BOOP
BY
MAX FLEISCHER
YES, BETTY, THE CHIEF WANTS TO STAR YOU IN "POLLY OF THE PLAINS"!
OH! I'D LOVE TO PLAY THAT PART!
BUT THERE'S ONLY ONE DRAW-BACK—THE PART CALLS FOR A BUXOM LASS AND—
I'M NO "PLUMP VENUS," BUT A LITTLE FATTENING DIET WOULD REMEDY THAT!
THAT'S WHAT I FIGURED—SO I'VE ORDERED A SPECIALIST TO MAKE UP A DIET FOR YOU!
HOPE HE INCLUDES NUT SUNDAES AND—
—ALSO YOU MUST DRINK LOTS OF MILK AND EAT PLENTY OF EGGS, CANDY, ICE CREAM, BANANA SPLITS, SUNDAES, CAKE AND——
THAT SOUNDS MORE LIKE A PICNIC THAN A DIET!
REMEMBER—YOU MUST FILL OUT PLENTY TO GET THE PART!
DON'T WORRY—I'LL COME BACK WITH MORE CURVES THAN A CORKSCREW!
TUES. WED. THUR. FRI. SAT. SUN. MON.
A WEEK PASSES—SO-O-O
HELLO, VON—I'M ALL READY FOR THE TEST SHOTS!
HM-M! GET ON THE SCALES FIRST!
??!! BUT YOU'VE LOST WEIGHT!
MY FATTENING DIET NEVER FAILED BEFORE—ARE YOU SURE YOU FOLLOWED IT RELIGIOUSLY?
YEP! RIGHT DOWN TO THE LAST DROP OF MILK!
BUT LISTEN—HOW COME YOU LOST INSTEAD OF GAINING WEIGHT ON A FATTENING DIET?
I DON'T KNOW—
—UNLESS IT WAS BECAUSE I USED TO SIT UP NIGHTS WORRYING ABOUT LOSING THE PART!
2·10

BETTY BOOP
BY MAX FLEISCHER
YES, BETTY- THIS IS A SEA GOING YACHT- SO DON'T BE 'SCARED!
OH! IT ISN'T THAT- BUT I'VE NEVER BEEN TO SEA BEFORE AND I'M AFRAID OF GETTING SEA SICK!
PIER
DON'T BE SILLY- JUST DON'T THINK ABOUT IT- "MAL DE MER" IS ONLY A MENTAL ----
WHAT-EVER IT IS, I'M AFRAID OF IT!
WAIT HERE AND I'LL HAVE THE CAPTAIN SHOW YOU HIS MEDICINE CABINET THAT OUGHT SATISFY YOU!
WELL, IT WILL HELP SOME!
IF THERE'S NOTHING TO BE AFRAID OF- WHY ALL THE CURES?
YOU SEE, MISS BOOP, WE HAVE ALL KNOWN CURES FOR SEA-SICKNESS-
BUT S'POSE IT GETS ROUGH?
WHY I'VE SAILED THE SEVEN SEAS, MA'M AND NEVER HUNG ON A RAIL YET!
BUT STILL I'M AFRAID OF GETTING SEA SICK!
NO SEA SICK, MISSY- FORGET UM!
STEWARD- WHEN IT'S ROUGH LIKE THIS- ISN'T THAT WHEN YOU GET SEA SICK? I'M SO 'SCARED!
-ER- WELL, A PRETTY HEAVY SEA IS RUNNING- BUT- ER- THERE'S NO CAUSE FOR WORRY!
UP AND DOWN- ISN'T IT JUST LIKE A "SEE-SAW"? AND LOOK AT THOSE BIG WAVES WITH THE PRETTY WHITE FOAM- THEY REMIND ME OF WHIPPED CREAM--
MY GOODNESS - WHAT MADE THEM ALL RUN LIKE THAT?
2-16
PLEASE BE PATIENT- I CAN ONLY ATTEND TO ONE AT A TIME!
WUR-R-R-RUP!
HURRY, BETTY- O-O-O-O-OH!
O-OH! O-OH!

BETTY BOOP
BY
MAX FLEISCHER
YOU SAY THE CHIEF IS GOING TO GIVE ME A CHANCE AT THE STAR PART?
YES WE'RE GOING TO TAKE TESTS OF YOU IN DIFFERENT COSTUMES!
I'VE ALWAYS WANTED TO STAR IN A REAL COSTUME PICTURE - CLOTHES MAY NOT MAKE A MAN" - BUT, OBOY! WHAT THEY DO FOR A WOMAN!
THIS PAJAMA SHOT OUGHT TO CLICK!
REAL CUTE, BETTY CAMERA!
HOW ABOUT TAKING A LITTLE NAP TO MAKE IT LOOK MORE NATURAL?
THAT'S IT, BETTY-VERY GOOD!
MY GOODNESS, WHAT CLOTHES! I'LL BE THE ANSWER TO WHAT THE WELL-DRESSED WOMAN SHOULD WEAR!
OKAY, CUT! NOW PUT ON THE ERMINE EVENING WRAP!
HOME, JAMES! -ER-BEG PARDON-THESE CLOTHES MAKE ME FEEL THAT WAY!
AND BELIEVE ME, BETTY-YOU LOOK THAT WAY!
STILL SOME MORE COSTUME SHOTS, HUH?
YES, A FEW IN SPORT CLOTHES-THEN YOU CAN REST WHILE WE GET "RUSHES" THROUGH
PHEW! TAKING THOSE TEST SHOTS WERE SOME STRAIN, BUT IT'LL BE WORTH IT TO GET THIS BIG PART!
LATER-
THE CHIEF OKAYED THE TEST SHOTS-YOU GET THE PART!
O-OH! I'M SO THRILLED!
NOW GO IN TO THE COSTUME DEPARTMENT-THEY HAVE YOUR COSTUME READY-WE'LL START SHOOTING RIGHT AWAY!
I'M SO ANXIOUS TO SEE THE COSTUMES!
NO MISTAKE, MISS BOOP, A BATHING SUIT IS THE COSTUME THE PART CALLS FOR!
HM-M! I SUPPOSE IF I'D TAKEN TEST SHOTS IN A BATHING SUIT-YOU'D HAND ME A FIG LEAF!
COSTUME LIST
© 1935, King Features Syndicate, Inc., Great Britain rights reserved.
2-23

BETTY BOOP
BY
MAX FLEISCHER
-AND HE FEARS NOTHING-BRAVE AS TWO LIONS AND NOT ONLY THAT-BUT HE'S GREAT PROTECTION AS A WATCH DOG!
NICE DOGGIE-I HAVE A FEW THINGS TO WATCH-I OUGHT TO HAVE A WATCH-DOG, TOO!
I WONDER WHAT COLOR WOULD FIT IN WITH THE COLOR SCHEME OF MY ROOMS?
SALE
SCOTTIES
BOSTONS
POODLES
MUTTS
THIS WAY, LADY, FOR THE WATCH-DOG DEPARTMENT!
I WANT ONE THAT KNOWS HIS WATCHING!
HOW'S ABOUT THESE?
NO! THEY'RE TOO BIG-WHY, YOU COULD PUT A SADDLE ON 'EM AND RIDE 'EM!
WELL, THEN CHOOSE YOUR OWN-WE HAVE EVERY TYPE, INCLUDING THE SCANDINAVIAN!
I'LL START WITH THESE!
LET'S SEE, NOW-EENY MEENY, MINEY, MOO---
WHY DON'T YOU TRY THE-"MY MOTHER TOLD ME TO TAKE THIS"? ONE?
YOU HAVE A REAL WATCH-DOG THERE-YOU BETTER WATCH HIM CLOSELY!
COME ON, HUGO-LET'S SEE YOU WATCH!
PUPS FOR SALE
HE MUST SEE SOMETHING THAT NEEDS WATCHING!
I HAVEN'T MUCH TO WATCH-SO I GOT A SMALL WATCH DOG!
WATCH-DOG-ER-YOU MEAN "WATCH-CHARM" DOG-DON'T YOU, BETTY?
SNIFF
HUGO! IS THAT NICE?
WHAT THA-~~?
WOOF!
AREN'T YOU ASHAMED OF YOURSELF, SCARING THAT POOR DOG LIKE THAT?
WUFF
WOOF/WARF
3-2

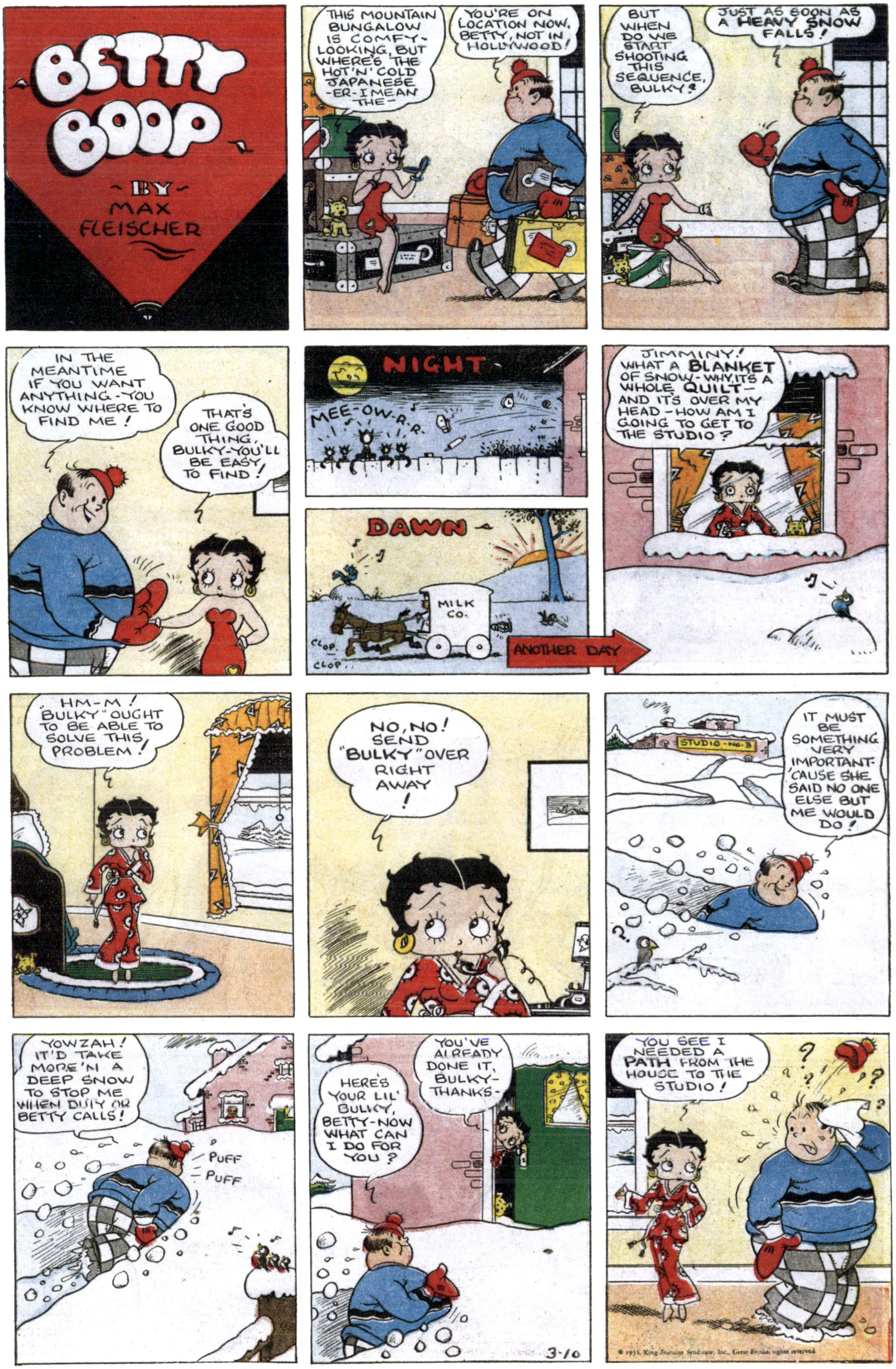
BETTY BOOP
BY MAX FLEISCHER
THIS MOUNTAIN BUNGALOW IS COMFY-LOOKING, BUT WHERE'S THE HOT 'N' COLD JAPANESE -ER-I MEAN THE-
YOU'RE ON LOCATION NOW, BETTY, NOT IN HOLLYWOOD!
BUT WHEN DO WE START SHOOTING THIS SEQUENCE, BULKY?
JUST AS SOON AS A HEAVY SNOW FALLS!
IN THE MEANTIME IF YOU WANT ANYTHING - YOU KNOW WHERE TO FIND ME!
THAT'S ONE GOOD THING, BULKY-YOU'LL BE EASY TO FIND!
NIGHT
MEE-OW-R-R.
DAWN
MILK CO.
CLOP. CLOP..
ANOTHER DAY
JIMMINY! WHAT A BLANKET OF SNOW-WHY, IT'S A WHOLE QUILT- AND IT'S OVER MY HEAD - HOW AM I GOING TO GET TO THE STUDIO?
HM-M! "BULKY" OUGHT TO BE ABLE TO SOLVE THIS PROBLEM!
NO, NO! SEND "BULKY" OVER RIGHT AWAY!
STUDIO - NO. 3
IT MUST BE SOMETHING VERY IMPORTANT-'CAUSE SHE SAID NO ONE ELSE BUT ME WOULD DO!
YOWZAH! IT'D TAKE MORE 'N A DEEP SNOW TO STOP ME WHEN DUTY OR BETTY CALLS!
PUFF
PUFF
HERE'S YOUR LIL' BULKY, BETTY-NOW WHAT CAN I DO FOR YOU?
YOU'VE ALREADY DONE IT, BULKY-THANKS-
3-10
YOU SEE I NEEDED A PATH FROM THE HOUSE TO THE STUDIO!
© 1935, King Features Syndicate, Inc., Great Britain rights reserved.

BETTY BOOP
BY MAX FLEISCHER
COMPETITION MAY BE OKAY IN BUSINESS, BUT IN LOVE IT'S JUST A BIG HEAD-ACHE AND I HAVE PLENTY OF BOTH WITH "VAN"!
HMM! THEY SAY THE BEST WAY TO A MAN'S HEART IS GOOD COOKING, BUT I CAN'T BOIL WATER WITHOUT BURNING IT~I KNOW-I'LL HIRE THE BEST COOK AVAILABLE!
YOU GET THE IDEA? DON'T LET HIM SEE YOU-I WANT HIM TO THINK I'M DOING THE COOKING!
I UNDERSTAND, MISS BOOP!
-AND HAVE TURKEY WITH ALL THE FIXINGS-HAVE IT ON THE TABLE READY TO SERVE!
I'LL COOK YOU A DINNER FIT FOR A KING!
EVERYTHING IS READY, MISS!
FINE! HERE HE COMES NOW-SO KEEP OUT OF SIGHT!
R-R-ING
LATER-
SNIFF! YOUR DINNER SURE SMELLS INVITING, BETTY!
I HOPE YOU'RE GOING TO ENJOY IT, VAN!
AIN'T HE GRAND?
CAN I HELP YOU TO MORE TURKEY, VAN?
I'LL SAY YOU CAN-IT'S SURE DELICIOUS-COOKED TO PERFECTION!
YUM-M! AND THIS PIE IS BETTER THAN EVEN MOTHER USED TO MAKE!
THANKS!
THAT WAS THE MOST PERFECT DINNER I'VE HAD IN AN AGE-WORDS FAIL ME IN TRYING TO DESCRIBE IT!
YOU FLATTER ME, VAN-REALLY!
?
-AND I'VE ALWAYS SAID-THE GIRL I MARRY MUST BE A GOOD COOK!
3-16
OH! MISTER VAN TWINKLE, WE WOULD MAKE A NICE COUPLE
© 1935, King Features Syndicate, Inc., Great Britain rights reserved.

BETTY BOOP
BY MAX FLEISCHER
MEET POICY TWINKLE, BETTY,- HE'S VAN'S KID BROTHER!
I'VE TAKEN QUITE A FAWNCY TO BILLY, MISS BOOP -I'D LIKE TO HAVE THE OLD DEAR OVER TO TEA!
SURELY, PERCY- NOW BILLY- DON'T PLAY ROUGH!
OH, DEAR! AN AMBULANCE AND A CROWD IN FRONT OF VAN'S HOUSE AND I TOLD BILLY NOT TO PLAY ROUGH!
BILLY!! WHAT HAPPENED?
AW! POICY DARED ME AND AH TOOK HIS DARE!
GANG-WAY!
OH, BILLY- HAVEN'T I ALWAYS SAID, ONLY FOOLS TAKE DARES- IF HE TOLD YOU JUMP OFF THAT ROOF WOULD YOU DO IT?
WELL, SIS- THAT'S WHAT HE DARED ME TO DO!
- AND YOU SAY HE'S UP AND AROUND PLAYING GAMES WITH THE NURSE, DOCTOR? I HOPE SHE'S A STRONG NURSE!
I'M SURPRISED AT PERCY- DARING BILLY TO JUMP OFF THE ROOF!
THE DOCTOR SAID WE COULD VISIT HIM TODAY!
REALLY, OLD DEAR- I'M DEUCEDLY SORRY!
LANDING ON HIS HEAD I GUESS SAVED HIM!
WELL, BILLY WAS ALWAYS A HARD-HEADED KID!
HOW IS HE DOING, DOCTOR?
THE LAST TIME I VISITED HIM HE ASKED THE NURSE TO PLAY SOME GAMES WITH HIM!
© 1935, King Features Syndicate, Inc., Great Britain rights reserved.
HIS GAMES ARE RAWTHER STRENUOUS AFFAIRS!
SH-H! HE MAY BE SLEEPING!
3-23
WHEN YO'ALL FEEL BETTER WE'LL PLAY SOME MORE, HUH, NURSIE?

BETTY BOOP
BY
MAX FLEISCHER
THIS "PERILS OF PEARL", SCRIPT CALLS FOR A LOT OF DANGEROUS STUNTS, BETTY- BUT DON'T WORRY- WE HAVE YOU COVERED WITH EVERY KIND OF INSURANCE!
WHY ARE YOU SO GOOD TO ME?
PERILS OF PEARL
YOU'RE SUPPOSED TO BE FALLING FROM A PLANE- RELAX - THAT INVISIBLE WIRE WON'T BREAK!
DON'T BE SCARED, BETTY- REMEMBER, IT'S ONLY A MOVIE STUNT!
B-B-BUT DO THE TIGERS KNOW THAT?
PLEASE DON'T WIGGLE THAT NET SO MUCH- IT MAKES ME NERVOUS!
OKAY, BETTY, JUMP!
DON'T WORRY, BETTY- THE TRAINER IS RIGHT BEHIND 'EM!
PLEASE DON'T MISS IT THIS TIME!
RIGHTO! NOW DIVE OUT, BETTY!
SHOW FEAR BETTY- REMEMBER, YOU'RE S'POSED TO BE IN A TOUGH SPOT-
YOU'RE TELLING ME!
OH, DEAR, WILL I BE GLAD WHEN THESE STUNTS ARE FINISHED!
TRY LANDING ON THE SKIS THIS TRIP!
CUT! YOU'VE USED THE WRONG STAR IN THESE SCENES- IT'S MISS LOVEWELL'S PART!
BUT, CHIEF- WE'VE MADE ALL OF THE SCENES--
?
THAT'S WHAT I SAID- SCRAP 'EM!
WHAT!
GIVE HER AIR!
WHEN SHE COMES TO-WE'LL HAVE TO START ON HER REAL SCRIPT!
3-30
© 1935, King Features Syndicate, Inc., Great Britain rights reserved

BETTY BOOP
BY MAX FLEISCHER
YES, VAN, I'VE DECIDED TO WEAR AN OLD-FASHIONED GOWN TO THE BIG COSTUME BALL!
I'LL BET YOU WILL LOOK STUNNING, MISS BOOP!
THE BUSTLE AND HOOP SKIRT HAVE ME KIND OF WORRIED THOUGH!
HERE'S YOUR COSTUME, MISS BETTY!
FINE! NOW YOU'D BETTER CALL IN SOME HELP TO GET ME INTO IT, CELESTE!
JUST A LITTLE MORE TO THE LEFT!
HOLD IT - LOWER AWAY!
ALL SET, VAN - CALL THE TAXI!
TAXI? YOU MEAN A MOVING VAN!
BUT BETTY - THEY'LL BE NO ROOM FOR ME?
GUESS YOU'LL HAVE TO PARK YOURSELF ON THE SPARE TIRE, VAN!
DON'T YOU THINK I'LL BE A HIT WITH THIS COSTUME, VAN?
YOU OUGHTA BE A BIG HIT, I MEAN!
OH! THERE GOES HALF OF MY SKIRT!
DON'T WORRY, BETTY - YOU STILL HAVE PLENTY LEFT!
R-RIP!
AND THERE GOES THE OTHER HALF!!
R-RIP!
WHAT NOW LIL' GAL?
SKIRT OR NO SKIRT - I'M NOT GOING TO MISS THAT BALL - DRIVE ON, JAMES!
THAT BIRD CAGE EFFECT WITH THE CUTE PANTELETTES IS STUNNING!
IT MUST BE SOMETHING VERY NEW!
FOR WEARING THE MOST UNIQUE - ORIGINAL - STRIKING COSTUME - MISS BOOP TAKES FIRST PRIZE!
4-6

BETTY BOOP
BY MAX FLEISHER
NOW, BILLY, WE'RE CALLING ON THE "TWINKLES" AGAIN AND I HOPE YOU WON'T MESS UP LITTLE PERCY LIKE YOU DID THE LAST TIME!
WELL, WHEN HE SAID, "LETS DO SOME HIKING," I THOUGHT HE SAID FIGHTING!
YOU MUST TRY TO BE A LITTLE GENTLEMAN — COPY HIS MANNERS — DO AS HE DOES!
OKEY DOKE!
THINK IT'S SAFE TO LEAVE 'EM ALONE?
OH, YES — I GAVE BILLY A GOOD TALK ON MANNERS 'N'EVERYTHIN'!
I SAY, OLD BEAN — I WISH YOU'D ACT AND DRESS LIKE A GENTLEMAN INSTEAD OF A BLOOMING TOFF!
OH, YEAH? WELL, ANY MUGG WHO WEARS A HIGH HAT, MONOCLE AND GLOVES, IS A SISSY!
? ? ?
THAT'S AN INSULT, SIR — AND I'M TREATING IT AS A GENTLEMAN SHOULD!
SPLAT
BUT, BILLY — THAT'S JUST AN OLD EUROPEAN CUSTOM!
MY HONOR IS SATISFIED, GOOD DAY, SIR!
LET ME AT HIM!
WELL, MY HONOR WON'T BE SATISFIED TILL I KNOCK HIM STIFF!
REMEMBER, GENTLEMEN DON'T HIT WITH THEIR FISTS — THEY USE THEIR GLOVES!
YASSUH! THAT'S OKAY BY ME!
STOP! WHERE ARE YOU GOING, BILLY?
THAT BIRD CAN'T GET AWAY WITH THAT GLOVE GAG ON ME, NO, SUH!
BILL-EE-E
HEY!
SO GENTLEMEN ONLY HIT WITH THEIR GLOVES, HUH?
BAM
WELL, THAT MAKES ME A GENTLEMAN!
4-13

BETTY BOOP
BY MAX FLEISCHER
GET READY, BETTY - WE'LL SHOOT THIS NEXT SCENE AT MY COUNTRY ESTATE!
SWELL. I'M ANXIOUS TO SEE YOUR PLACE!
I S'POSE YOU HAVE EXTENSIVE GROUNDS, TOO?
HAVE I? WAIT'LL YOU SEE MY BEAUTIFUL LAWN!
DID YOU SAY COUNTRY ESTATE? WHAT COUNTRY?
IT WON'T BE LONG NOW - WHY, IT'S ONLY A TEN MINUTE WALK FROM THE STATION - IF YOU RUN!
OW! LOOK AT WHAT THOSE CHICKENS DID TO MY SWELL LAWN?
KEEP OFF
MAIL
VON SCRIPT
SHOO! WHOSE CHICKENS ARE THEY?
THE FARMERS NEXT DOOR AND HE REFUSES TO KEEP 'EM OFF MY LAWN!
AND IT WAS MY TURN TO KEEP CHICKENS THIS YEAR, TOO!
COME ON, I'VE GOT AN IDEA!
ARE THOSE EGGS STRICTLY FRESH?
WHY THEY'RE STILL WARM, MA'AM!
FRESH EGGS
THAT'S IT - PLACE 'EM ALL AROUND THE LAWN!
I STILL DON'T GET YOUR IDEA, BETTY!
PS-ST! LOUDER, BETTY!
OH, VON WHAT BEAUTIFUL EGGS!
YEAH - I GET ABOUT A DOZEN A DAY FROM THOSE CHICKENS NEXT DOOR!
?
OH! THE FARMER TOOK A HINT - -
4-20

BETTY BOOP
BY MAX FLEISCHER
HELLO! YOU SAY MY BROTHER "BUBBY'S" SCREEN TEST CAME OUT SWELL AND HE GETS THE PART? FINE! I'LL HAVE HIM RIGHT DOWN!
STOP! COME HERE, "BUBBY"-THE STUDIO JUST PHONED FOR YOU!
TELL 'EM - MISTER BOOP REGRETS, HE CANNOT APPEAR TODAY!
EXPRES
WHY CAN'T I GO AS I AM?
LISTEN, "BUBBY"-THIS ISN'T A SLUM PICTURE!
BUT THIS AIN'T SATURDAY NIGHT!
SCRUB YOURSELF GOOD-THIS IS A BIG CHANCE FOR YOU TO BECOME FAMOUS!
FAMOUS FOR WHAT?
AS A GREAT MOVIE STAR-WHY, YOUR FACE WILL BECOME KNOWN ALL OVER THE WORLD!
AND MY PICTURE WILL BE ON ALL THE BILLBOARDS, TOO?
YES! AND IN ALL THE PAPERS FROM COAST TO COAST-YOU'LL BE THE MALE "CURLY KEMPLE"!
HM-M! YES, HE LOOKS OKAY FOR THE PART-I'LL MEASURE HIM TO MAKE SURE!
WITH HIS EXPRESSIVE EYES AND CLASSIC PROFILE I KNOW HE'LL BE A HIT!
YEP! HE'S JUST THE RIGHT SIZE!
I'M SURE HE'LL SCREEN SWELL AND HIS ROGUISH SMILE OUGHT TO GO OVER BIG!
NOW JUST DO AS THE DIRECTOR TELLS YOU, "BUBBY"!
WAIT HERE, BETTY-WHILE I TAKE HIM IN FOR HIS COSTUME!
OH! I'M SO ANXIOUS TO SEE HIM IN HIS PART!
WELL, COME ON, BETTY-THEY'RE ALL READY TO SHOOT! THE KID HAS THE LEAD IN THIS "UGLY DUCKLING" COMEDY.
MY FACE WILL BE FAMOUS-BAH!
OKAY, "BUBBY"-NOW PUT ON THE HEAD-CAMERA, READY!

BETTY BOOP
BY MAX FLEISCHER
THIS "JUNGLE JANE" IS ALL ADVENTURE IN THE JUNGLE - DON'T BE 'SCARED OF THE ANIMALS - THE TRAINERS AND HUNTERS WILL TAKE CARE OF THEM!
BUT WHO'S GOING TO TAKE CARE OF ME?
JUNGLE JANE
CAMERA! DON'T WORRY, BETTY - "BIG BERTHA" IS WELL TRAINED!
THAT'S IT, BETTY - ACT NONCHALANT - JUST PRETEND YOU DON'T SEE HIM STALKING YOU!
OKAY, BETTY - THE TRAINER HAS "BO-BO" UNDER CONTROL!
YOU WOULDN'T FOOL ME, WOULD YOU?
NOW TOSS YOUR SPEAR AND THEN RUN FOR COVER - THE HUNTERS WILL STOP HIM!
IT'LL BE JUST TOO BAD IF THEY MISS!
DON'T BE 'SCARED - REMEMBER - IT'S ONLY A MOVIE STUNT!
DON'T WORRY, BETTY - IF THEY GET TOO CLOSE THE HUNTERS WILL SHOOT 'EM!
WHAT! ARE THEY WAITING TO SEE THE WHITES OF THEIR EYES BEFORE THEY SHOOT?
CAMERA! RUN, BETTY - YOU CAN BEAT 'EM TO THE STOCKADE GATE!
B-BUT S'POSE IT'S A TIE?
YES, SIR - YOU'LL GO DOWN AS THE MOST FEARLESS ACTRESS OF ALL TIME - NOW GO INTO THE TENT AND REST 'TILL THE "BLACK PANTHER" SCENE!
NO. 3.
YOU WOULD MAKE IT A BLACK ONE!
QUICK! THAT'S BETTY CALLING FOR HELP!
GRAB YOUR GUNS AND SPEARS, MEN!
EE-E-EEK! HALP!
© 1935, King Features Syndicate, Inc., Great Britain rights reserved
O-OH! I JUST SAW A MOUSE!

BETTY BOOP
BY MAX FLEISCHER
GOOD GRIEF! WHO BLUE PENCILED THIS COSTUME LIST OF MINE?
THE FRONT OFFICE-THEY'RE CUTTING PRODUCTION COSTS RIGHT DOWN TO THE BONE!
WHY, WE'VE GOT TO USE IMITATION FOOD IN THE BIG BANQUET SCENE!
THAT WON'T MAKE ME MAD-I'M ON A DIET!
BUT THE PALATIAL YACHT SHOT-IS THAT CUT, TOO?
YES, THAT'S CHANGED TO A ROW-BOAT!
AND YOU SAY THE SWANKY NIGHT CLUB SEQUENCE IS OUT?
AND HOW-WE'RE USING YOU SITTING ON A PIANO INSTEAD!
COSTUMES SET III.
THAT'S CARRYING THIS ECONOMY THING TOO FAR!
BUT THE WORST CUT OF ALL IS THE BIG MOB SCENE IS OUT ENTIRELY!
WHAT! WHY, THAT'S THE MOST IMPORTANT SCENE OF THE PICTURE-OH! YOU MUST SAVE IT-OR THE PICTURE IS A FLOP!
YOU'RE TELLING ME-IF THEY ONLY LEFT THAT SHOT IN WE'D PULL THROUGH BUT THE COST OF EXTRAS AND-
OH, DEAR! THERE MUST BE SOME WAY TO SAVE THAT IMPORTANT MOB SCENE!
ULTOMATO FILM STUDIO
B.B.
OH! THERE'S BETTY BOOP!
GIVE US YOUR AUTOGRAPH BETTY?
I SAW HER FIRST!
???
OH! BETTY-PUL-EESE!
DON'T LET HER GET AWAY!
YOO-HOO! VON SCRIPT-GET YOUR CAMERAS READY!
B.B.
HERE'S YOUR MOB SCENE!
GREAT! LEAD 'EM OVER TO SET SIX!
B.B.

BETTY BOOP
BY MAX FLEISCHER
YOU SAY, THE FIRST RUSHES OF "BUBBY" ARE SWELL AND YOU WANT HIM DOWN RIGHT AWAY FOR THE NEXT SCENES? OKAY!
ALLAY OOP! JUMP!
NOW SCRUB YOURSELF GOOD, "BUBBY"- YOU MUST LOOK YOUR BEST!
WHY ALL OVER? THIS AIN'T A NUDIST PICTURE- IS IT?
NOW THIS NEXT SCENE CALLS FOR HIM TO LAUGH HEARTY AND LOUD!
THAT'S EASY. LAUGH, BIG BUBBY!
?
I'LL MAKE SOME FUNNY FACES TO GET HIM LAUGHING. LOOK, "BUBBY"!
GUESS YOU'LL HAVE TO TRY SOME OTHER WAY!
BAH-WAW-WA-A-
WEE-EE! LOOKIT THE MONKEY, "BUBBY"!
OH, SEE! ISN'T THAT FUNNY, DEAR?
WHY DON'T YOU BEHAVE- I'M NO SISSY!
TOYS
"NOT CRY, BUBBY- YOU MUST LAUGH- THE SCRIPT CALLS FOR IT!
I'LL BRING IN ONE OF THE COMEDIANS FROM THE OTHER SET- WE MUST GET HIM LAUGHING!
SNIFF- SNIFF-
OH! HE FLEW THROUGH THE AIR---
LOOK AT THE FUNNY MANS, DEAR!
OW! HE'S YAWN ING!
HO-HUM-M
NOPE! IT'S NO USE NOTHING SEEMS TO STRIKE HIM FUNNY!
WAIT! I'LL DO THE COMEDY ACT I DID YEARS AGO- IT USED TO LAY 'EM IN THE AISLES!
THIS NEXT STUNT OUGHTA MAKE HIM BUST RIGHT OUT LAUGHING- WATCH NOW, "BUBBY- WEE-E-E-
IT SOUNDS FUNNY ANY WAY!
?
HA-HA-HO-HO-HAR-HAW HEE-HEE
BAM
SWELL! DO IT AGAIN, BUBBY "THINKS THAT STUNT IS VERY FUNNY!
HE WOULD
HA HA HA HA HA HA HA HAR
5-18

BETTY BOOP
BY MAX FLEISCHER
YEP! BETTY-YOU'VE BEEN SELECTED FOR THE LEAD IN "CAPT. KIDD, JR.," THE PIRATE PICTURE!
OH! I LOVE THAT-I'VE ALWAYS WANTED TO PLAY A SEA-GOING PART!
"MY ANCESTORS WENT DOWN TO THE SEA IN SHIPS"-IT'S IN MY BLOOD-I'LL REHEARSE THIS GOOD!
"-BELAY THERE YOU LUBBERS-FOLLOW ME-BOARD 'EM AND GIVE NO QUARTER---"
"AVAST THERE-GIVE 'EM A BROADSIDE-EVERY MAN FOR HIMSELF"
NEXT DAY
AND I HAVE MY PART LETTER PERFECT!
FINE! GET INTO YOUR PIRATE CAPTAIN'S COSTUME-WE'RE LEAVING FOR THE SHIP RIGHT AWAY!
NOW THIS STORM SCENE IS THE MOST IMPORTANT AND EXPENSIVE SHOT OF THE PICTURE AND I DON'T WANT ANY HITCH IN IT!
SOUND TRACKS-CAMERAS-'N'EVERYTHIN' ARE READY-GET INTO YOUR PLACES! ARE YOU READY, BETTY?
AYE, AYE, SIR!
ALL SET! START THE WIND AND WAVE MACHINES!
JOLLY ROGER
OKAY! CAMERA!
5-25
WELL, I'LL BE--- CUT!

BETTY BOOP
BY
MAX FLEISCHER
WHAT! YOU SAY "BUBBY" IS CAST FOR A LEADING PART IN "OUT IN THE COLD AGAIN"? HOW THRILLING!
AM I TO BE THE COMIC DONKEY AGAIN, SIS?
NO DEAR, YOU'RE BEING CO-STARRED WITH "PARK CABLE" THE BIG CHARACTER ACTOR - YOU'RE MADE BUBBY!
I'VE REHEARSED HIM TILL HE HAS HIS PART DOWN PAT - HE'LL BE A SURE HIT!
FINE! GET HIM INTO HIS COSTUME - WE'RE SHOOTING RIGHT AWAY!
YES, BETTY, WE'VE DECIDED TO HAVE YOU DO THE DIRECTING!
ME? WELL, AT THAT - I GUESS HE'LL ACT BETTER FOR ME THAN ANYBODY ELSE!
NOW DON'T FORGET - YOU'RE S'POSED TO BE JUST A HOMELESS WAIF AND DO JUST AS I TELL YOU!
NOW REMEMBER YOUR PART, BUBBY! READY? CAMERA!
SO YOU REFUSE TO DO "FAGIN'S" BIDDIN', HUH? WELL, GET OUT AND NEVER DARKEN MY DOOR AGIN--
OUT IN THE COLD, BRAT - BEFORE I PUT THE ZING ON YUH - OUT! SCR-R-RAM!
WAM
"BUBBY", WHY DID YOU DO THAT? NOW YOU'VE SPOILED THE SCENE!
YOU'RE S'POSED TO BE SCARED AND ACT TIMID - NOT BELLIGERENT - WHEN "FAGIN" ORDERS YOU OUT IN THE COLD!
OH, YEAH?
WELL, HE ACTED LIKE HE MEANT IT!
6-1

BETTY BOOP
BY
MAX FLEISCHER
YES, BETTY—THIS NEXT SCENE MUST BE FINISHED TODAY—IS THE SOUND-TRACK, LIGHTS 'N' EVERYTHIN' OKAY, JOE?
YES, CHIEF—EVERYTHING'S OKEY DOKE!
QUIET! READY, BETTY? CAMERA!!
ALL SET, VON!
HEY! WHAT TH'-- CUT!
"BUBBY"! YOU MUSTN'T BREAK IN ON A SCENE!
SIC 'IM SPUNKY!
AFTER ALL OUR CAREFUL PREPARATION-SOMEBODY LET THAT DAWGONE KID BUST IN ON THE SHOT!
SH-H!—CHIEF! HE'S BETTY'S KID BROTHER AND SHE'S VERY TOUCHY ABOUT HIM!
EVERYTHING IS READY AGAIN AND SEE THAT NOTHING INTERFERES WITH THE SHOOTING-OR ELSE--
I'LL PLACE A DOUBLE GUARD 'ROUND THE SET!
READY, BETTY? CAMERA!! WELL, I'LL BE~ CUT!
TSK-TSK! "BUBBY," WHAT DID I TELL YOU?
GR-R-R-- NOW THAT'S THE FIFTH TIME THAT KID'S SPOILED THE SCENE-'S GOT ME WACKY!
BUT WE DON'T DARE TO PUT THE ZING ON HIM-BETTY WOULD GET SORE—THERE'S NOTHING TO DO, BUT TO WRITE IN A PART FOR THE KID!
YEAH! THEY'RE CHANGING THE SCRIPT AND WRITING IN A PART FOR BROTHER "BUBBY"!
OH! I LOVE THAT!
HOURS LATER
'S'ALL FINISHED AT LAST, BETTY!
SOME PART-IT'LL MAKE THE PICTURE!
I'M SO THRILLED-I KNOW "BUBBY" WILL BE A HIT!
WHAT!! YOU CAN'T FIND HIM?
WE'VE GOT TO HAVE HIM NOW-HAVE ALL THE SPECIALS AND EVERYBODY SEARCH THE GROUNDS!
IT'S ONE OF THE BEST PARTS WE EVER WROTE, TOO!
?
NOZIR! CHIEF-WE CAN'T FIND HIM ANYWHERE!
THE GATEMAN SAID HE SAW HIM LEAVE ON THE SPARE TIRE OF A CAR!
OW! AFTER ALL THAT WORK-NOW WE'VE GOT TO CHANGE THE SCRIPT BACK AGAIN!
6-9
© 1935, King Features Syndicate, Inc., Great Britain rights reserved.

BETTY BOOP
BY
MAX FLEISCHER
YOUR SCREEN TESTS WERE OKAY, BETTY— YOU GET THE LEAD IN THIS BIG FEATURE "FLIRTING WITH DEATH"!
SWELL! A VAMP "DRAMA, HUH?
NO! IT'S AN ADVENTURE PICTURE, FULL OF THRILLS AND ACTION - WAIT! I'LL READ YOU A FEW SCENES!
?
-AND IN THE NEXT SCENE YOU RIDE OFF A CLIFF ON THE BACK OF A WILD MUSTANG---
YOU MEAN MY "DOUBLE" WILL!
DOUBLE, ME EYE— THERE'S A VERY SMALL CHANCE OF YOU GETTING HURT!
THAT'S TOO BIG FOR ME-BESIDES MY CONTRACT FORBIDS ME TO TAKE CHANCES!
ALLRIGHT, CALL IN YOUR LAWYERS!
HELLO! YES -YOU MUST COME OVER - IT'S A MATTER OF LIFE AND DEATH!
YOU SAY, THE SCRIPT READS LIKE A "DEATH WARRANT" TO YOU, BETTY? WELL--
HERE IT IS, BOYS- READ IT AND WEEP!
-AND YOU MUST USE A DOUBLE IN THIS "FLYING TRAPEZE" SCENE, TOO!
THAT IS RATHER RISKY— OKAY! WE'LL USE A DOUBLE IN THAT SHOT!
HM-M! ALSO IN THIS CHASE BY WILD TIGERS AND THE FIGHT WITH THE GIANT PYTHON AND THE---
B-BUT LISTEN--
HOW ABOUT THE BURNING PLANE SHOT AND THE BIG MAN-EATING SHARK BATTLE AND THE THRILLING EXPLOSION SCENES?
YOU'LL HAVE TO USE A "DOUBLE" IN ALL THOSE SCENES, TOO!
THAT'S WHAT I SAID - I'M STARRING THE "DOUBLE"!
? ? ? ? ?

BETTY BOOP
BY
MAX FLEISCHER
YES, BETTY-YOUR BROTHER "BUBBY" GETS THE LEAD IN "LITTLE LORD FAUNTLEROY"-WE START SHOOTING THIS AFTERNOON!
SWELL! BUT THAT'S RATHER A SHORT NOTICE!
I'LL HAVE TO WORK FAST-"BUBBY" MUST HAVE THE PART DOWN PAT!
BUBBY!! HE WOULD BE MISSING AT A TIME LIKE THIS--OH-OH---
SOCK IT OVER THE FENCE, BUBBY!
COME QUICK, BUBBY-IT'S VERY IMPORTANT!
OH, YEAH? WELL, SO IS THIS!
THE IDEA-HERE'S A CHANCE FOR YOU TO MAKE A BIG HIT IN THE MOVIES AND--
AND BUBBY'S OUR BEST HITTER, TOO!
YES, AND I HAD A SWELL CHANCE TO MAKE A HIT AND WIN THE GAME!
WE'LL JUST GO OVER THAT LAST SCENE ONCE MORE-STOP THAT YAWNING!
HO-HUM-M! IT SOUNDS LIKE A BEDTIME STORY!
-AND HE KNOWS ALL HIS LINES AND SCENES PERFECTLY!
FINE! GET HIM INTO HIS COSTUME TILL I SEE HOW HE LOOKS!
STAND UP, BUBBY-THE DIRECTOR WANTS TO OKAY YOUR COSTUME!
YES, SIR-HE'S A PERFECT LITTLE LORD FAUNTLEROY!
HIM OKAY IT? SHOW ME A MIRROR TILL I OKAY IT FIRST!
YES, DEAR-THE CURLS GO WITH THE PART!
WHY, I LOVE THOSE CURLS!
SPLAT!
WELL, TAKE 'EM THEN!
© 1935, King Features Syndicate, Inc., Great Britain rights reserved.
"HURRY UP, "SPIKE"-I'M BATTING NEXT!
FOR SALE
HOORAY! WE'LL WIN NOW-"BUBBY" IS BACK!
6-23
LUCKY BUCKS
PLAY MONEY
2 BUCK

BETTY BOOP
BY
MAX FLEISCHER
GOOD AFTER-NOON, ARE YOU READY TO REHEARSE MY SONGS?
READY? WE'VE BEEN READY AND WAITING FOR YOU SINCE MORNING!
...AND THAT'S WHY I'M WACKY OVER YOU...
FINE! YOU SURE HAVE 'EM ALL DOWN PAT AND YOU'RE IN GOOD VOICE, TOO!
NOW REMEMBER WE MUST FINISH RECORDING EM ALL BY TOMORROW NIGHT!
OKEY DOKE!
OH, SURE - BRING YOUR FRIENDS RIGHT OVER - I'D LIKE TO HAVE YOU HEAR MY NEW SONGS!
AND HERE'S ANOTHER I SING IN THE NIGHT CLUB SCENE!
I LOVE TO DO THE RHUMBA WITH A SWELL LIL NUMBER...
OBOY! WHAT A VOICE!
HERE'S ANOTHER TORCH SONG I SING IN THE FINALE!
I'LL ALWAYS BE THAT WAY ABOUT YOU AND...
WOW! BROADWAY STARS COULDN'T DO BETTER!
BRAVO! THAT LAST ONE WAS A PIP!
OH! ALLRIGHT I'LL SING THEM ALL OVER AGAIN ONCE MORE AND THAT'S ALL!
WE COULD LISTEN TO YOU ALL NIGHT, BETTY!
THANKS, BETTY!
GOOD NIGHT ALL - I'M GLAD YOU LIKED MY SONGS!
LIKED 'EM? I NEVER HEARD YOU SING BETTER!
YOU WERE IN PERFECT VOICE, BETTY, AND HOW!
NEXT DAY
RIGHT ON TIME, HUH? WELL THE BIG CHORUS 'N'EVERYTHIN' IS ALL READY FOR YOUR RECORDING AND---
AHEM! BUT LISTEN- WHISS-S-S-S-S-S
WOZZAT?
AHEM! I SAID MY-S-S WHISS-S-S-S-S...
© 1936 King Features Syndicate, Inc. World rights reserved.
THAT'S WHAT I SAID - IT'S A CASE OF VOICE STRAIN. SHE WON'T BE ABLE TO SING FOR AT LEAST A WEEK!
SKWISH
PLOP

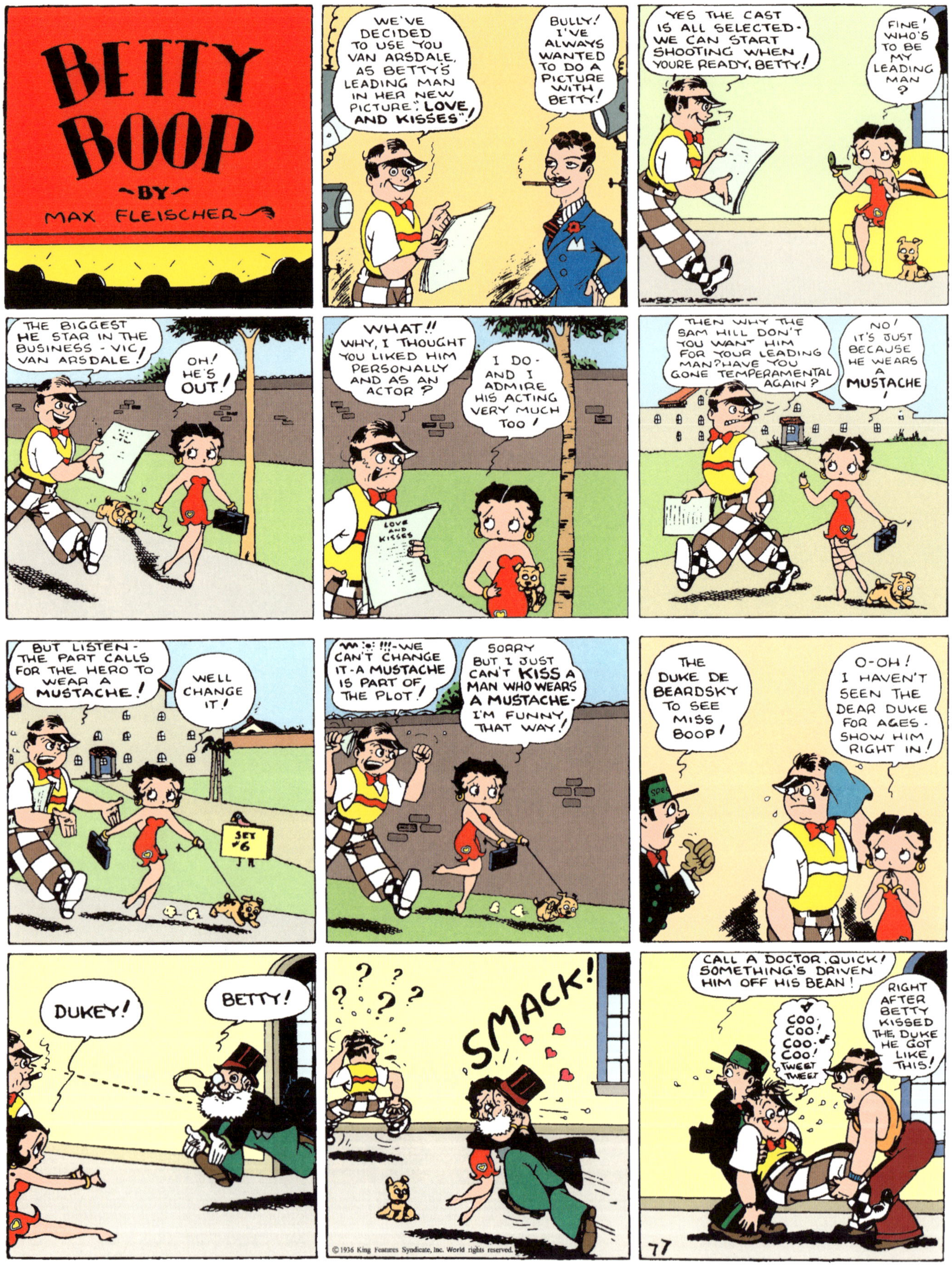
BETTY BOOP
BY
MAX FLEISCHER
WE'VE DECIDED TO USE YOU VAN ARSDALE, AS BETTY'S LEADING MAN IN HER NEW PICTURE, "LOVE AND KISSES"!
BULLY! I'VE ALWAYS WANTED TO DO A PICTURE WITH BETTY!
YES THE CAST IS ALL SELECTED - WE CAN START SHOOTING WHEN YOU'RE READY, BETTY!
FINE! WHO'S TO BE MY LEADING MAN?
THE BIGGEST HE STAR IN THE BUSINESS - VIC VAN ARSDALE!
OH! HE'S OUT!
WHAT!! WHY, I THOUGHT YOU LIKED HIM PERSONALLY AND AS AN ACTOR?
I DO - AND I ADMIRE HIS ACTING VERY MUCH TOO!
LOVE AND KISSES
THEN WHY THE SAM HILL DON'T YOU WANT HIM FOR YOUR LEADING MAN? HAVE YOU GONE TEMPERAMENTAL AGAIN?
NO! IT'S JUST BECAUSE HE WEARS A MUSTACHE!
BUT LISTEN - THE PART CALLS FOR THE HERO TO WEAR A MUSTACHE!
WELL CHANGE IT!
SET #6
!!!-WE CAN'T CHANGE IT - A MUSTACHE IS PART OF THE PLOT!
SORRY BUT I JUST CAN'T KISS A MAN WHO WEARS A MUSTACHE - I'M FUNNY THAT WAY!
THE DUKE DE BEARDSKY TO SEE MISS BOOP!
O-OH! I HAVEN'T SEEN THE DEAR DUKE FOR AGES - SHOW HIM RIGHT IN!
DUKEY!
BETTY!
SMACK!
© 1936 King Features Syndicate, Inc. World rights reserved.
CALL A DOCTOR, QUICK! SOMETHING'S DRIVEN HIM OFF HIS BEAN!
COO-COO! COO-COO! TWEET TWEET
RIGHT AFTER BETTY KISSED THE DUKE HE GOT LIKE THIS!
77

BETTY BOOP
BY
MAX FLEISCHER
IT'S A PERFECT PART FOR "BUBBY"-THIS LEAD IN THE "OLD SWIMMIN' HOLE" AND YOU DIRECT IT!
WE CAN USE HIS PALS FOR THE OTHER PARTS!
ALL YOU HAVE TO DO IS JUST THE THINGS YOU DO WHEN YOU GO SWIMMING!
SWELL! I'LL GET MY GANG!
ALL SET-WHERE'LL WE LEAVE OUR CLOTHES!
OH, YOU MUST WEAR BATHING-SUITS-YOU'LL FIND THEM IN THERE!
YEAH! THIS AIN'T A NUDIST FILM!
NOW FIRST WE MUST REHEARSE THE SCENE TILL IT'S PERFECT!
I CAN DO MY TRICK DIVE WITHOUT A REHEARSEL!
OKEY DOKE!
GEE! MOVIE ACTORS-OBOY!
NOW YOU DO YOUR DIVE, BUBBY!
GANGWAY! GANGWAY!
HIT IT HARD, BUBBY!
DO YOUR BEST, BUBBY-REMEMBER YOU'RE THE STAR OF THE PICTURE!
MARVELOUS WOW! WHAT A TRICK!
I NEVER KNEW HE WAS SO GOOD!
BAM
WOT TH--
HA-HA! TRY LANDING IN THE WATER THE NEXT TIME!
HA-HA-HA-HA-HA-HA-HA-HA-
IT WAS FUNNY, BUT--
HA-HA! WRITE THAT STUNT INTO THE SCRIPT-IT'LL MAKE THE PICTURE!
THAT STUNT WOULD MAKE ANY PICTURE!
THE OLD SWIMMIN HOLE
BUT, BUBBY, DEAR, YOU MUST DO IT OVER AGAIN-THAT WAS ONLY THE REHEARSEL!
OH, YEAH? WELL, THAT'S JUST TOO BAD!
ICE BOX
© 1935, King Features Syndicate, Inc., Great Britain rights reserved.
LUCKY BUCKS PLAY MONEY 2
LUCKY BUCKS PLAY MONEY 2
LUCKY BUCKS PLAY MONEY 2

BETTY BOOP
BY MAX FLEISCHER
OKAY-BETTY, NOW DIVE INTO THE RIVER!
BUT LISTEN----
SORRY, BETTY-BUT WE MUST DO A RETAKE ON THAT STUNT-YOU GOT OUT OF FOCUS!
CUT! NO, NO, THAT WON'T DO!
YOU DIDN'T LOOK SCARED ENOUGH WE'VE GOT TO RETAKE IT!
I-I W-WAS TOO FRIGHTENED TO LOOK S-SCARED!
CAMERA!!--- CUT! NO DICE!
WHAT!! ANOTHER RETAKE?
YEAH! AND BEFORE THE JUNGLE SCENE-YOU DIDN'T STAY ON LONG ENOUGH!
CAMERA! MAKE IT LOOK CLOSE, BETTY!
OW! THEY JUST MISSED ME-IT SURE WAS A CLOSE ONE!
I KNOW-BUT NOT CLOSE ENOUGH-WE MUST RETAKE THE SHOT!
NOW THE NEXT SHOT IS A CLOSE-UP KISS WITH VAN TWINKLE!
O-OH! -ER- ONLY ONE?
SMACK!
SWELL! GREAT! PERFECT! OKAY, CUT!
WHAT! NO RETAKE?
7-20
© 1935, King Features Syndicate, Inc., Great Britain rights reserved

BETTY BOOP
BY
MAX FLEISCHER
THAT'S ALL ON THIS TRIP, MISS BOOP!
WHAT! NO FAN MAIL?
U.S.M.
LOOK AT THE SWELL NOTICES THE OUT OF TOWN PAPERS GIVE YOUR NEW PICTURE, BETTY!
YEAH, BUT THERE'S NO FAN REACTION- SNIFF!
TALK ABOUT THE "FORGOTTEN MAN"- MY PUBLIC MUST HAVE WRITER'S CRAMPS - ALL I GOT WAS A FLOCK OF BILLS!
THERE, THERE. PULL YOURSELF TOGETHER - NO NEWS IS GOOD NEWS - YOU KNOW!
A CONVENTION - OR ARE THEY MOVING THE POST OFFICE?
MUST BE A GANG OF EXTRAS FOR THE OTHER SET!
MAIL FOR MISS BETTY BOOP!
U.S.M.
OFCOURSE, THEY'RE ALL FAN MAIL!
WELL, I KNOW THEY CAN'T BE BILLS - 'CAUSE I DON'T OWE THAT MANY PLACES!
THERE'S A COUPLE O' MORE TRUCK-LOADS OUTSIDE!
U.S.M.
BETTY BOOP
SHE SHOULD BE HAPPY NOW! WOW! WHAT A PILE OF LETTERS - THEY BREAK ALL RECORDS!
BOO-HOO! BOO-HOO!
WHAT THA~??
WHY, YOU OUGHT TO BE JUMPING WITH JOY-GETTING ALL THAT FAN MAIL!
SNIFF! FAN MAIL - ME EYE-
THEY'RE "CHAIN LETTERS" AND EACH ONE ASKS ME TO SEND A DOLLAR!
LUCKY BUCKS PLAY MONEY 2 BUCK
LUCKY BUCKS PLAY MONEY 2 BUCK
LUCKY BUCKS PLAY MONEY 2 BUCK

BETTY BOOP
BY MAX FLEISCHER
AND NOT ONLY THAT - BUT OTHER STARS ARE IN THE PAPERS AS REGULAR AS THE WEATHER REPORT!
WAIT! I'LL PUT THE **ZING** ON THAT PUBLICITY OUTFIT, PRONTO!
YEAH! WHAT HAS BETTY GOT TO DO TO GET INTO THE PAPERS - COMMIT "**HARA KIRI**" OR SOMETHING?
I'M JUST WORKING ON A COLOSSAL STUNT FOR BETTY RIGHT NOW - LOOK!
THE MIRROR
STAR ADOPTS BABY
IT'S STUPENDOUS! GET IT? IT'LL MAKE YOUR NAME A HOUSE-HOLD WORD - HOP OVER TO THE ORPHANAGE AND PICK OUT A **QUINTET** OF KIDDIES!
ADOPT A QUINTET OF BABES?
THE MIRROR
STAR ADOPTS TWINS
P.D.Q. STAR ADOPTS BABY
BETA DARBO ADOPTS BABY
PICK OUT THE **FIVE CUTEST** IN THE PLACE AND I'LL USE 'EM IN YOUR NEXT PICTURE!
LEAVE IT TO ME - I JUST ADORE KIDDIES!
A **QUINTET**! MAYBE THEY'LL BECOME AS FAMOUS AS THE "**DIONNE QUINTUPLETS**"!
YOU WISH TO ADOPT **FIVE**? WELL, TAKE YOUR PICK, MISS BOOP!
KITCHEE-KITCHEE! AREN'T THEY THE CUTEST DEARS?
NOW HERE IN WARD SIX YOU HAVE EVERY TYPE!
OH! THEY'RE ALL SUCH LIL' DARLINGS - IT'S HARD TO MAKE A SELECTION!
YOU MIGHT TRY - "EENY, MEENY, MINEY, MOO"!
?
GA-GOO-GA-
GA-GA-
GOO-
GA-
GOO-
THEY'RE ALL SO CUTE I JUST COULDN'T PICK OUT THE **FIVE CUTEST** - SO I ADOPTED THE WHOLE **ORPHANAGE**!
© 1935, King Features Syndicate, Inc., Great Britain rights reserved.
LUCKY BUCKS
PLAY MONEY
2
LUCKY BUCKS
PLAY MONEY
2
LUCKY BUCKS
PLAY MONEY
2

BETTY BOOP
BY MAX FLEISCHER
THE PAPERS ARE SURE PLAYING UP MY ADOPTION OF THE "QUINTET" OF KIDDIES—WOW! WHAT PUBLICITY!!
THE DAILY
BETTY BOOP ADOPTS FIVE BABIES!
WHAT! YOU WANT ALL FIVE KIDDIES DOWN FOR A SCREEN TEST?
NOW SCRUB YOURSELVES GOOD WHILE I GET YOUR CLEAN CLOTHES!
—AND IF YOUR TEST IS OKAY YOU GET PARTS IN MY PICTURE—WHY, YOU'LL BE AS FAMOUS AS THE "DIONNE QUINTUPLETS"!
"YOU MAY SHOOT WHEN READY, GRIDLEY"!
SWELL! THE SOUND-TRACKS AND CAMERAS ARE ALL READY!
THEY'RE SO INTERESTED IN THE LIGHTS AND EVERYTHING!
NO, NO! LOOK THIS WAY—HEY! LOOK AT THE CAMERA AND SMILE!
LOOK, CHILDREN! PS-ST! SEE THE LITTLE BIRDIE!
NO SOAP! HEY! 'S NO USE! YOU SIT ON THE CAMERA. MAYBE THAT WILL MAKE 'EM LOOK!
GET DOWN—WE'VE GOT TO TRY SOMETHING ELSE—WHERE'S THE HEAD SETS?
LOOK! THE DARLINGS WANT TO PLAY!
OH-OH! THIS WILL NEVER DO!
TAKE 'EM OFF! I'VE GOT A SCHEME TO ATTRACT THEIR ATTENTION TOWARD THE CAMERA!
BA-WA-BA-WA-
BANG!
OKAY! CAMERA!
WELL, I'LL BE—
© 1935, King Features Syndicate, Inc. Great Britain rights reserved
LUCKY BUCKS PLAY MONEY 2
LUCKY BUCKS PLAY MONEY 2
LUCKY BUCKS PLAY MONEY 2

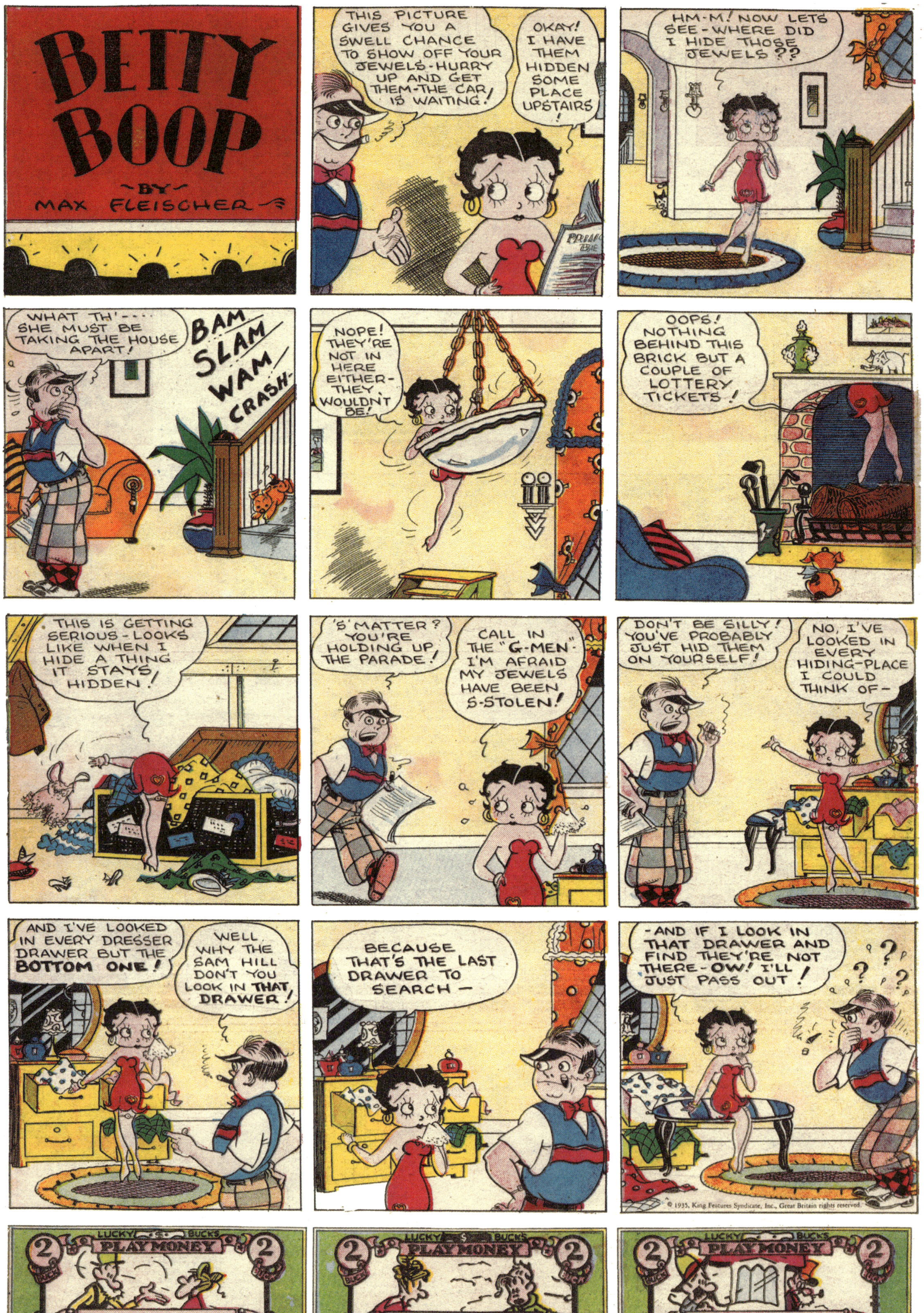
BETTY BOOP
BY
MAX FLEISCHER
THIS PICTURE GIVES YOU A SWELL CHANCE TO SHOW OFF YOUR JEWELS-HURRY UP AND GET THEM-THE CAR IS WAITING!
OKAY! I HAVE THEM HIDDEN SOME PLACE UPSTAIRS!
HM-M! NOW LETS SEE-WHERE DID I HIDE THOSE JEWELS??
WHAT TH'--- SHE MUST BE TAKING THE HOUSE APART!
BAM
SLAM
WAM
CRASH
NOPE! THEY'RE NOT IN HERE EITHER-THEY WOULDN'T BE!
OOPS! NOTHING BEHIND THIS BRICK BUT A COUPLE OF LOTTERY TICKETS!
THIS IS GETTING SERIOUS-LOOKS LIKE WHEN I HIDE A THING IT STAYS HIDDEN!
'S MATTER? YOU'RE HOLDING UP THE PARADE!
CALL IN THE "G-MEN" I'M AFRAID MY JEWELS HAVE BEEN S-STOLEN!
DON'T BE SILLY! YOU'VE PROBABLY JUST HID THEM ON YOURSELF!
NO, I'VE LOOKED IN EVERY HIDING-PLACE I COULD THINK OF-
AND I'VE LOOKED IN EVERY DRESSER DRAWER BUT THE BOTTOM ONE!
WELL WHY THE SAM HILL DON'T YOU LOOK IN THAT DRAWER!
BECAUSE THAT'S THE LAST DRAWER TO SEARCH-
-AND IF I LOOK IN THAT DRAWER AND FIND THEY'RE NOT THERE-OW! I'LL JUST PASS OUT!
© 1935, King Features Syndicate, Inc., Great Britain rights reserved.
LUCKY BUCKS
PLAY MONEY
2
LUCKY BUCKS
PLAY MONEY
2
LUCKY BUCKS
PLAY MONEY
2

BETTY BOOP
BY MAX FLEISCHER
-AND NOT ONLY THAT, BUT IT'S AN IMPORTED, EXCLUSIVE MODEL OF DARING DESIGN-THE LAST WORD IN ULTRA-FASHIONS!
IT MUST BE A GORGEOUS GOWN-I'LL TAKE SPECIAL CARE OF IT, MISS BOOP!
"CLOTHES MAY NOT MAKE THE MAN"-BUT A WOMAN, OH, BOY! THIS NEW CREATION WILL MAKE ME A SENSATION IN MY NEXT PICTURE!
?
CONGRATULATE US, BETTY-WE'VE SECURED THE MOVIE RIGHTS TO "THE GIRL IN GREEN"!
"THE GIRL IN GREEN"
THE GIRL IN GREEN?
YES-WE OUT-BID ALL COMPETITORS AND IT COST US PLENTY-WE'RE DOING IT IN COLOR-A SUPER COLOR SPECIAL!
-ER-CAN'T YOU CHANGE IT TO "THE GIRL IN BLUE"?
DON'T BE SILLY-THE PLOT IS BUILT AROUND A GREEN GOWN-IT'S THE THEME OF THE PICTURE AND-
NO USE ARGUING-YOU'LL JUST HAVE TO CHANGE IT TO BLUE-THAT'S FINAL!
OW! AFTER ALL THE EXPENSE AND EVERYTHING, NOW YOU'RE GOING TEMPERAMENTAL ON US!
-AND SHE INSISTS ON HAVING IT CHANGED TO "THE GIRL IN BLUE" OR NO DICE!
EGAD! HAS SHE GONE WACKY?
BUT HER CONTRACT! GET AN INJUNCTION-SUE!
"WHAT'S THIS-YOU GOT THE BLUES OR SUMPIN'?
THE AIR WILL BE BLUE IF YOU REFUSE TO PLAY "THE GIRL IN GREEN"!
IT'S LIKE ASKING A LEOPARD TO CHANGE HIS SPOTS!
DON'T YOU UNDERSTAND? YOU MUST WEAR A GREEN GOWN-THAT'S THE PLOT!
SO Y'WON'T TALK-ER-I MEAN Y'WON'T PLAY THE PART AS IS, HUH?
LISTEN-HAVE YOU ANY SANE REASON FOR WANTING IT CHANGED FROM "THE GIRL IN GREEN" TO "THE GIRL IN BLUE"?
I'LL SAY I HAVE!
I JUST BOUGHT THE MOST GORGEOUS, MOST STUNNING-EXQUISITE BLUE GOWN YOU EVER SAW!
© 1935, King Features Syndicate, Inc., Great Britain rights reserved.
2 BUCK LUCKY BUCKS PLAYMONEY 2 BUCK
2 BUCK LUCKY BUCKS PLAYMONEY 2 BUCK
2 BUCK LUCKY BUCKS PLAYMONEY 2 BUCK

BETTY BOOP
-BY-
MAX FLEISCHER
PUBLICITY? TAKE A GANDER AT THAT- A FULL PAGE IN EVERY PAPER IN THE COUNTRY!
WHAT! NO MAGAZINES?
DAILY BLAH
DON'T MISS- BETTY BOOP
-IN- BEACHED!
COME ON- YOU AIN'T SEEN NOTHIN' YET- I'LL SHOW YOU BOOSTIN' THAT IS BOOSTIN'!
YES, SIR- YOU'RE THE TOPS - YOU TOP EVERY BUILDING IN EVERY TOWN!
LOOKIE! A CHAIN BILL-BOARD "PLUG" FROM COAST TO COAST!
HOPE NOBODY BREAKS IT!
BETTY BOOP!
-IN- BEACHED!!
STUPENDOUS! COLOSSAL!
Betty Boop
TALK ABOUT BOOSTING YOU TO THE SKIES- HOW'S ABOUT THAT?
BOOP
-IN- BEACHED!
SEE! A BANNER ACROSS EVERY MAIN STREET IN THE COUNTRY!
EVEN BOOSTING YOU IN ALL THE PARADES AND--
COLOSSAL
STUPENDOUS
"THE PARADE OF THE WOODEN SOLDIERS" TOO?
NO, SIR- BETTY- WE DIDN'T OVER-LOOK A PLACE TO GIVE YOU A BOOST!
OH, YEAH?
HOW ABOUT MY SALARY?
LUCKY BUCKS
PLAY MONEY

BETTY BOOP
BY
MAX FLEISCHER
FINE! NOW LOOK AT THE CAMERA!
YES, WE'LL DO THAT SHOT ONCE MORE JUST TO MAKE SURE!
WHAT DO YOU MEAN- WE?
I HOPE THAT'S THE LAST OF THE HIGH-DIVING SHOTS!
RIGHT! WE GO OUT TO THE DESERT ON LOCATION FOR THE NEXT SCENES-WE'LL BE GONE FOR TWO WEEKS!
OH, SWELL! IT'LL BE SUCH FUN ROUGHING IT!
YEAH! JUST TAKE ALONG THINGS THAT YOU ABSOLUTELY NEED!
WELL, I MUST TAKE MY MAID!
MAID? OH, ALLRIGHT!
-AND I JUST COULDN'T GET ALONG WITHOUT MY HAIR-DRESSER!
BUT WE'RE GOING TO ROUGH IT- LIVE IN TENTS 'N' EVERYTHIN'!
WHY, I'D BE LOST WITH-OUT MY CHAUFFEUR AND CARS!
OH, ALLRIGHT- TAKE 'EM ALONG!
AND BEING ON A SPECIAL DIET- I MUST TAKE ALONG MY OWN COOK!
WHAT TH'-- NOW LISTEN, BETTY--
BUT I MUST TAKE MY PETS ALONG, TOO- I COULDN'T BEAR BEING AWAY FROM THEM TWO WEEKS!
OKAY! I GUESS A COUPLE OF PETS WON'T MAKE MUCH DIFFERENCE!
ALL SET! I'M SENDING MY PET PONY BY PLANE!
OW! PETS!! LOOKS LIKE YOU ROBBED THE ZOO!
STUDIO NO. 35
9-14

BETTY BOOP
BY MAX FLEISCHER
Y'SAY, THE TESTS ARE OKAY AND I GET THE LEADING PART? YIP-PEE!!
AT LAST I'M CAST FOR A PART WHERE I CAN SHOW 'EM THAT I CAN WEAR SWELL GOWNS!
NO PARKIN
STOP
YES-AND IN THE BIG SCENE YOU WEAR THE LATEST CREATION OF THE FAMOUS "DE STILE"- GO IN AND SEE IF IT FITS YOU!
OBOY! I'LL HAVE A FIT IF IT DOESN'T FIT ME!
IT'S GORGEOUS! -ER- BUT THE TRAIN FEELS LIKE A FREIGHT TRAIN- O-OW! IT'S SO HEAVY!
OH! WE HAVE A COUPLE OF KIDS TO CARRY YOUR TRAIN!
NOW REHEARSE WALKING!
I STILL CAN HARDLY WALK IN IT!
I'M SORRY- BUT YOU'LL HAVE TO CHANGE THE SCRIPT TO JUST STANDING- WALKING IN THIS GOWN IS OUT!
ALLRIGHT! I GUESS THE TRAIN IS TOO HEAVY FOR WALKING!
LOOK! WHAT ARE ALL THE GIRLS RUNNING FOR?
"VAN HART"-THE NEW LEADING MAN, HAS JUST ARRIVED!
OH! HERE HE COMES!
LOOK! EVEN THE SCRUB-WOMEN ARE RUSHING TO SEE HIM -YOU'RE THE ONLY FEMALE ON THE LOT WITH ANY SENSE!
ISN'T HE JUST STUNNING? A-AH!
O-OH! THEM EYES- THEM LIPS THEM---
WOT D'YE MEAN, YOU CAN'T WALK IN IT?
YEAH? BUT WHO SAID ANYTHING ABOUT RUNNING? GANGWAY!!
OUCH! STOP THAT !!* CROWDING!
O-OH! AIN'T HE GRAND? YOO-HOO!
© 1935, King Features Syndicate, Inc., Great Britain rights reserved.
IT'S VERY SWEET OF YOU, MISS BOOP, TO GO TO ALL THE TROUBLE TO GREET ME IN COSTUME!
AW! YOU'RE ONLY TRYING TO BE NICE TO ME!
LUCKY BUCKS PLAY MONEY 2
LUCKY BUCKS PLAY MONEY 2
LUCKY BUCKS PLAY MONEY 2

BETTY BOOP
BY MAX FLEISCHER
I'VE GOT PICTURES OF ALL THE BIG STARS FOR YOU TO PICK OUT A LEADING MAN FOR YOUR NEXT OPUS!
THAT'S A SWELL IDEA!
WELL, HOW'S ABOUT "JOE FABLE"-HOLLYWOOD'S GIFT TO WOMEN-STAR ACTOR AND---
NO! HE'S OUT, TOO!
AH! "CURLY CUE," THE ANSWER TO A MAIDEN'S PRAYER AND A GREAT ACTOR!
HM-M! NO DICE - HE'D CRAMP MY STYLE!
YES, SIR-A QUARTET HARD TO BEAT-ALL PERSONALITY BOYS-YOU CAN'T MISS ON EITHER OF 'EM!
POOEY! THEY LOOK LIKE A LOT OF SISSIES!
BUT LISTEN-THEY'RE ALL THE BIGGEST STARS IN THE BUSINESS. WHY---
NO SOAP! THEY JUST WON'T DO!
MAYBE YOU'RE RIGHT THEY MAY LOOK BETTER IN THE FLESH THEY CAN'T LOOK ANY WORSE!
COME ON-I HAVE 'EM ALL LINED UP IN THE "PROP" ROOM!
LOOK 'EM OVER-EVERY TYPE-ALL STARS! YOU CAN'T GO WRONG ON ANY OF 'EM-TAKE YOUR PICK, BETTY!
?
PROP. ROOM
YOU PICK-WHICH?
THAT ONE-ON THE RIGHT-BY THE PLANT!
??????
PROP. ROOM
'AT'S WOT I SAID-THAT'S A "PROP" DUMMY!
WELL, AT THAT-HE'S THE LIVEST-LOOKING ONE OF THE BUNCH!
LUCKY BUCKS
2 PLAY MONEY 2
BUCK BUCK

BETTY BOOP
BY MAX FLEISCHER
YOUR BROTHER BOBBY'S TESTS ARE OKAY - NOW WE'RE GOING TO GIVE HIM A REAL BUILD-UP!
O-OH! HOW THRILLING!
THE PUBLICITY DEPARTMENT HAS ARRANGED WITH A BIG WRITER TO INTERVIEW HIM!
INTERVIEW! SUPPOSE HE WON'T TALK?
MISS DE SKRIBBLE WILL BE OUT TO SEE THE KID - NOW TELL HER PLENTY - YOU KNOW - THE OLD HOKUM!
RIGHTO! IF I TOLD HER THE REAL TRUTH ABOUT THAT KID - SHE'D CALL A COP!
WOW! WHAT A SWELL BREAK FOR BUBBY - IT'LL MAKE HIM FAMOUS!
THERE SHE IS NOW - HEY! DON'T YOU DARE RUN AWAY!
R-R-ING
-AND NOW TELL ME - HAS HE ANY IDIOSYNCRASIES?
OH! MY, NO! HE'S NEVER HAD THOSE THINGS - WHY, HE'S NEVER HAD THE MEASLES EITHER!
HERE ARE SOME MORE PICTURES OF HIM! THAT'S HIM IN THE MIDDLE!
I'M SO ANXIOUS TO SEE HIM - HE'S JUST ADORABLE - I COULD KISS HIM TO PIECES!
HE WAS HERE A MOMENT AGO! YOO-HOO! WHERE ARE YOU, BOBBY!
KISS ME TO PIECES, HUH?
COME DOWN HERE AND MEET "MISS DE SKRIBBLE" D'YE HEAR?
I HEAR YOU UP THERE - COME DOWN HERE THIS MINUTE!
AWRI' AWRI'! I'LL BE READY IN A JIFFY!
King Features Syndicate, Inc., Great Britain rights reserved.
HOW D'YE DO MISS DE SKRIBBLE?
LUCKY BUCKS
PLAY MONEY
2 BUCK
LUCKY BUCKS
PLAY MONEY
2 BUCK
LUCKY BUCKS
PLAY MONEY
2 BUCK

BETTY BOOP
BY
MAX FLEISCHER
WELL, IF YOU'VE TAKEN OFF ENOUGH POUNDAGE YOU GET THE PART, BETTY!
I MUSTA LOST PLENTY. I'VE BEEN ON THAT STRICT DIET ALL WEEK!
OW! WHY, YOU AIN'T LOST A POUND, BUT GAINED A COUPLE-HOW COME?
GUESS I'M ONE OF THOSE POOR LOSERS YOU HEAR ABOUT!
THAT SPECIAL DIET IS SUPPOSED TO BE INFALLIBLE-ARE YOU SURE YOU ATE NOTHING BUT WHAT THE DIET CALLED FOR?
YES-THAT IS, OUTSIDE OF MY REGULAR MEALS!
THAT'S WHAT I SAID-COME ON-I'M GONNA TAKE CHARGE OF YOUR REDUCING, PERSONALLY!
YOU'RE GOING TO HAVE ME DO ROAD WORK?
YES, THAT'S A SURE WAY OF TAKIN' OFF WEIGHT-IF YOU GET TIRED WALKIN' YOU CAN RUN!
WHAT D'YE MEAN IT WAS A ONE-WAY RIDE?
"YOU'RE GOIN' TO TOWN"-KID-AND IT'S JUST A TEN-MILE JAUNT!
HEY! NOT SO FAST-I'M NO "OMAHA"!
TO CITY 10 MILES
THIS IS ONE TIME THAT YOU WALK BACK FROM A RIDE!
PF-F-F-F! YOU OLD MEANY!
TO CITY 10 MILES
I'LL BE SEEIN' YOU AT THE STUDIO-TA-TA!
HM-M! NOT BACK YET? FORCIN' BETTY TO DO A TEN-MILE WALK IS RATHER A DRASTIC METHOD OF REDUCIN', BUT-
THE POOR KID-I'LL DRIVE BACK AND GET HER-IT'S BREAKIN' MY HEART JUST THINKIN' OF HER AWAY OUT THERE WALKIN' BACK HOME!
WELL, I'LL BE--
TO CITY 10 MILES
LUCKY BUCKS PLAY MONEY 2
LUCKY BUCKS PLAY MONEY 2
LUCKY BUCKS PLAY MONEY 2

BETTY BOOP
BY
MAX FLEISCHER
YES, BETTY, YOUR NEXT PICTURE IS "CLEOPATRA"!
O-OH! AT LAST I AM TO PLAY A COSTUME PICTURE!
YEAH! TAKE A GANDER AT THE EXOTIC COSTUMES YOU'RE TO WEAR!
QUICK! LET ME SEE THEM!
WHAT D'YE MEAN - IS IT A NUDIST OPUS OR A "STRIP ACT"?
THAT'S WHAT I SAID - WHERE ARE THE FANS OR THE BUBBLE BALLOONS THAT GO WITH 'EM?
BUT LISTEN - THE PART OF "CLEOPATRA" CALLS FOR COSTUMES LIKE THOSE --
-AND NOT ONLY THAT- BUT WHAT WOULD MY PUBLIC THINK IF I APPEARED IN SUCH SCANT ATTIRE?
WELL, YOU CAN'T PLAY THE PART OF "CLEOPATRA" IN FORMAL CLOTHES!
AND I'M NOT GOING TO PLAY IT IN THAT DARING MAKEUP EITHER!
THERE IS NO HAPPY MEDIUM - THE COSTUMES ARE HISTORICALLY CORRECT!
WELL, HERE'S ONE TIME HISTORY DOESN'T REPEAT - NOT ON ME!
MODESTY IS A BEAUTIFUL VIRTUE - BUT ART ---
WHY, WE'VE SPENT A FORTUNE ON THOSE COSTUMES ---
YOU SHOULD HAVE GOTTEN MORE FOR YOUR MONEY!
BUT LISTEN, BETTY ---
I'M SORRY, BUT MODESTY FORBIDS ME TO DISPLAY MY CHARMS IN SUCH A BRAZEN MANNER!
PHEW! I'VE GOT TO GO TO THE BEACH TO COOL OFF - STILL I CAN'T BLAME BETTY - HER MODESTY IS REFRESHING!
OH! SO DARING - BUT SO STUNNING!
WELL, I'LL BE ---
THOSE NEW BATHING SUITS MAKE EVE LOOK OVER-DRESSED!
© 1935, King Features Syndicate, Inc., Great Britain rights reserved.
LUCKY BUCKS PLAY MONEY 2
LUCKY BUCKS PLAY MONEY 2
LUCKY BUCKS PLAY MONEY 2

BETTY BOOP
BY MAX FLEISCHER
GET PACKED UP—WE'RE MAKING THE NEXT SHOTS ON THE INDIAN RESERVATION OF THE SCHNOZZLE TRIBE!
OH! THAT INDIAN LOVE SCENE, HUH?
HERE WE ARE—THEY'VE SET UP THE STUDIO RIGHT SIDE OF THE INDIAN VILLAGE—THAT'LL HELP!
YES, CHIEF, WE'RE ALL READY TO SHOOT THE INDIAN LOVE SCENE. WHERE'S THE INDIAN?
WHY-ER-- THAT'S THE CATCH—WE HAVEN'T GOT ONE YET!
WHY, THAT OUGHT TO BE EASY!
SCENE IV
THE SCRIPT CALLS FOR AN INDIAN BRAVE TO KISS YOU—I'M AFRAID WE'RE GOING TO HAVE TROUBLE TO GET ONE!
WHAT D'YE MEAN-TROUBLE?
INDIANS DON'T MAKE LOVE LIKE US—WE'VE GOT TO FIND A MODERN ONE WITH NO SCRUPLES ABOUT KISSING—Y'SEE THEY RUB NOSES OR---
OH! THAT'S WHY THEY HAVE SUCH BIG SCHNOZZLES
MAYBE THE BIG CHIEF WILL ORDER ONE TO ACT THE PART IF YOU ASK HIM!
I'LL STEP RIGHT OVER TO HIM AND WATCH ME GET MY MAN!
HM-M! SHE'S A LONG TIME—GUESS THE POOR KID IS HAVING TROUBLE TO GET AN INDIAN TO PLAY THE LOVE SCENE!
BACK AT LAST, HUH? HOW'D YOU MAKE OUT?
OH, SWELL! I THINK YOU HAVE YOUR INDIAN CUSTOMS ALL WRONG!
ME ME! UGH! ME. OR ELSE— ME UGH ME! ME ME!
THERE'S THE WHOLE TRIBE—CHIEF AND ALL, TO SELECT ONE FROM!
-ER-SELECT ONE, ME EYE-
'AT'S WOT I SAID—TELL 'EM I'VE CHANGED THE SCENE TO A RACE TO THE CANADIAN BORDER!
LUCKY BUCKS PLAY MONEY 2
LUCKY BUCKS PLAY MONEY 2
LUCKY BUCKS PLAY MONEY 2

BETTY BOOP
-BY-
MAX FLEISCHER
SWELL! MARVELOUS! PERFECT CASTING -YOU LOOK JUST LIKE A HAWAIIAN PRINCESS!
AND I FEEL LIKE A NUDIST!
NOW WE WILL REHEARSE THE "HULA-HULA" DANCE -JUST DO AS MADAM WAH KIKI SHOWED YOU!
DO YOU WANT ME TO GET ARRESTED?
THIS "HULA-HULA" SEQUENCE MUST BE GOOD-IT'S THE BIG SHOT OF THE PICTURE!
DON'T YOU THINK I OUGHTA HAVE A FAN OR SUMPIN' TO GO WITH THIS COSTUME
NOW GO INTO YOUR DANCE- NO! NO! THIS AIN'T AN ADAGIO OR A TANGO- WIGGLE! SHAKE! GET GOING!
THAT'S WHAT I SAID-YOU'VE GOT TO PUT MORE HOOTCH INTO IT---
WHAT IS IT- A SPEAK-EASY SCENE?
WE'LL GO OUT ON THE "HAWAIIAN SET" MAYBE THE TROPICAL ATMOSPHERE WILL PUT YOU INTO THE MOOD!
IT'LL HAVE TO BE TROPICAL OR IT'LL PUT ME IN BED WITH PNEUMONIA
OKAY! BETTY- CAMERA! BE LOOSE- SHAKE THOSE SHOULDERS!!
THATA BABY! BEAR DOWN ON IT-YOU'RE DOING GREAT! MARVELOUS!!
WOW! WHAT WIGGLIN'- THIS SHOT WILL MAKE THE PICTURE!
© 1935, King Features Syndicate, Inc., Great Britain rights reserved.
CUT! OKAY, BETTY! WONDERFUL! I NEVER SAW SUCH SWELL "HULA-HULA" STUFF!
HULA-HULA S-STUFF, ME EYE ~
11-3
? ? ?
BRR-R-R- I WAS ONLY SHIVERING FROM THE COLD!
LUCKY BUCKS
PLAY MONEY
2
LUCKY BUCKS
PLAY MONEY
2
LUCKY BUCKS
PLAY MONEY
2

BETTY BOOP
BY
MAX FLEISCHER
WHAT! Y'SAY BUBBY'S SCREEN TEST TURNED OUT SWELL? OH! I'M SO THRILLED!
-AND YOU WON THE CONTEST FOR MAKING THE FUNNIEST FACES OVER ALL THE KIDS!
OH, YEAH? WHY, I WASN'T EVEN PLAYING!
SO YOU'RE GIVING BUBBY THE LEAD IN THE "KID KOMEDY"?
YES- THAT IS IF HE CAN DO A FEW CUTE LITTLE KID STUNTS!
OH! I'M SURE HE CAN DO ANY KID STUNT!
WELL, WE'LL TRY HIM OUT FIRST WITH STANDING ON HIS HANDS!
?
THAT OUGHT TO BE EASY FOR HIM — COME ON, BUBBY- STAND ON YOUR HANDS!
NO! THAT'S OUT!
WHY, I'VE SEEN YOU DO THAT OFTEN!
COME ON, KID- WE MUST HAVE A REHEARSAL!
NOPE! CAN'T DO IT!
SEE HOW SIMPLE IT IS- NOW YOU DO IT!
LOOKIE-LOOKIE-BUBBY!
NO DICE!
WHY, ANY KID CAN DO THAT STUNT!
OFCOURSE! THE SCRIPT CALLS FOR YOU TO STAND ON YOUR HANDS -COME ON--
NO SOAP!
DON'T BE SO STUBBORN, BUBBY!
LISTEN - WON'T YOU AT LEAST TRY TO DO IT?
NO! NO! A THOUSAND TIMES. NO!
WHAT! YOU'RE GOING TEMPERAMENTAL ON US, HUH?
GOING TEMPERA-MENTAL, ME EYE!
? ? ?
I'VE GOT A RIP IN MY PANTS!
© 1933, King Features Syndicate, Inc., Great Britain rights reserved.
LUCKY BUCKS PLAY MONEY 2 2
LUCKY BUCKS PLAY MONEY 2 2
LUCKY BUCKS PLAY MONEY 2 2

BETTY BOOP
BY MAX FLEISCHER
HO-HUM! BEING A MOVIE STAR IS NO BARGAIN! UP WITH THE SUN AFTER PRACTISING HALF OF THE NIGHT!
WELL, I OUGHT TO HAVE ALL OF THE DANCES PERFECT - I PRACTISED THEM TILL TWO A.M.!
WELL, THEY MUST BE PERFECT, BETTY - I'LL CALL A REHEARSAL!
NO, NO! YOU'RE DOING THAT SCARF DANCE LIKE A "TOREADOR" TEASING A BULL!
HOW AM I DOIN'?
NOT SO HOT! YOUR TIMING IS AWAY OFF - TRY IT AGAIN!
WHAT! NOT RIGHT YET?
NO! AND THESE DANCES MUST BE RIGHT BEFORE WE SHOOT 'EM - THEY'RE THE BIG FEATURES OF THE PICTURE!
NOW LET'S DO THAT "TRUCKIN' DOWN" NUMBER OVER JUST ONCE MORE!
TAP
TAPITY TAP
HOURS LATER
SWELL! PERFECT! YOWZAH! YOU HAVE ALL OF THE DANCES DOWN PAT AT LAST!
NOW WE CAN SHOOT ALL OF THE DANCE SCENES! CAMERAS AND SOUND TRACKS ARE ALL READY!
-AND I'M ALL READY, TOO - TO FAINT FROM EXHAUSTION!
COSTUME SCENE III
YOU'LL JUST HAVE TO POSTPONE THE SHOOTING - OH! I COULDN'T DANCE ANOTHER STEP - I'M DANCED OUT!
OKAY! WE'LL SHOOT THE BEDROOM SEQUENCES THEN - WE CAN'T LOSE ANY TIME ON THIS PICTURE
THIS SLEEPING SCENE OUGHT TO BE NATURAL - THAT'S IT - CAMERA!
WHAT A LIFE -
THEY EVEN HAVE YOU WORK WHILE YOU SLEEP - BZ-Z-Z -Z-Z-
BZ-Z
BZ-Z
BZ-Z-Z
? ? ?
© 1935, King Features Syndicate, Inc., Great Britain rights reserved.
LUCKY BUCKS PLAY MONEY 2 BUCKS
LUCKY BUCKS PLAY MONEY 2 BUCKS
LUCKY BUCKS PLAY MONEY 2 BUCKS

BETTY BOOP
BY MAX FLEISCHER
BUBBY! COME HERE AND GET DRESSED - WE'LL BE LATE FOR AUNT TILLIE'S TRAIN!
YOU CAN'T BE LATE ENOUGH FOR ME!
THE IDEA - AFTER ALL - SHE'S YOUR AUNT TILLIE!
WELL I AIN'T BRAGGIN' ABOUT IT!
YOO-HOO! BETTY! HERE'S YOUR AUNT TILLIE - UP HERE WITH MY FRIEND, CASEY, THE ENGINEER!
PODUNK SHORT LINE
P.R.R.
O-OH! IN THE ENGINE CAB!
SHE WOULD!
NOW WE'LL GO TO THE STUDIO FIRST FOR A REHEARSAL!
FINE! BUT IF IT'S ALL THE SAME TO YOU, BETTY - I'LL TAKE MINE "STRAIGHT"!
ON THIS SET WE'LL SHOOT THE BIG JUNGLE SEQUENCE!
YEAH? BIG GAME STUFF, HUH? SHOOTIN DUCKS IS MY LIMIT-
JUNGLE SET DO NOT FEED ANIMALS
PARIS, KY.
YES, I PUT HER UP ON A CAMERA PLATFORM - SO SHE WON'T BE SCARED OF THE TIGERS!
FINE! AUNT TILLIE HAS NEVER SEEN A MOVIE SHOT - I KNOW SHE'LL ENJOY IT!
ALL READY FOR THE BIG CHASE SCENE! LET THE TIGERS LOOSE - CAMERA!
I'LL LEAD THEM PAST AUNT TILLIE - IT'LL GIVE HER A BIG THRILL!
WHAT THA-? HEY! LAY OFF! GET BACK, YOU ~!!-*?
HEY! STOP!
WHAT D'YE MEAN - YOU BIG OVER-GROWN TOMCATS?
AUNT TILLIE! IT'S ONLY ACTING - JUST A MOVIE STUNT--
BAM
© 1935, King Features Syndicate, Inc., Great Britain rights reserved.
OH, YEAH? BUT DO THE TIGERS KNOW THAT?
OW
© 1935, King Features Syndicate, Inc., Great Britain rights reserved.
LUCKY BUCKS PLAYMONEY 2
LUCKY BUCKS PLAYMONEY 2
LUCKY BUCKS PLAYMONEY 2

BETTY BOOP
BY MAX FLEISCHER
OH! AUNT TILLIE, THE DIRECTOR WANTS TO KNOW IF YOU'LL TAKE A PART IN MY PICTURE!
TELL 'IM YES, YES, A THOUSAND TIMES YES!
CASTOR OIL
DON'T WORRY, BETTY, I'LL DO AS THE DIRECTOR SAYS!
THAT'S IT-JUST KEEP IN MIND THAT YOU'RE NOT AT HOME NOW AND HE'S NOT "UNCLE DINNY"!
YES, SHE'S JUST THE TYPE-SOPHISTICATED AND FULL OF APPEAL!
I'M WHAT?
I'LL SAY SHE IS!
I AIN'T HAD A DRINK TODAY-YOU INSULTIN' OLD BUZZARD-LET ME AT 'IM!
WHY, AUNT TILLIE, HE'S COMPLIMENTING YOU, LISTEN-
I THOUGHT HE WAS INCINERATIN' THAT I WAS PLASTERED!
EXPLAIN THE PART TO HER, VON!
-ER-YES-Y'SEE, YOU TAKE THE PART OF A WAITRESS -AUNT TILLIE AND YOU--
QUIET PLEASE-OKAY! CAMERA!
HOW AM I DOIN'?
WHAT TH'--- CUT!
OOPS!
OH, OH!
WAS SHE PUSHED OR DID SHE FALL? HA-HA-HA-!
WHO THREW THAT?
IS THERE A DOCTOR IN THE HOUSE?
UPSIDAISY! HA-HA! THAT FALL WAS A WOW! I'LL HAVE IT WRITTEN INTO THE SCRIPT!
IT WAS VERY FUNNY, BUT--
© 1933, King Features Syndicate, Inc., Great Britain rights reserved.
IT'LL MAKE THE PICTURE-COME ON, AUNT TILLIE, DO THAT FALL OVER AGAIN!
WHAT! WHY, YOU CRACKPOT-I'LL YU!!
YOU CAN COME OUT NOW. THE GUARDS HAVE HER UNDER CONTROL!
YOU WOULDN'T FOOL ME, WOULD YOU
LUCKY BUCKS PLAY MONEY
LUCKY BUCKS PLAY MONEY
LUCKY BUCKS PLAY MONEY

BETTY BOOP
-BY-
MAX FLEISCHER
Registered U.S. Patent Office
OH, OH! IT MUST BE A FIRE!
OUCH! STOP CROWDIN' YOU ~
ONE SIDE PUL-LEEZE!
CRACKPOTS!
WHAT'S THE PLOT-SHOOTING A MOB SCENE OR SUMPIN'?
NO! OUR NEW STAR, VAL VELOUR, IS DUE TO ARRIVE N'EVERY FEMALE IN THE STUDIO HAS GONE WACKY!
BEG PARDON!
I TAKE IT BACK-THANK GOODNESS THERE'S ONE IN THE STUDIO WITH SOME SENSE!
I SHOULD RUSH ANY NEW STAR, WHY, LISTEN--
I ADMIRE YOU FOR IT, BETTY-WELL, I'VE GOT TO GO MEET HIM!
THE IDEA! WHY, I WOULDN'T CROSS THE STREET TO SEE THE BIGGEST STAR IN THE BUSINESS AND NOT ONLY THAT, BUT--
HM-M! AT THAT, IF HE'S HALF AS HANDSOME AS HIS PICTURE-HE'S SOME HEART-THROBBER
Val Velour
I WONDER IF HE IS THAT GOOD-LOOKING~ -ER--????
THAT'S WHAT I SAID-BRING THE TELESCOPE UP WITH YOU!
LOOKIE! LOOKIE! SEE STARS 5¢ A LOOK
PS-ST! YOU'RE POINTIN' IT THE WRONG WAY-THE BIG STARS ARE UP---
OH, YEAH? WELL, I'M LOOKING RIGHT AT THE BIGGEST STAR IN THE WHOLE UNIVERSE!
LOOKIE! LOOKIE! SEE STARS 5¢ A LOOK!
HEY!
GANGWAY! GANGWAY!
© 1935, King Features Syndicate, Inc., Great Britain rights reserved.
YOO-HOO!
STAND BACK!
WOT THA-IT'S BETTY!
LUCKY BUCKS PLAY MONEY 2
LUCKY BUCKS PLAY MONEY 2
LUCKY BUCKS PLAY MONEY 2

BETTY BOOP
BY
MAX FLEISCHER
-AND WE'RE SHOOTING YOUR SCENES WITH VAN TWINKLE TOMORROW-SO GET DOWN EARLY FOR A REHEARSAL!
I'LL REHEARSE THEM TONIGHT TO MAKE SURE!
YES, VAN, YOU MUST COME OVER--
WELL, Y'CAN'T HATE ME FOR TRYIN'-C'MERE, Y'LIL IMP!
OH, "AUNT TILLIE"-CAN'T YOU DO SOMETHING TO KEEP "BUBBY" QUIET?
DON'T WORRY, I'LL KEEP HIM IN BED IF I HAVE TO SIT ON HIM TO DO IT!
DO THAT-'CAUSE THESE SCENES ARE VERY IMPORTANT AND WE MUSTN'T BE BOTHERED!
-ER-WE'LL GO OVER THE LOVE SCENE FIRST--
OH! YOU MEAN WHERE I KISS YOU GOOD-BYE?
?
SMACK!
YES, BETTY, I THOUGHT THAT WAS VERY GOOD!
YES-ER-BUT YOU KNOW PRACTICE MAKES PERFECT!
?
SMACK!
DON'T YOU THINK WE COULD PUT A LITTLE MORE FERVOR-ER-YOU KNOW IT'S THE BIG SHOT OF THE PICTURE!
RIGHTO! WE MUST GET PLENTY OF FERVOR INTO IT!
WAIT! LET ME SHOW YOU HOW TO PUT THAT FERVOR STUFF INTO IT!
?
AUNT TILLIE!!!
IS THAT NICE? STOP!! BREAK!!
SMACK! SMACK! SMACK! SMACK SMACK
YES, DOCTOR-PLEASE COME RIGHT OVER!
FAINTIN'-THE BIG SISSY!
TO TOWN
© 1935, King Features Syndicate, Inc., Great Britain rights reserved.
LUCKY BUCKS
PLAY MONEY
2

BETTY BOOP
BY MAX. FLEISCHER
Registered U. S. Patent Office
BRING SISTER A GLASS OF WATER, BUBBY, PLEASE!
WITH PLEASURE, SIS - AND WITH ALACRITY!
THANKS, BUBBY!
DON'T MENTION IT-ANYTHING ELSE YOU WANT JUST CALL FOR IT!
YES, BUT YOU MUST ADMIT HE'S BEEN A PERFECT DEAR ALL DAY!
-AND LOOK, AUNT TILLIE - HE'S TAKING HIS BATH WITHOUT BEING TOLD!
I STILL SAY THERE'S A METHOD IN HIS MADNESS!
-ER-SIS- CAN I HAVE A DOLLAR FOR A NEW FOOTBALL?
WHAT? DON'T BE SILLY-THE LAST TIME YOU KICKED IT THROUGH THE GROCER'S WINDOW
BESIDES, THAT GAME IS TOO ROUGH FOR YOU - AUNT TILLIE WILL TAKE YOU TO THE ZOO!
AW! WHY DON'T YOU BEHAVE?
HE'S BEEN SITTING THERE THAT WAY FOR AN HOUR!
MEET MY FOOTBALL TEAM, SIS - THEY ALL WANT YOUR AUTOGRAPH!
OFCOURSE, I'LL GIVE THEM MY AUTOGRAPH - I FEEL VERY FLATTERED!
HM-M! THERE'S A CATCH IN IT SOMEWHERE!
THEY DO ACT A LITTLE OVER-JOYED!
YEA, BO! LE'S GO!!
WOW! THANKS, SIS!
WE'LL MAKE BUBBY CAPTAIN FOR THIS!
GIVE ME ONE!
I'LL TAKE TWO!
BETTY BOOP'S AUTOGRAPHS - TEN CENTS APIECE!
COUPLA MORE SALES 'N' THE FOOTBALL IS OURS!
© 1935, King Features Syndicate, Inc., Great Britain rights reserved.
PLAY MONEY
PLAY MONEY
PLAY MONEY

BETTY BOOP
-BY-
MAX FLEISCHER
Registered U. S. Patent Office
YEP! ALL THE CAST IS SELECTED BUT SOMEBODY FOR THE "CRYIN' ANNIE" PART!
WHY NOT TEST MY AUNT TILLIE FOR THAT PART?
OKAY, BRING HER IN FOR A TEST!
THERE SHE IS NOW-BATTLING WITH THE GATE-MEN! YOO-HOO! AUNT TILLIE!!
GREAT! SHE LOOKS THE PART OF "CRYIN' ANNIE" WITHOUT THE MAKEUP-GET HER INTO COSTUME FOR A TEST!
IS THAT A KNOCK OR A BOOST-YOU BIG DUMBCRACK?
WHY DON'T YOU BEHAVE?
PERFECT! NOW YOU'RE S'POSED TO BE "CRYIN' ANNIE", THE APPLE-SELLER - LET'S SEE YOU CRY!
???
GO ON, AUNT TILLIE, CRY!
WHAT'S THE DELAY? BEGIN, COMMENCE, START CRYIN'- WHAT! YOU WON'T CRY, HUH?
THINK OF SOMETHING SAD!
????
THE PART CALLS FOR YOU TO CRY!
HA-HA! IT SEEMS SO SILLY IT MAKES ME LAUGH HA-HA!!
THIS IS NO LAUGHING MATTER-I'LL GET THE SOB VIOLINIST TO HELP YOU CRY!
THIS GUY COULD MAKE A LAUGHIN' HYENA CRY-WHY--ER-...
GET HOT-PLAY IT FASTER AND I'LL SHOW YOU HOW I CAN JIG!
AUNT TILLIE, IS THAT NICE?
THAT SCRIPT IS SAD ENOUGH TO MAKE A LANDLORD BREAK OUT CRYING-SNIFF!
--IT'S SNOWIN'-NOBODY WILL BUY ONE OF YOUR APPLES-YOUR CHILDREN ARE AT HOME HUNGRY-COLD-FREEZIN'----
HA-HA! STOP! YOU'LL GIVE ME HYSTERICS
LISTEN-WHS-S-S-S-S-S-
YES-YES-IT MAY WORK AT THAT!
WHY, I CAN'T REMEMBER ANYTHING THAT EVER MADE ME CRY-CAN'T YOU CHANGE IT TO A LAUGHIN' PART?
YEAH? WELL, HOW'S ABOUT WHEN YOU WAS A BIT OF A KID AND THEY TOLD YOU THERE WASN'T ANY SANTA CLAUS?
OH, OH! 'DEED I REMEMBER IT AS THO' IT WAS YESTERDAY-SNIFF-SNIFF!
QUICK! HOOK UP THE SOUND TRACK-GET THE CAMERAS IN PLACE---
BOO-HOO-BAW-WAW-BOO-HOO-BAW-WAW
© 1935, King Features Syndicate, Inc., Great Britain rights reserved.
LUCKY BUCKS PLAY MONEY 2 2
LUCKY BUCKS PLAY MONEY 2 2
LUCKY BUCKS PLAY MONEY 2 2

BETTY BOOP
BY MAX FLEISCHER
Registered U. S. Patent Office.
HEY! HEY! WHERE ARE YOU GOING WITH THAT COVER?
AW! WE'RE PLAYIN' INDIAN AND WE'VE GOT TO HAVE A "TEEPEE," AIN'T WE?
NOT WITH MY NEW SATIN CHAISE LONGUE COVER! WHY, THE IDEA!
HAVE A HEART, SIS - WE CAN'T PLAY INDIAN WITHOUT A "TEEPEE"
SURELY, YOU CAN! PLAY AN INDIAN WAR DANCE OR BUFFALO HUNT - USE FIDO FOR THE BUFFALO---
TSK! TSK! SUCH A WACKY IDEA!
HOW'S ABOUT A SHEET OR SUMPIN?
WHAT! NO TEEPEE?!
PLAYIN' INDIAN WITHOUT A TEEPEE IS LIKE PLAYIN' BALL WITHOUT A BALL!
HOLD EVERY-THIN', I'VE GOT AN IDEA - WAIT HERE!
NOW WE CAN SLIP OVER TO MRS. DE SWANK'S "TEA" - BUBBY WILL BE BUSY PLAYING INDIAN --
PLAYIN' INDIAN? THAT KID'S SO WILD ALL HE HAS TO DO IS ACT NATURAL!
WOULD YOU WEAR MY NEW GOWN WITH THE SLIT SKIRT, IF YOU WAS ME?
OF COURSE! YOU WANT TO LOOK YOUR BEST AND THAT SLIT SKIRT IS THE LATEST THING!
YEAH! THAT'S WHY I WAS SAVIN' IT FOR THE GLASS-BLOWERS' BALL!
YOU WOULD! WELL, HURRY AND DRESS. WE MUSTN'T BE LATE!
OW! 'S GONE! HELP! POLICE! CALL ALL CARS -
OH! OH! NOW WHAT?
'S GONE! STOLEN! OW! MY BEAUTIFUL NEW GOWN WITH THE SLIT SKIRT ~ OW!
- ER - YOU DON'T THINK BUBBY WOULD - ER -
EEK
THAT'S WHAT I SAID - BRING IN AUNT TILLIE'S NEW GOWN RIGHT THIS MINUTE!
PLOP
AW! WHY DON'T YOU BEHAVE?
© 1936, King Features Syndicate, Inc., Great Britain rights reserved.
LUCKY BUCKS PLAY MONEY 2
LUCKY BUCKS PLAY MONEY 2
LUCKY BUCKS PLAY MONEY 2

BETTY BOOP
BY MAX FLEISCHER
Registered U. S. Patent Office
YES, BUBBY- AUNT TILLIE IS GOING TO BE BEAUTIFIED!
AIN'T THAT CUTE? YES, THAT'S ALL IT IS, BUBBY!
-ER- WHAT'S THAT CRACK ABOUT BEAUTY BEIN' ONLY SKIN DEEP?
WELL, I'LL BET THEY'LL HAVE TO GO DEEPER THAN THAT ON YOU!
OH, YEAH? WELL, FRESHIE, WE'LL GO VERY DEEP INTO THAT MATTER WHEN I GET BACK!
-AND THE DIRECTOR SAID I'D GET THE PART IF I GOT BEAUTIFIED UP A BIT?
YES, AND I'M TAKING YOU TO A "BEAUTY SPECIALIST" THAT COULD MAKE AN UGLY DUCKLING LOOK LIKE A SWAN!
B.B.
-AND I WANT YOU TO BEAUTIFY AUNT TILLIE!
HM-M! I'M ONLY A BEAUTICIAN NOT A MAGICIAN!
PAGE A MORTICIAN - I'M GOING TO KNOCK THIS INSULTING SAP LOOSE FROM HIS WHISKERS!
WHY DON'T YOU BEHAVE?
HOLD STILL- PIERRE IS GOING TO PLUCK YOUR EYEBROWS FIRST!
OH! ZAY LOOK LIKE ZE MUSTACHE- I MUST PLUCK ZEM TO ZE LINE!
GO EASY, WHISKERS- OR I'LL PLUCK YOU LIKE A LONG ISLAND DUCK!
WHOA! YOU MUST HOLD YOUR PUNCHES, AUNT TILLIE!
OW! I SAID PLUCK 'EM OUT NOT DIG 'EM OUT- SILLY!
WAIT! I NEED HELP- I WILL CALL ZE WHOLE STAFF!
ZE HOT TOWELS, QUEEK! OW! HURRY! NOW TURN ON ZE FACIAL MACHINE OW! OW! HOLD HER, EVERYBODY- NOW ZE HAIR WAVER ~~ OW!!
OH, OH! THE PANIC IS ON!
OW! WHAT TORTURE I WENT THROUGH, BUT IT WAS WORTH IT!
I'LL SAY IT WAS- WAIT TILL THE DIRECTOR SEES YOU NOW!
BUT DON'T YOU NOTICE ANY DIFFERENCE IN AUNT TILLIE?
WHAT DIFFERENCE?
WHAT DIFFERENCE, HUH? ARE YOU BLIND, YOU BIG DUMBCRACK?
CALL ALL CARS!
HE IS NOW!
NOW IS THAT NICE?
© 1935, King Features Syndicate, Inc., Great Britain rights reserved.
LUCKY BUCKS PLAY MONEY 2
LUCKY BUCKS PLAY MONEY 2
LUCKY BUCKS PLAY MONEY 2

BETTY BOOP
BY MAX FLEISCHER
Registered U. S. Patent Office
WHY, BUBBY-YOU SHOULD BE THRILLED TO WATCH AUNT TILLIE DO HER SCENES!
AW! WHY DON'T YOU BEHAVE?
TO SET NO. 350
OH! I DIDN'T KNOW THE SCRIPT CALLED FOR AN AMBULANCE IN AUNT TILLIE'S SCENES!
CLANG CLANG
THEY OUGHTA USE A HEARSE-SHE'LL KILL THE PICTURE
HOW IS SHE DOING? HAS SHE FINISHED THE FIRST SCENE YET?
OW! I'LL SAY SHE FINISHED IT!
THAT WAS THE ONE WHERE SHE THROWS THE DUMMY OFF THE CLIFF, HUH?
YEAH! SHE THREW THE VILLAIN OFF THE CLIFF INSTEAD OF THE DUMMY!
HOW'D SHE DO IN THE "PLAYING TAG" SHOT WITH THE HERO?
OH! SHE WRECKED THAT TOO - SHE TAGGED HIM SO HARD HE'S STILL OUT!
YOU SAY SHE KILLED THE FIRE RESCUE SHOT, TOO?
SHE MURDERED IT! INSTEAD OF JUMPING INTO THE NET-SHE LANDED ON THE FIREMEN WHO WERE HOLDING IT!
TO SET NO. 6 1/2
AND YOU CUT THAT SCENE OUT, HUH?
WE HAD TO-WE RAN OUT OF FIREMEN!
NOW THEY'RE SHOOTING THE JUNGLE SCENES WITH HER AND USING REAL WILD ANIMALS IN THE BIG CHASE SHOT!
O-OH! THAT SOUNDS DANGEROUS-I HOPE THEY'RE NOT TOO WILD!
SHE'LL BRING 'EM BACK TAME!
WHOA! STOP! HALT! HEY! AUNT TILLIE!
BUT THEY'RE S'POSED TO CHASE YOU-NOT YOU CHASE THEM!
WELL, I HAVE TO THINK OF ME PUBLIC-THEY'D THINK I WAS GOING SOFT IF I LET A LOT OF OVER-GROWN TOMCATS CHASE ME AROUND
© 1936, King Features Syndicate, Inc., Great Britain rights reserved. 1·18
LUCKY BUCKS PLAY MONEY 2
LUCKY BUCKS PLAY MONEY 2
LUCKY BUCKS PLAY MONEY 2

BETTY BOOP
BY
MAX FLEISCHER
Registered U. S. Patent Office
YOO-HOO! AUNT TILLIE-THE DIRECTOR JUST 'PHONED THAT THE PART IS YOURS IF--
OH! THERE'S A CATCH IN IT, HUH? WAIT'LL I GIVE BUBBY HIS CASTOR OIL!
AND HE ASKED ME IF YOU WERE A GOOD SINGER-'COURSE, I SAID YES!
WELL MAYBE I CAN'T SING GOOD, BUT I CAN SING LOUD!
I'VE ENGAGED PROFESSOR OCTAVE-HE CAN TEACH A FROG TO SING LIKE A NIGHTINGALE!
I'M NO FROG, BUT---
YOU'VE GOT TO BE ABLE TO SING FAIRLY WELL TO GET THE PART!
IF NOT-IT'S "FARE THEE WELL" TO THE PART, HUH?
YES, PROFESSOR-THIS IS THE LADY YOU ARE TO TEACH HOW TO SING!
HM-M! WELL, YOU CAN'T HATE A GUY FOR TRYING!
NOW TELL ME-WHAT REGISTER DO YOU SING IN!
TO TELL YOU THE TRUTH, PROF ABOUT THE ONLY PLACE I SING IN IS THE BATHROOM!
OR IN THE RAIN HUH?
BEFORE WE START-NOW HOW'RE YOU ON THE SCALES?
LISTEN, SILLY! IT'S NONE OF Y'BUSINESS WHAT I WEIGH!
NOW JUST DO AS THE "PROF" SAYS, AUNT TILLIE!
YES JUST SING THE SCALE LIKE THIS-DO-RE-MI-FA-SO-LA-SI-DO-
DO-RAY-MEE-E-FAW-SO-O-O-O-LA SEE-E-DO-O-
WHAT D'YE MEAN-TERRIBLE? I SANG IT EXACTLY LIKE YOU DID, SILLY!
WELL ONE OF US IS ROTTEN-NOW TRY IT OVER AGAIN IN YOUR OWN WAY!
BEE-E-UTIFUL! MARVELOUS-SUCH TONE-WONDERFUL! HOLD IT!
O-O-OW! YEOW! O-OW! YEE-E-O-OW!!
© 1936, King Features Syndicate, Inc., Great Britain rights reserved
I CAN'T UNDERSTAND WHY SHE ASSAULTED ME-WHY, I WAS COMPLIMENTING HER ON HER BEAUTIFUL SINGING!
YOU WOULDN'T FOOL ME, WOULD YOU?
LUCKY BUCKS PLAY MONEY 2
LUCKY BUCKS PLAY MONEY 2
LUCKY BUCKS PLAY MONEY 2

BETTY BOOP
BY MAX FLEISCHER
Registered U S Patent Office
AUNT TILLIE – THE STUDIO WANTS YOU ON THE WIRE!
THAT'S OUT! NO MORE WIRE OR FLYING TRAPEZE ACTS FOR ME!
AND THEY WANT TO KNOW IF YOU CAN RIDE A HORSE!
NO! BUT YOU CAN'T HATE ME FOR TRYIN'
TO SET 3
HE MAY BE A LIL' FRISKY - Y'SEE, THIS'LL BE THE FIRST TIME HE'S EVER BEEN RODE!
WELL IT'LL BE THE FIRST TIME I EVER RODE A HORSE SO WE START EVEN!
KEEP YOUR EYE ON THE BALL - I MEAN THE HORSE!
WAIT'LL I PIN UP MY SKIRT SO I CAN RIDE HIM STRADDLE-LEGGED!
?
BAM!
AUNT TILLIE!! WHY DON'T YOU BEHAVE?
THAT'S WHAT I SAID - IS THAT ANY WAY TO TREAT A LADY, YOU MUG?
WAM
HEY! I SAID RIDE HIM - NOT RASSLE HIM!
HOLD STILL - OR I'LL SLAP YOU BOW-LEGGED!
LET HIM UP - YOU WIN!
OOPS! SO YOU WON'T WALK, HUH?
PLOP
SWOONIN' - THE BIG SISSY!
AT THAT - IT WASN'T JUST THE RIGHT KIND OF A MOUNT FOR HER!
MOUNT? SHE NEEDS A MOUNTAIN! WAIT!
YES - I'VE HAD THE SCRIPT CHANGED TO A "PACHYDERM" - ELEPHANT TO YOU!
AH! YOU'RE ONLY TRYING TO BE NICE TO ME!
© 1936, King Features Syndicate, Inc., Great Britain rights reserved
LUCKY BUCKS PLAY MONEY 2
LUCKY BUCKS PLAY MONEY 2
LUCKY BUCKS PLAY MONEY 2

BETTY BOOP
BY MAX FLEISCHER
NOW, BUBBY - YOU PLAY WITH THE GOLD FISH WHILE SISTER STEPS OVER TO SEE AUNT TILLIE GO THROUGH HER SCENES!
I'LL BET SHE GOES RIGHT THROUGH 'EM, TOO!
KEEP OFF
HOW IS AUNT TILLIE'S COMEDY LOVE SCENE COMING ALONG?
COMEDY? SHE'S MAKIN' A TRAGEDY OUT OF IT!
WELL, THE PART CALLS FOR HER TO BE ROUGH, DOESN'T IT?
YES, IT'S S'POSED TO BE A ROUGH AND TUMBLE COMEDY LOVE SCENE, BUT NOT THAT ROUGH!
MAYBE I CAN MAKE HER SOFTEN IT DOWN A BIT!
IF YOU DON'T - WE'LL RUN OUT OF ACTORS! WOW! WHAT A ROUGH GAL!
WHY, IT LOOKS LIKE YOU'RE "FILMING THE BATTLE OF THE MARNE"!
IT'S WORSE THAN THAT - SHE'S USED UP ALL THE ACTORS THOSE SHE AIN'T KNOCKED OUT ARE HIDING!
CAST
THE BIG SISSIES!
IF THAT'S THE WAY YOU MAKE LOVE - I'D HATE TO SEE YOU IN A FIGHT!
CLANG
TO SET
THE SHOW - I MEAN THE PICTURE MUST GO ON - IT'S THE BIG SHOT OF THE PICTURE!
WELL, GET ME AN ACTOR THAT WON'T FALL APART WHEN I PUT ON THE HEAVY LOVE SCENE!
YOU'VE USED 'EM ALL UP - NONE OF 'EM COULD STAND UP UNDER SUCH ROUGH STUFF!
WHY NOT LET HER BRING HER BOY FRIEND?
THAT'S IT! I'LL GET MY SWEETIE - "HUNKY DORY" - HE'S WAITING OUTSIDE FOR ME!
I'VE NEVER SEEN "HUNKY" BUT HE MUST BE SOME MAN - THE WAY SHE RAVES ABOUT HIM!
OBOY! HE MUST BE A MAN MOUNTAIN - THE SCENE WILL MAKE THE PICTURE!
MEET THE BOY FRIEND, "HUNKY DORY"!
WHAT? IS HE WALKING ON HIS KNEES?
I DIDN'T KNOW THE "STINGER MIDGETS" WERE IN TOWN!
© 1936, King Features Syndicate, Inc., Great Britain rights reserved
LUCKY BUCKS
PLAY MONEY
2
LUCKY BUCKS
PLAY MONEY
2
LUCKY BUCKS
PLAY MONEY
2

BETTY BOOP
BY MAX FLEISCHER
Registered U.S. Patent Office
YOUR PICTURE IS A SMASH HIT-ALL THE PAPERS PLAY YOU UP ON THE FRONT PAGE!
AIN'T THAT GRAND? JUST AS THOUGH I ROBBED A BANK OR SOMETHIN'!
YOU OUGHT TO BE THRILLED RECEIVING ALL THIS FAN MAIL!
BUT MY BOY FRIEND, "HUNKY DORY," IS SO JEALOUS-I'LL HAVE TO SAY THEY'RE CHAIN-LETTERS
-AND YOU'RE ON ALL THE BILL-BOARDS IN TOWN!
WHAT! NO SANDWICH SIGNS?
COLOSSAL! AUNT TILLIE
YOO-HOO! GIVE US YOUR AUTOGRAPH, AUNT TILLIE?
LOOK! MUST BE A FIRE SOME PLACE!
AUTOGRAPH-HUNTERS-YOU'RE FAMOUS!
MY PUBLIC! YOU FLATTEN ME-TO SAY THE LEAST!
WATCH OUT THEY DON'T SLIP IN A CHECK ON YOU!
OBOY! SHE CAN WRITE LEFT-HANDED, TOO!
AMBIDEXTROUS! SEE! WHEN MY RIGHT GOES LAME I CAN USE MY LEFT!
I WISH YOU'D USE YOUR HEAD-YOU'RE OVER-DOING IT!
OW! I CAN'T WRITE ANOTHER LINE-MY BOTH HANDS ARE KILLING ME!
HEY! WAIT-AUNT TILLIE!
QUICK! INTO THE STUDIO DOCTOR'S OFFICE!
WHAT D'YE MEAN, I CAN'T USE MY HANDS FOR A WEEK?
'CAUSE YOU HAVE A SEVERE CASE OF WRITERS' CRAMP!
OH-OH! AUNT TILLIE WITH BOTH HANDS IN A SLING-WHAT A SWELL BREAK!
I FEEL AS HELPLESS AS A FISH OUT OF WATER!
IT ISN'T FAIR TO BAWL HER OUT IN HER HELPLESS CONDITION!
OH, YEAH? WELL, I'VE WAITED FOR THIS CHANCE WHERE SHE COULDN'T HIT BACK!
SAYS WHO?
WAM
© 1936, King Features Syndicate, Inc., Great Britain rights reserved
2 LUCKY BUCKS PLAY MONEY 2
2 LUCKY BUCKS PLAY MONEY 2
2 LUCKY BUCKS PLAY MONEY 2

BETTY BOOP
BY
MAX FLEISCHER
Registered U.S. Patent Office
GETTING THE MALE LEAD IN YOUR NEW COMEDY-"ON THE LAST LAP" WAS A SWELL BREAK FOR YOUR BOY FRIEND!
YEAH! THE PART WAS MADE FOR "HUNKY"-I MADE THE DIRECTOR GIVE IT TO HIM!
HAS YOUR SWEETIE, "HUNKY DORY," HAD ANY STAGE EXPERIENCE?
I'LL SAY HE HAS-HE PLAYED THE FRONT END OF A HORSE, IN "HORSES"!
TO SET 6¾
YOU BOTH OUGHTA BE A HIT IN THIS COMEDY, "ON THE LAST LAP"-YOU BOTH HAVE FAT PARTS!
WELL, I MAY BE A LITTLE PLUMP, BUT LISTEN, SILLY—
"ON THE LAST LAP"
NOW GET INTO POSITION FOR THE COMEDY LOVE SCENE WHILE I CALL THE CAMERAS
I'LL ARRANGE THEM!
HEY! DIDN'T I TELL YOU TO GET INTO POSITION-WHAT'S THE DELAY?
WE'RE FOLLOWING THE SCRIPT TO A "T"!
WHAT'S THAT LAST CRACK-
WHAT D'YE MEAN-AM I PLAYING THIS LOVE SCENE ALONE? YOU CRACKPOT!
WELL, WHERE'S "HUNKY DORY"?
? ?
HERE I AM, SUH!
?
LISTEN, THIS AIN'T AN X-RAY PICTURE-NOR A GAME OF "HIDE-AND--GO-SEEK"-
HM-M! DIDN'T YOU SAY TO SIT ON HUNKY'S LAP-OR AM I TOO LOUD?
YES, BUT HOW ARE WE GOING TO SHOOT THE SCENE WHEN WE CAN'T SEE HUNKY? AND IT'S THE BIG SHOT OF THE PICTURE!
? ? ?
WHY DON'T YOU BEHAVE?
DON'T YOU UNDERSTAND, AUNT TILLIE YOU BOTH MUST BE SEEN AND-
FILM CAN NO. 45
2-22
WELL, HOW'S ABOUT THIS?
GREAT! HOLD IT! CAMERA!
"ON THE LAST LAP"

BETTY BOOP
BY
MAX FLEISCHER
Registered U.S. Patent Office.
YES, AUNT TILLIE, YOUR BOY FRIEND, HUNKY DORY, IS OUT OF YOUR PICTURE!
WHAT! SAYS WHO?
THE CASTING DIRECTOR!
WHY, WHEN I SHOWED THAT "HUMPTY DUMPTY" HUNKY'S PHOTO HE SAID HE WAS THE PERFECT TYPE!
I KNOW-BUT THAT WAS ONLY A PHOTO OF HIS FACE AND HEAD!
WHAT DOES THE CRACKPOT WANT- A MAP OF HIM OR SUMPIN'?
I JUST PASSED AUNT TILLIE-SHE LOOKED AS SORE AS A WET HEN!
HER BOY FRIEND WAS TURNED DOWN FOR THAT COMEDY PART!
CALL ALL CARS-SHE'S ON A RAMPAGE!
SHE WOULD!
POW! SOCK! BAM! PLOP!
CASTING OFFICE
WHAT D'YE MEAN YOU SOCKED THE CASTING DIRECTOR?
WHY DON'T YOU BEHAVE?
YEAH! HE SAYS HUNKY'S FACE WAS PERFECT BUT THAT HE LOOKED LIKE HE WAS WALKIN' ON HIS KNEES!
WELL, HUNKY IS-ER RATHER SHORT!
-AND REMEMBER, AUNT TILLIE, THE CASTING DIRECTOR HAS THE LAST WORD!
HE'S HAD HIS LAST WORD FOR SOME TIME!
AND NOT ONLY THAT BUT THE PART CALLS FOR A VERY TALL MAN!
WAIT! I'LL HAVE HUNKY GET HIS BIG TWIN BROTHER!
HUH- I'VE BEEN REJECTED BY BETTER STUDIOS THAN THIS!
NOW DO AS I SAY- GET YOUR TWIN BROTHER, WACKY AND COME BACK- AND LISTEN-BZ-Z-Z-Z-Z-Z
HUNKY'S TWIN BROTHER- HOW'S ABOUT HIM?
GREAT! PERFECT FACE, SIZE 'N'EVERYTHIN'! -HE'S HIRED!
PS-ST! 'MEMBER I GET HALF THE SALARY?
BIG TWIN BROTHER BAH!
© 1936, King Features Syndicate, Inc., Great Britain rights reserved
LUCKY BUCKS
PLAY MONEY
2 BUCK
LUCKY BUCKS
PLAY MONEY
2 BUCK
LUCKY BUCKS
PLAY MONEY
2 BUCK

BETTY BOOP
BY MAX FLEISCHER
Registered U. S. Patent Office
THE BIG CHIEF HAS DECIDED TO GIVE AUNT TILLIE THE LEAD IN "TIGER GAL"!
SWELL- SHE JUST LOVES ANIMALS!
TIGER GAL
YEAH? WELL THESE BABIES ARE REAL WILD TIGERS AND THE PART CALLS FOR HER TO GO INTO THE CAGE WITH 'EM!
O-OH! THAT'S ASKING TOO MUCH OF HER-YOU WILL HAVE TO FAKE THAT SCENE!
CAN'T FAKE IT — IT'S THE BIG SHOT OF THE PICTURE!
THAT'S WHAT I SAID-I'M GOING TO ADVISE HER TO REFUSE THE PART!
DON'T BE SILLY- 'COURSE I'M TAKING THE PART-WHAT'S A FEW TIGERS MORE OR LESS!
BUT THEY'RE REAL WILD MAN-EATING TIGERS!
MAN-EATING TIGERS, HUH? WELL ME BEING A WOMAN-THAT MAKES ME SAFE!
YOU WOULD JEST AT A TIME LIKE THIS!
SET 6⅞
OFCOURSE WHILE YOU'RE IN THE CAGE WE'LL HAVE YOU WELL PROTECTED BY EXPERIENCED HUNTERS —
AND WHO'S GOING TO PROTECT THE TIGERS?
WHY DON'T YOU BEHAVE?
TIGER GAL
NOW 'MEMBER YOUR INSTRUCTIONS-LOOK 'EM STRAIGHT IN THE EYE AND-
DON'T WORRY- IF THEY TRY TO BITE ME-I'LL BITE 'EM RIGHT BACK!
GR-R-R-R
GR-R-R-R
QUICK! WHAT'S HAPPENED TO POOR AUNT TILLIE?
'S'NO USE-WE CAN'T SHOOT THE TIGER SCENES!
HA-HA! ROUGH, TOUGH AUNT TILLIE SCARED OF THE TIGERS, HUH?
© 1936, King Features Syndicate, Inc., Great Britain rights reserved
SCARED OF 'EM- ME EYE -
?
?
FOR THE LAST TIME- ARE YOU OVER-GROWN TOMCATS COMING OUT OR WILL I HAVE TO GO IN AFTER YOU?
LOOK!
LUCKY BUCKS
PLAY MONEY
2
2
BUCK
LUCKY BUCKS
PLAY MONEY
2
2
LUCKY BUCKS
PLAY MONEY
2
2

BETTY BOOP
BY
MAX FLEISCHER
THINK OF THAT, AUNT TILLIE - BUBBY IS TO PLAY THE LEAD IN "BABY DUMPLIN'"!
SWELL! MAYBE I COULD PERSUADE 'EM TO GIVE ME THE "NURSE PART"!
?
HE WAS HERE JUST A MOMENT AGO - YOO-HOO! BUBBY!
AND THE LIL' TIKE AIN'T HIDIN' UP THE CHIMNEY NEITHER!
THAT'S WHAT I SAID - WHAT GOES UP MUST COME DOWN!
LOOK-OUT THAT DOESN'T GO DOUBLE - AUNT TILLIE!
WHO KNOWS - YOU MAY TURN OUT TO BE A HANDSOME MATINEE IDOL
AW! WHY DON'T YOU BEHAVE?
THIS PART WILL MAKE YOU FAMOUS, BUBBY!
THE KID IS PERFECT FOR THE PART, BUT AUNT TILLIE IS OUT - SHE'S TOO ROUGH - ALWAYS SOCKING SOMEBODY!
GIVE HER ANOTHER CHANCE. SHE PROMISED TO BEHAVE!
OKAY! YOU GET THE PART IF YOU PROMISE TO CUT THE ROUGH STUFF - GET INTO YOUR COSTUMES!
I'LL BE MILDER THAN THOSE DOVES YOU HEAR ABOUT!
SHE'S THE ONLY ONE WHO CAN HANDLE BUBBY, ANYWAY!
THE PARTS WERE MADE FOR THEM!
PERFECT CASTING, IF I DO SAY SO!
HOW'RE WE DOIN'?
CAST
DOESN'T BUBBY MAKE THE CUTEST BABY?
YES-SUH, HE'S CUTER THAN THE QUINTUPLETS - KITCHEE - KITCHEE!
YOU'LL THINK HE'S QUINTUPLETS IF YOU DON'T LAY OFF THAT STUFF!
NOW IS THAT NICE ?
SOCK
YOU'RE WACKY - LISTEN, SILLY - IF I SOCKED YOU - YOU'D STAY SOCKED!
PEEP! PEEP!
HONEST - IT WAS BUBBY WHO HIT YOU!
THE BIG FAKIR NOBODY CAN PULL THAT "KITCHEE-KITCHEE" STUFF ON ME AND GET AWAY WITH IT!
HOLLYWOOD
STATE LINE
© 1936, King Features Syndicate, Inc., Great Britain rights reserved.
3-15
LUCKY BUCKS PLAY MONEY 2
LUCKY BUCKS PLAY MONEY 2
LUCKY BUCKS PLAY MONEY 2

BETTY BOOP
BY
MAX FLEISCHER
FOR THE 'STEENTH TIME, YOU HALF-PINT - NO! Y'CAN'T SEE THE CASTING DIRECTOR!
CASTING DIRECTOR
I'VE BEEN TOSSED OUT OF BETTER STUDIOS THAN YOURS - YOU
STOP! IT'S HUNKY DORY - AND HE'S GIVING SOMEBODY THE RAZZBERRY!
HE DOES SEEM A BIT RUFFLED!
AND THE BIG BOHUNKS GAVE ME THE QUICK RUSH!
OH! YEAH? WELL JUST A MINUTE - I'LL TAKE THE MATTER UP WITH THOSE TOUGH GUYS, PRONTO!
AUNT TILLIE - MAYBE HUNKY IS TOO SHORT FOR THE PART!
WON'T LET HIM IN TO SEE THE CASTING DIRECTOR - HUH?
'MEMBER I'M RIGHT BEHIND YOU - M'DEAR!
BUT THE PART MAY CALL FOR A TALLER MAN!
WAIT - I'LL GIVE THEM MY CARD!
I'LL GIVE 'EM MY CARD RIGHT ON THE KISSER!
NO DICE!
NO SOAP!
ONE SIDE, SUH!
YOUR METHOD IS RATHER CRUDE, AUNT TILLIE, BUT-
IT GETS RESULTS - Y'GOT TO ADMIT THAT, BETTY!
DERN TOOTIN'!
HE SAYS YOU MUST HAVE AN APPOINTMENT OR-
DON'T TELL ME HE WON'T SEE ME OR I'LL SHAKE YOU LOOSE FROM YOUR EARS!
IT'S GETTING TOO ROUGH FOR ME - I'LL WAIT OUTSIDE!
-AND TELL HIM TO COME OUT OR I'LL COME IN!
GULP! YES-SIR - I MEAN YES MA'AM!
- - AND I THINK MY BOY FRIEND, HUNKY DORY, HERE IS JUST THE ONE FOR THAT PART!
THAT NOSE - THAT HANDLE-BAR MUSTACHE ARE PERFECT - DOESN'T EVEN NEED A MAKE UP!
DO WHAT?
I SAID FOR HIM TO STAND UP TILL I SEE IF HIS HEIGHT IS OKAY!
SIR-R-!
CALLING ALL CARS
STEP ON IT - OW! IT LOOKS LIKE A POLICE PARADE BEHIND US!
YOU'VE GOT TO LEARN YOU CAN'T WRECK STUDIOS LIKE THAT!

BETTY BOOP
BY MAX FLEISCHER
Registered U.S. Patent Office
YOUR NOTICES ARE MARVELOUS. THEY HAIL YOU AS A WONDERFUL COMEDY PROSPECT —CALL YOU 'A DIAMOND IN THE ROUGH'!
WELL, MAYBE I AM A LIL' ROUGH IN MY WAYS, BUT—
AUNT TILLIE SENSATIONAL HIT!!!
THEY ALSO RAVE OVER YOUR SIMPLICITY AND NAIVETÉ!
WELL, AFTER ALL—YOU GOT TO ADMIT I AIN'T GOT THE WORST FIGGER IN THE WORLD!
ALL THESE FLATTERING NOTICES ARE GOING TO BRING A HORDE OF ADVENTURERS AND FORTUNE-HUNTERS!
WELL, IF ANY OF 'EM CAN FIND A FORTUNE AROUND ME I'LL SPLIT WITH 'EM!
COUNT MEEYOUT CALLING, MA'AM
OH! FOR AUNT TILLIE? SHOW HIM IN, PEEVES!
YEAH! AND I'LL SHOW HIM OUT!
ADORED ONE—ON MY BENDED KNEES, I ASK YOU—WILL YOU MARRY ME?
WELL, OF ALL THE STUPENDOUS, COLOSSAL NERVE!
HOW ROMANTIC!
NO! NO! A THOUSAND TIMES, NO! YOU TOSSPOT!
BUT YOU SHOULDN'T REJECT HIS PROPOSAL IN SUCH AN EMPHATIC MANNER!
THAT'S THE ONLY KIND OF A REJECTION THOSE TITLED FURRINERS UNDERSTAND!
AGAIN I ASK YOU, MY BEAUTIFUL 'HIBISCUS' WILL YOU BE MINE?
'HIBISCUS,' ME EYE—YOU DUMBCRACK—FOR THE 'STEENTH TIME, NO!
WHY DON'T YOU BEHAVE?
THAT BEWHISKERED COUNT WILL MAKE ME LOSE MY TEMPER YET!
HERE'S YO' LAUNDRY, MA'AM!
BUT YOU PROMISED TO TRY AND CONTROL YOUR TEMPER!
COUNT TEN, AUNT TILLIE!
YES—OVER THIS NO ACCOUNT—FOR THE LAST TIME, SILLY—WHY, I WOULDN'T MARRY YOU IF YOU WAS THE LAST MAN ON EARTH!
AM I TO TAKE THIS AS A REFUSAL?
WELL, YOU CAN USE YOUR OWN JUDGMENT!
LUCKY BUCKS
PLAY MONEY
LUCKY BUCKS
PLAY MONEY
LUCKY BUCKS
PLAY MONEY

BETTY BOOP
BY
MAX FLEISCHER
Registered U. S. Patent Office
THEY ADVERTISED FOR A SHORT MAN - LOOKS, VOICE AND EXPERIENCE UNNECESSARY!
WELL, HUNKY HAS ALL OF THOSE QUALIFICATIONS!
NOW WE MUST HORN HUNKY IN WITH INFLUENCE BACKED UP BY FORCE!
OH, NO! HE MUST APPLY FOR THE PART IN THE REGULAR MANNER!
SORRY, HUNKY - BUT IT LOOKS LIKE YOU'LL HAVE TO GET IN LINE!
GET IN LINE, ME EYE - WHY, IT LOOKS LIKE THE "BIG PARADE"!
THAT'S WHAT I SAID - I'M DOING THE CASTING - CASTING YOU TOSSPOTS ON YOUR WAY!
CASTING DIRECTOR
WHAT! ONLY ONE APPLICANT? HM-M! BUT I GUESS YOU'LL DO!
IM THE LONE APPLICANT, SUH! THANK YOU SUH!
SAY, "AH"! LEG LENGTH N' WEIGHT OKE!
HEIGHT OKE!
OKEY DOKE!
CONGRAT-ULATE ME. I WON THE PART!
HOW COULD YOU MISS? AUNT TILLIE ELIMINATED ALL COMPETITION!
WELL, ALL IS FAIR IN LOVE AND THE MOVIES!
WHO KNOWS? HUNKY MAY BE ANOTHER "PARK FABLE"!
THINK OF IT - YOU'LL BE SEEN AND ADMIRED BY THE VAST PUBLIC - YOUR FACE WILL BE AS FAMOUS AS THE "FACE ON THE BAR-ROOM FLOOR"!
AW! YOU'RE ONLY TRYING TO BE NICE TO ME!
IT'LL BE SHOWING A NEW PERSONALITY TO THE PUBLIC!
AND WHEN THE PUBLIC TAKES A GANDER AT THEM EYES 'N' THEM MUSTACHE - THEY'LL GO WACKY OVER HIM!
COME ON, WE'LL GO OVER AND SEE HUNKY REHEARSE!
I'M PROUD TO THINK I'VE DISCOVERED A NEW FACE FOR THE MOVIES!
SET 1,456
King Features Syndicate, Inc., Great Britain rights reserved
ON WITH COSTUMES! CAMERA!
SEEN AND ADMIRED - WHAT IS THIS, AN XRAY PICTURE? BAH!
LUCKY BUCKS
PLAY MONEY
2
LUCKY BUCKS
PLAY MONEY
2
LUCKY BUCKS
PLAY MONEY
2

BETTY BOOP
BY
MAX FLEISCHER
Registered U. S. Patent Office
"HUNKY DORY", MIND LITTLE BUBBY - I'D LIKE TO GO OVER AND SEE AUNT TILLIE DO HER BIG SCENE!
WELL, DON'T MISS IT IF YOU CAN HELP IT
YOU SAY HE'S AN ACTOR FROM AUNT TILLIE'S SET?
BEG PARDON- HE WAS!
TO BE EXPLICIT- HE'S CASUALITY NUMBER NINE!
OW! ANOTHER ONE "NON COMPOS MENTIS" - WHY WON'T SHE BEHAVE?
CLANG CLANG CLANG
-ER- AUNT TILLIE'S TREATIN' 'EM ROUGH AGAIN, HUH?
AND HOW! I TOLD HER TO PUT PLENTY OF PUNCH INTO HER PART AND SHE TOOK ME LITERALLY - LOOKS MORE LIKE A SCENE FROM THE "BATTLE OF THE MARNE" THAN A MELODRAMA!
CAST
NOW MEMBER, YER ONLY TO STRUGGLE A BIT BEFORE THE VILLAIN OVER-POWERS YOU AND-
GIMME THEM PAPERS - ME PROUD BEAUTY OR ELSE --
STAN' BACK- MARMADUKE WHIFFLETREE SUBSIDE --
NOW WHAT ARE WE GOING TO DO - YOU'VE KNOCKED 'EM ALL BOWLEGGED!
WHAT! NO MORE VILLAINS LEFT?
AT'S WHAT I SAID THAT MAKES IT UNANIMOUS — SHE'S GONE THROUGH OUR FULL LIST OF VILLAINS LIKE A CYCLONE THROUGH A KANSAS HAMLET!
THEY CAN'T TAKE IT, HUH? THE BIG SISSIES!
CAN'T YOU ADVERTISE OR SOMETHIN?
CAST
OUR ONLY CHANCE IS TO HAVE THE X.Y.Z COMPANY LOAN US THEIR VILLAIN!
OH, DEAR! LET'S HOPE THEY WILL!
TELL 'EM OOEYPAY IF THEY DON'T!
SET 15673
CONGRATULATE ME - THE X.Y.Z COMPANY'S VILLAIN AGREES TO TAKE THE PART AND SAYS HE'LL FURNISH HIS OWN COSTUME!
CONSIDER Y'SELF CONGRATULATED, SILLY!
THAT'S SWELL!
ALL SET LE'S GO!
?
? ?
SOUND STAGE QUIET!
© 1936, King Features Syndicate, Inc., Great Britain rights reserved
LUCKY BUCKS
2 PLAY MONEY 2
LUCKY BUCKS
2 PLAY MONEY 2
LUCKY BUCKS
2 PLAY MONEY 2

BETTY BOOP
BY MAX FLEISCHER
Registered U S Patent Office
I'LL MEET YOU AT YER GIRL FRIEND'S -BROTHER HUNKY- I'D LIKE TO MEET HER!
OKAY! BROTHER WACKY- SHE'S A DIAMOND IN THE ROUGH- VERY ROUGH!
BUT MY DEAR, THEY GAVE ME THE BIG RUSH-SAID I WAS TOO SMALL FOR AN EXTRA AND TOO BIG FOR A MIDGET!
AND YOU'RE TOO DUMB TO BE MY BOY FRIEND- SO THAT MAKES IT UNANIMOUS-SCRAM!
NOW IS THAT NICE, AUNT TILLIE?
TAKE IT ON THE LAM, YOU TOSSPOT, BEFORE I LOSE MY TEMPER!
BUT I THINK YOUR WAY OF BREAKING UP YOUR ENGAGEMENT IS RATHER CRUDE!
OH, YEAH? WELL, I'LL BREAK UP HIS MUSTACHED MUGG IF HE EVER GETS WITHIN HITTIN' DISTANCE OF ME AGAIN
WHY DON'T YOU BEHAVE?
WELL, I'LL BE ~~
GREETINGS AND SALUTATIONS!
?
AND IF YOU COME BACK AGAIN, YOU DUMBCRACK, I'LL TAKE YOU APART!
IT'S ALL A TERRIBLE MISTAKE, WACKY. AUNT TILLIE THOUGHT YOU WERE YOUR TWIN BROTHER, HUNKY, BACK AGAIN!
NO, THAT WASN'T HUNKY YOU HIT - IT WAS HIS TWIN BROTHER!
TWIN BROTHER?! OH! JUST WAIT TILL I LAY MY HANDS ON THAT SHRIMP, HUNKY-GR-R-R-
I WON'T MAKE THAT MISTAKE AGAIN - I'LL KNOW THE ONE WITHOUT THE BLACK EYE IS "HUNKY"!
DO AS I SAY- BELT ME IN THE EYE AND THE $10 IS YOURS!
IT'S A CRAZY WAY TO EARN A "SAWBUCK," BUT Y'ASKIN' FOR IT!
GOOD AFTERNOON, LADIES!
© 1936, King Features Syndicate, Inc. Great Britain rights reserved
LUCKY BUCKS
PLAY MONEY
2
LUCKY BUCKS
PLAY MONEY
2
LUCKY BUCKS
PLAY MONEY
2

BETTY BOOP
-BY-
MAX FLEISCHER
Registered U.S. Patent Office
YOU SAY AUNT TILLIE'S NEW CONTRACT IS ALL READY FOR HER SIGNATURE? SWELL!
EVEN THE DIRECTORS WANT MY AUTOGRAPH, HUH?
UGH! I CAN'T TAKE IT!
COLD CURE
OH, SURE. THEY'LL MAKE ANY CONCESSIONS WITHIN REASON---
I'LL LET THEM REASON THAT OUT WITH MY BOY FRIEND "HUNKY DORY," HE'S MY MANAGER!
GLUB GLUB
MY STARS! WHAT DOES HUNKY KNOW ABOUT LAW?
LISSEN, HE'S BEEN MIXED UP WITH IT SO OFTEN HERE AND THERE, THAT HE KNOWS ALL THE ANSWERS!
THIS IS A CONTRACT, NOT A PLEASURE TRIP!
AND SEE THAT YOU GET ME A VACATION AND OTHER CONCESSIONS-
MY DEAR- YOU'LL HAVE MORE CONCESSIONS THAN THE WORLD'S FAIR!
BUT YOU SHOULD HAVE A REAL LAWYER REPRESENT YOU!
DON'T WORRY- HE'LL OUT-SMART THOSE "APSAYS"- HE SAYS HE'LL 'PHONE WHEN EVERYTHING IS OKEY DOKE!
QUICK! THAT MUST BE HUNKY ALREADY!
OBOY! AIN'T HE SOME FAST WORKER?
R-R-RING!
?
WHAT!! THEY GAVE YOU THE BIG RUSH AND YOU'RE IN THE HOSPITAL-? WELL, I'LL BE---
I'LL TAKE 'EM APART- THEY CAN'T DO THAT TO MY MANAGER AND GET AWAY WITH IT!
HUNKY MUST HAVE DONE SOMETHING TO GET SUCH ROUGH TREATMENT-
NOW WAIT TILL YOU HEAR THEIR SIDE OF THE STORY!
IT BETTER BE GOOD OR ELSE--
BUT YOUR MANAGER'S DEMANDS WERE IMPOSSIBLE-
© 1936 King Features Syndicate, Inc. Great Britain rights reserved
WHY, HE SAID HE ONLY DEMANDED A VACATION FOR ME-
YES, THE TOSSPOT INSISTED ON YOU HAVING A SIX-MONTHS VACATION-
? ?
TWICE A YEAR!
LUCKY BUCKS
PLAY MONEY
2
LUCKY BUCKS
PLAY MONEY
2
LUCKY BUCKS
PLAY MONEY
2

BETTY BOOP
BY MAX FLEISCHER
Registered U. S. Patent Office.
Y'SAY THEY ARE SENDING UP THE CONTRACT FOR MY APPROVAL?
YES, HUNKY DORY IS BRINGING IT OVER - YOU'LL BE A REAL MOVIE STAR AT LAST!
SPINACH! UGH! I CAN'T TAKE IT, I TELL YOH!
YOUR CONTRACT, TILLIE - READ IT AND WEEP WITH JOY!
OH! I'M SO ANXIOUS TO READ IT!
IT BETTER BE GOOD!
HM-M! AND LOOK AT CLAUSE #23, PARAGRAPH #44 - IT SAYS YOU CAN'T MARRY OR - - -
AND LOOKIT THIS CLAUSE #56 - WHY, THE INSULTING TOSSPOTS - I COULD SUE 'EM FOR THAT - OW! AND LOOKIT -
JUST SKIP IT TILLIE!
WHY DON'T YOU BEHAVE?
SUCH COLOSSAL, STUPENDOUS NERVE - TRYING TO TIE ME UP TO SUCH CLAUSES - WHY - - -
AFTER ALL THE STUDIO IS ENTITLED TO SOME RIGHTS!
DON'T WORRY - THEY'LL GET 'EM AND SOME LEFTS, TOO - I'LL WRITE UP MY OWN CONTRACT - -
AHEM! DON'T FORGET TO SLIP IN MY PERCENTAGE, TILLIE!
I DON'T NEED A LAWYER TO REPRESENT ME - I CAN TAKE CARE OF MYSELF ANYWHERE, ANY PLACE OR ANY TIME!
YES, PERHAPS PHYSICALLY, BUT -
'AT'S WHAT I SAID - HERE'S MY CONTRACT - SIGN IT OR ELSE -
SORRY, MADAM - BUT YOU MUST TAKE THAT MATTER UP WITH MY LEGAL DEPARTMENT!
PRESIDENT
YES I'M MY OWN LAWYER - LEAD ON, BOYS!
TO THE CONFERENCE-ROOM MADAM - THIS WAY!
BUT I DON'T THINK IT'S FAIR - AUNT TILLIE ALONE AGAINST YOUR WHOLE LEGAL FORCE!
HEH, HEH! WHEN MY MASTER MINDS GET THROUGH WITH HER SHE'LL BE SIGNED UP TO OUR CONTRACT AND LIKE IT!
YES SIR! SHE CONVINCED US HER CONTRACT WAS FAR SUPERIOR TO OURS!
? ? ? ? ?
© 1936, King Features Syndicate, Inc., Great Britain rights reserved.
LUCKY BUCKS PLAY MONEY 2 BUCK
LUCKY BUCKS PLAY MONEY 2 BUCK
LUCKY BUCKS PLAY MONEY 2 BUCK

BETTY BOOP
BY MAX FLEISCHER
WHY ALL THE SLICKIN' UP. THEY AIN'T NO SCHOOL TODAY?
I'M TAKING YOU DOWN TO THE STUDIO TO SEE AUNT TILLIE DO HER "BABY DUMPLING" SCENES!
WHY DON'T YOU BEHAVE? "BABY DUMPLIN'?" SHE MIGHT BE ABLE TO PLAY HER GRAND-MOTHER!
YOU SEE, BUBBY, IT'S A BURLESQUE ON "BABY DUMPLIN'"— COMEDY STUFF!
WHY, I THOUGHT AUNT TILLIE'S PICTURE WAS IN PRODUCTION ON THIS SET?
IT IS- BUT SHE AIN'T!
SET 6
WAIT THERE, BUBBY- IT LOOKS LIKE AUNT TILLIE HAS GONE TEMPERA-MENTAL ON 'EM!
NO! NO! A THOUSAND TIMES, NO!
AW! HAVE A HEART, AUNT TILLIE- PUL-LEESE!
QUIET! SET #6
AND YOU SAY SHE REFUSES TO COME OUT?
AND NOT ONLY THAT, BUT SHE'S HOLDING UP THE WHOLE CAST-OW! WHAT A WOMAN!
HEAR THAT? I'M LEAVING- BUT FAST!
DON'T BE SILLY- WAIT! EVERY-THING WILL BE OKEY DOKE!
FOR THE LAST TIME- GIVE ME MY CLOTHES OR ELSE-
YOO HOO! DON'T BE LIKE THAT- OPEN UP- THIS IS BETTY!
COSTUME DEPT.
KNOCK NOCK NOK
BUT LOOKIT THE MAKEUP- THEY'LL HAVE ME CUTTING OUT PAPER DOLLS NEXT!
HM-M! BUT THE PART CALLS FOR THAT MAKEUP, AUNT TILLIE!
TEE-HEE!
HA-HAR! "BABY DUMPLIN'!" OW! SOME BABY!
HA-HA! SHE'S A RIOT- SHE'LL MAKE THE PICTURE!
HA HA
HA- HA-
GIVE ME THE HA-HA STUFF, HUH? WELL, LAUGH THAT OFF, YOU TOSSPOTS!
CALLING ALL CARS.
WELL, NO MUGGS CAN LAUGH AT ME AND GET AWAY WITH IT!
THEY WERE PAYING YOU A BIG COMPLIMENT- REMEMBER, YOU'RE PLAYING A COMIC PART!
© 1936, King Features Syndicate, Inc., Great Britain rights reserved.
LUCKY BUCKS
2 PLAY MONEY 2
2 BUCKS

BETTY BOOP
BY MAX FLEISCHER
YOU SAY THEY TRIED OUT TEN ACTORS FOR THE PART IN YOUR NEW COMEDY, "DANCING ON YOUR FEET"?
YEAH! AND MY BOY FRIEND, "HUNKY DORY," BEAT 'EM ALL OUT FOR IT!
'COURSE, IT'S A COMEDY - BUT I WOULDN'T THINK THEY'D SELECT HUNKY - HE'S SO SHORT AND - - - -
WELL, TO TELL THE TRUTH - I HELPED EM WITH THE SELECTION BY KNOCKING OUT THE OTHER ASPIRANTS
CUT! THAT'S ALL FOR TODAY, BETTY - NOW WE'LL GO OVER AND SEE HOW AUNT TILLIE IS DOING!
I'D LOVE TO - WAIT TILL I CHANGE MY COSTUME!
ALL SET! DID YOU KNOW HUNKY DORY IS CO-STARRING WITH AUNT TILLIE?
YES - SHE SAYS THE PART FITS HIM LIKE A GLOVE - GUESS SHE MEANS A BOXING GLOVE!
PICKING THAT LIL' SQUIRT AS A LEAD FOR HER IS VERY BAD CASTING!
THERE WAS NOTHING ELSE TO DO - SHE SCARED OFF ALL OF THE OTHER APPLICANTS
OH, OH! LOOKS LIKE THE PANIC IS ON!
?
OW! LISSEN, AUNT TILLIE - WHY DON'T YOU BEHAVE? WE OUGHTA TITLE THIS PICTURE "RETAKE" - WELL, I'LL BE -
SHE AND HER HALF-PINT BOY FRIEND HAVE MESSED UP EVERY SCENE - I TURNED OVER THE DIRECTING TO CASEY!
WHAT HAVE YOU GOT AGAINST CASEY?
AND I SUPPOSE SHE'LL RUIN THE BIG COMEDY RHUMBA DANCE SHOT, TOO!
WELL, SHE SAYS HUNKY IS A SWELL RHUMBA PARTNER!
CUT! LISSEN, ARE YOU TRYING TO GRAB THIS BIG DANCE SCENE?
'AT'S WHAT I SAID - THE SCRIPT DOES NOT CALL FOR A SOLO DANCE!
WHAT D'YE MEAN - SOLO DANCE?
© 1936, King Features Syndicate, Inc., Great Britain rights reserved.
LUCKY BUCKS
PLAY MONEY
2

BETTY BOOP
BY MAX FLEISCHER
THERE'S AUNT TILLIE WITH THAT PRIZE-FIGHTER AGAIN AND SHE SEEMS BADLY SMITTEN!
I'VE BEEN WACKY OVER YOU, BABY, SINCE DE FOIST TIME I TOOK A GANDER AT YER WIDE OPEN PAN!
AW! MISTER MUGG, YOU'RE ONLY TRYING TO BE NICE TO ME - TEE-HEE-!
P-POOR HUNKY DORY!
THERE, THERE, HUNKY, DON'T TAKE IT SO HARD!
SNIFF-SNIFF-SLUP-SNIFF!
BUCK UP, HUNKY - THIS MISTER MUGG MAY BE JUST A PASSING FANCY!
YEAH? WELL, HE AIN'T GOIN' TO HAVE NO CHANCE TO MAKE ANY PASSES AT ME - SNIFF-
WHAT! Y'SAY HUNKY IS GOING AROUND AND AROUND LIKE A WATCHMAN IN A "ROUND-HOUSE," HUH?
WELL, YOU CAN'T BLAME HIM FOR BEING JEALOUS AT THE WAY YOU'RE CARRYING ON WITH THAT MISTER MUGG!
THE POOR BOY IS ALL BROKEN UP - IT'S DANGEROUS TO TRIFLE WITH A MAN'S AFFECTIONS LIKE THAT!
CAN I HELP IT IF THEY ALL GO "WACKY" OVER ME?
IT'S NO LAUGHING MATTER - WHY, THE DESPERATE LOOK IN POOR HUNKY'S EYES AND --- O-OH! LOOK!
GULP! OW! HE'S GOT A GUN!
OH, DEAR! I TOLD YOU HE HAD A TRAGIC LOOK IN HIS EYES! HURRY!!
TO THINK HE'D DESTROY HIMSELF OVER LOVE FOR ME. HOLD IT! STOP!!
OH, HUNKY, D-DON'T!
HUNKY, DEAR - DON'T DO IT! DON'T DO IT!
BEG PARDON!
I BEG OF YOU, HUNKY - PUL-LEEZE DON'T SHOOT Y'SELF!
?
DON'T BE SILLY. THIS IS ONLY A "PROP" GUN I'M USING IN THE MOB SCENE
5-24
WHAT D'YE MEAN - BY FOOLING ME LIKE THAT - YOU TOSSPOT?
WHY DON'T YOU BEHAVE?
© 1936, King Features Syndicate, Inc., Great Britain rights reserved.
LUCKY BUCKS
PLAY MONEY
2
LUCKY BUCKS
PLAY MONEY
2
LUCKY BUCKS
PLAY MONEY
2

BETTY BOOP
BY MAX FLEISCHER
GIVE US YER AUTOGRAPH, AUNT TILLIE-
WILL I? OBOY! YOU FLATTER ME, KIDS!
AND EVEN THE KIDS ON THE STREET MOBBED ME FOR MY AUTOGRAPH!
JUST LOOK AT THE BIG PLAY THE PAPERS GAVE YOU!
MOVIE STUPENDOUS COLOSSAL! AUNT TILLIE BIG HIT!
SEE? THAT MEANS YOU'RE FAMOUS — YOU WERE THE BIGGEST THING IN THE PICTURE!
HM-M! I DO LOOK A LITTLE STOUT IN IT- DON'T I?
FAN MAIL FOR AUNT TILLIE!
PHEW! WHAT A SCARE-I THOUGHT THEY WERE BILLS!
YOUR BILL TROUBLES ARE OVER!
YEAH! IT LOOKS LIKE A MOB SCENE AT THE STUDIO GATE-ALL ASKING FOR TILLIE!
PUBLIC, HERE I COME
TO THINK I'VE WAITED ALL MY LIFE FOR A LIL' ADMIRATION-WOW! AND LOOK WHAT I GET!
SEE! THEY ALL HAVE PAPERS OR BOOKS-THEY ALL WANT YOUR AUTOGRAPH!
NOW DON'T LET THIS SUDDEN FAME GO TO YOUR HEAD!
HEAD? I'M THRILLED FROM HEAD TO FEET-SUCH ADMIRATION MUST BE DESERVED!
AND ACT DIGNIFIED-REMEMBER, YOU'RE A BIG MONEY STAR NOW!
I NEVER DREAMED MY NAME WOULD BE SOUGHT AFTER LIKE THIS!
WELL, OF ALL THE CRUST —WHY, YOU TOSSPOTS, I'LL---
WHY DON'T YOU BEHAVE? THAT'S NO WAY TO TREAT POOR AUTOGRAPH-COLLECTORS!
OH, YEAH?
BUT THOSE MUGGS WANTED ME TO AUTOGRAPH A FLOCK OF SALE SLIPS FOR CARS, HOUSES 'N' LOTS-STOCKS 'N' BONDS 'N' WHAT-NOT!
?
© 1936, King Features Syndicate, Inc., Great Britain rights reserved
LUCKY BUCKS PLAY MONEY 2
LUCKY BUCKS PLAY MONEY 2
LUCKY BUCKS PLAY MONEY 2

BETTY BOOP
BY MAX FLEISCHER
OH, DEAR! I'M ALL OF A FLITTER - "HUNKY" JUST 'PHONED THAT HE'S COMING UP AND SAYS HE HAS GREAT NEWS!
MAYBE HE GOT A JOB!
WHY DON'T YOU BEHAVE?
AND Y'SAY YOU HAVE A CHANCE FOR THE COMIC LEAD IN "FISH-FACE FAGIN"?
NOTHIN' DIFFERENT, MY DEAR - BUT HERE'S THE CATCH - - LISTEN - -
BOO-HOO-O BEE-HEE- SLUP- - SNIFF-SNIFF!
WHY, YOU OUGHT TO BE HAPPY THAT "HUNKY" GOT SUCH A BIG PART!
YEA, BUT AT WHAT A PRICE - WHAT A SACRIFICE - BOO-HOO! H-HE MUST SHAVE OFF HIS MUSTACHE - BOO-HOO!
WE MUST SACRIFICE FOR ART'S SAKE, Y'KNOW?
SNIFF! I FELL IN LOVE THE FIRST TIME I SAW HIM AND HIS WONDERFUL HANDLE-BAR MUSTACHE - THE BIGGEST IN WAHOO COUNTY - -
IT MAY IMPROVE HIS LOOKS, MAKE HIM LOOK YOUTHFUL AND - -
MAYBE YOU'RE RIGHT - BUT THINK OF ALL THE YEARS OF GROWING THAT GORGEOUS MUSTACHE, WASTED!
BUT THINK OF HOW IT HID ALL HIS OTHER FEATURES!
DON'T BE SO FIDGETY, AUNT TILLIE. HUNKY WILL BE HERE ANY MOMENT NOW!
I CAN'T HELP IT WHEN I THINK OF HUNKY MINUS "OLD HANDLE-BARS"!
AT LAST! WOW! YOU'VE GOT ME ALMOST AS ANXIOUS TO SEE HIM AS YOU ARE!
IF YOU WAS HALF AS MUCH, BETTY, YOU'D BE "WACKY"!
R-RING
PULL YOURSELF TOGETHER, AUNT TILLIE!
OW!! IS THAT A BUTTON-HOLE OR A MOUTH?
BEG PARDON!
HIDING A MUGG LIKE THAT ON ME ALL THESE YEARS WHY, YOU - - -
THIS BEAUTIFUL "HANDLE-BAR" MODEL, YES, SIR! GOING IN DISGUISE, HUH?
NO! GOING OUT OF DISGUISE, SUH!
WIGS
TOUPEE
NON SKID TOUPEE
LUCKY BUCKS
PLAY MONEY
2
LUCKY BUCKS
PLAY MONEY
2
LUCKY BUCKS
PLAY MONEY
2

BETTY BOOP
BY MAX FLEISCHER
SINCE HUNKY DORY SHAVED OFF HIS MUSTACHE, AUNT TILLIE HAS BEEN LIKE THAT!
WHY DON'T SHE BEHAVE?
BOO-HOO-BEE-HEE-SNIFF. SNIFF.
THERE, THERE. PULL YOURSELF TOGETHER, AUNT TILLIE!
OW! WHEN I THINK OF HUNKY SHAVING OFF HIS GORGEOUS MUSTACHE—BOO-HOO!
BUT THERE'S ONE CONSOLATION—IT MAKES HIM LOOK YOUNG!
YES, LIKE A YOUNG MACKEREL—OR A PLUCKED DUCK!
WE MUST SACRIFICE FOR ART'S SAKE AND IT WON'T BE IN VAIN IF HE GETS THE PART!
BUT WHAT A SACRIFICE—"THE BIGGEST "HANDLE-BAR" MUSTACHE IN SEVEN COUNTIES!
AND AFTER ME SHAVIN' OFF MY MUSTACHE THEY TURNED ME DOWN FOR THE "FISH-FACE FAGIN" PART!
E-EEK!!
OH! SHE'S FAINTED—CATCH HER!
"OLD HANDLE-BARS"—GONE! AND NO PART—BOO-HOO!
BE BRAVE, TILLIE—I'VE BEEN TURNED DOWN BY BETTER STUDIOS THAN THAT!
'MEMBER, THERE ARE OTHER STUDIOS, AUNT TILLIE!
WHAT D'YE MEAN—HUNKY WAS "TYPED" WITH THAT BEAUTIFUL FULL-BLOWN MUSTACHE?
WITHOUT IT HE LOOKS SO YOUTHFUL HE HAS MORE CHANCES FOR PARTS!
TRY THIS DIRECTOR FIRST, BUT DON'T BE TOO TRYING!
I'LL COME OUT WITH A PART FOR HIM OR ELSE
HM-M! A JUVENILE, HUH?
OR ANYTHING YOU'VE GOT HANDY!
SORRY, BUT WE AIN'T CASTING TODAY—BRING BACK YOUR LITTLE SON A WEEK FROM SOME TUESDAY!
MY WHAT?
NO GUY CAN PULL A CRACK LIKE THAT ON ME—
BUT YOU SHOULDN'T HAVE WRECKED THE PLACE JUST FOR THAT!
CALLING ALL CARS
© 1936, King Features Syndicate, Inc., Great Britain rights reserved
LUCKY BUCKS
2 PLAY MONEY 2
LUCKY BUCKS
2 PLAY MONEY 2
LUCKY BUCKS
2 PLAY MONEY 2

BETTY BOOP
BY MAX FLEISCHER
Registered U.S. Patent Office
SNIFF! TO THINK HUNKY DORY'S BEAUTIFUL "HANDLE-BARS" MUSTACHE IS GONE-SACRIFICED FOR ART-THE BIGGEST MUSTACHE IN "WAHOO COUNTY," TOO - SNIFF!
PULL YOURSELF TOGETHER AUNT TILLIE. IT'S LOSS IS THE MOVIE INDUSTRY'S GAIN!
SNIFF! HE LOOKS LIKE A NUDIST WITHOUT IT-SNIFF-I LOVED EVERY HAIR OF THAT MUSTACHE-NOW IT'S GONE-SNIFF!
BUT IT TYPED HIM! WITH IT OFF HE LOOKS YOUTHFUL AND CAN TAKE JUVENILE PARTS!
YEP! TILLIE, I'M CAST FOR THE COMIC BABY IN YOUR NEXT COMEDY, "BABY DARLIN'"!
YEAH? THEY MUST THINK YOU'RE IN YOUR SECOND CHILDHOOD, HUH?
-ER-YOU DO LOOK YOUTHFUL, BUT--
TUT, TUT TILLIE, YOU MUST BE BROAD-MINDED IN THE MOVIES!
'AT'S WHAT I SAID-IF I CATCH YOU MESSING AROUND WITH THOSE BLONDES ON THE SET I'LL SLAP YOU BOW-LEGGED!
YOU MUSTN'T BE SO JEALOUS, AUNT TILLIE!
GET INTO YOUR COSTUMES-OBOY! YOU'RE PERFECTLY CAST-YOU BOTH FIT THESE DUMB ROLES TO A "T"
LISSEN, MUGG-IS THAT A KNOCK OR A BOOST?
SOUNDS LIKE BOTH TO ME!
THAT'S IT-JUST ACT NATURAL-WOW! YOUR DUMB-LOOKING PANS ARE KNOCKOUTS, THAT'S ALL-CUT!!
WE'LL LEAVE HUNKY THERE WHILE WE TAKE SOME CLOSE-UPS OF YOU, TILLIE!
I DON'T LIKE TO TRUST HIM OUT OF MY SIGHT, BUT~
HE SURE MAKES A CUTE BABY!
OH, LOOK! A NEW BABY STAR!
ISN'T HE JUST DARLING? LOOK AT THOSE EYES AND-
I ADORE BABY STARS!
O-OH! I COULD JUST HUG HIM TO PIECES!
HE'S TOO SWEET FOR WORDS!
KITCHEE-KITCHEE COO
GOO GA-A-GOO!
OW! WELL, OF ALL THA----
GA-A-GOO-GA-A-GOO-!
SMACK
SMACK
WHY DON'T YOU BEHAVE?
AND IF I HEAR ANYMORE "GA-A-GOO-ING" OUT OF YOU-I'LL TAKE YOU APART!
SLAP
© 1936, King Features Syndicate, Inc. Great Britain rights reserved
LUCKY BUCKS PLAY MONEY 2
LUCKY BUCKS PLAY MONEY 2
LUCKY BUCKS PLAY MONEY 2

BETTY BOOP
-BY-
MAX FLEISCHER
Registered U. S. Patent Office
SNIFF! SHAVING OFF THE BEAUTIFUL "HANDLE-BARS" MUSTACHE WAS AN AWFUL SACRIFICE, FOR ARTS SAKE!
AUNT TILLIE-THINK HOW YOUTHFUL-LOOKING HE LOOKS WITH-OUT IT - HE'S A JUVENILE TYPE NOW!
IT WAS THE BIGGEST MUSTACHE IN "WAHOO COUNTY" WITH THE BIGGEST WING-SPREAD - A RECORD LENGTH FROM STEM TO STERN!
YES, BUT IT HID HIS FEATURES COMPLETELY HE LOOKED LIKE HE WAS HIDING BEHIND A BUSH!
CONGRATULATE ME! SALUTE ME -'CAUSE I'M TO BE STARRED!
OW! LOOK AT THAT NAKED-LOOKIN' PAN-LOOKS LIKE A PLUCKED DUCK!
?
YOU SAY YOU'RE TO PLAY "COUNT MEEOUTSKY" IN THE RUSSIAN COMEDY-"RUSSIAN AROUND"?
A STAR! YES, SUH-I'LL ADMIT IT WAS WORTH SACRIFICING "OLD HANDLE-BARS"!
I WAS HIDING MY LIGHT UNDER A FLOWING MUSTACHE!
I WON'T CRY ABOUT LOSING YOUR MUSTACHE ANY MORE. I CAN SEE IT WAS ALL FOR THE BEST!
'COURSE, IT WAS - IT COVERED TOO MUCH GROUND - IT CRAMPED HIS STYLE!
SMACK
THAT MUSTACHE WAS A GREAT WORRY 'N' CARE, ANY-HOW - IT WAS GETTING OUT OF CONTROL!
TO THINK IT HID THAT FACE ON ME FOR ALL THESE YEARS!
THAT FACE WILL BE FAMOUS SOON!
THINK OF IT-HIS FACE WILL BE FAMOUS THE WORLD OVER ON BILL-BOARDS, FAN MAGAZINE COVERS 'N' EVERYTHIN'!
YES, HIS FACE WILL BE HIS FORTUNE!
GET INTO YOUR MAKEUP, "HUNKY DORY"-YOU'RE HOLDING UP THE PICTURE!
AH! THE BEGINNING OF A NEW FACE FOR THE PUBLIC TO IDOLIZE!
AND WHAT A FACE!
BEG PARDON!
SET 3
FUNNY-HUNKY HAS THE STAR PART, TOO!
I'M COCKEYED LOOKING FOR HIM-THIS IS THE RUSSIAN SET, AIN'T IT?
NO! I DON'T SEE HIM IN THAT SCENE EITHER!
MAY BE THEY AIN'T SHOOTING HIS SCENES YET-OH, OH, LOOK!
SET 3 QUIET
6-28
OW! IT'S "HUNKY DORY"!
MY FACE WILL BE FAMOUS-BAH!
© 1936, King Features Syndicate, Inc., Great Britain rights reserved.
LUCKY BUCKS
PLAY MONEY
2

BETTY BOOP
-BY-
MAX FLEISCHER
Registered U. S. Patent Office
LOOK, AUNT TILLIE — HUNKY DORY IS SPREAD ALL OVER THE PAPER LIKE A PRESIDENTIAL CANDIDATE!
WHAT! HAS THE CRACKPOT BEEN IN ANOTHER FIGHT?
MOVIE PAGE
HUNKY DORY NEW STAR COLOSSAL! STUPENDOUS!
OH! THAT MEANS HIS PICTURE IS A HIT AND THAT HUNKY IS A STAR — OR AM I TOO LOUD?
I HOPE ALL THIS SUDDEN FAME AND ADULATION DOESN'T GO TO HIS HEAD!
MOVIE PAGE
"HUNKY DORY" IN "TOSSPOT"
DON'T MISS IT IF YOU CAN!
IF IT DOES — I'LL SOON KNOCK IT OUT OF HIS PUDDIN' HEAD!
WHAT BILLING! THE WORLD WILL KNOW HUNKY HAS ARRIVED!
LOOK! THERE MUST BE A MOB SCENE IN ONE OF THE PICTURES!
DON'T BE SILLY — THEY'RE AUTOGRAPH HUNTERS AND THEY'RE ASKING FOR HUNKY!
WE WANT HUNKY DORY!
I THOUGHT THE "CHAIN LETTER" CRAZE WAS OVER!
THAT'S "FAN MAIL" FOR HUNKY — A SURE SIGN OF FAME!
MAIL
THAT WAS THE MOST FAN MAIL I EVER SAW ONE STAR RECEIVE!
LOOKED LIKE THE POST OFFICE MADE HUNKY'S DRESSING-ROOM A SUB-STATION!
WHY, THIS OUGHT TO BE THE HAPPIEST MOMENT OF YOUR LIFE!
SNAP OUT OF IT — YOU TOSSPOT — WHY, WITH THAT RECORD-BREAKING BATCH OF FAN MAIL —
FAN MAIL — ME EYE —
THEY'RE ALL BILLS!
FORGET THOSE BILLS — LOOK AT ALL THOSE ADORING FANS — CALLING TO PAY YOU HOMAGE!
YEAH? WELL, WHATEVER THEY PAY — MEMBER, HUNKY, WE'RE 50-50!
WE WANT HUNKY DORY!
YOU MUST SEE THEM — YOU OWE IT TO YOUR PUBLIC!
HIS PUBLIC — AH! WHAT MAGIC IN THEM THERE WORDS — HIS PUBLIC!!
MY PUBLIC!
© 1936, King Features Syndicate, Inc., Great Britain rights reserved.
?
GANGWAY!! HIDE ME QUICK — THEY'RE A FLOCK OF BILL-COLLECTORS!
STOP 'IM!
7-5
LUCKY $ BUCKS
PLAY MONEY
2 BUCKS

BETTY BOOP
-BY-
MAX FLEISCHER
Registered U. S. Patent Office
AUNT TILLIE, YOU'D BETTER HURRY, HUNKY DORY IS HOLDING UP THE SCENE WITH THE "HICCOUGHS"!
TEMPERAMENTAL HUH? WELL, TELL THE "HICKOFFS" TO GO ON WITHOUT THE LIL' CHEESE!
NONO! HUNKY HAS A TERRIBLE CASE OF "HICCOUGHS" AND THEY CAN'T STOP THEM!
OH, YEAH? I'LL STOP HIS HICKIN' OR ELSE-
HIC- HIC- HIC- HIC-
BUT HE SEEMS TO BE HICCOUGHING MUCH EASIER THAN HE WAS
WELL, HE OUGHTA- HE'S BEEN PRACTISIN FOR THE LAST HOUR AND WE'VE TRIED EVERY CURE ON HIM-BUT NO DICE!
HIC- HIC- HIC-
THAT'S IT- CLOSE YOUR EYES, OPEN YOUR KISSER, HOLD YOUR BREATH AND KEEP SWALLOWIN'!
HOPE IT WORKS- 'CAUSE THE PICTURE MUST GO ON!
GULP. HIC- HIC- HIC- HIC-
IF IT DOESN'T- SHE'S GOING TO TRY THE "SCARE CURE"!
OW! IF THAT DON'T SCARE 'IM LOOSE FROM HIS HICKIN'- I'LL GIVE UP!
BOO!
HIC- HIC- HIC- HIC- HIC
HM-M! GOING TO SHAKE 'EM OUT, HUH? NOT A BAD IDEA!
WELL, YOU CAN'T HATE ME FOR TRYING!
HIC HIC HIC HIC HIC
WHAT! IS THE LIL' CRACKPOT STILL "HICKIN'"?
NOW HE'S HICKIN' WORSEN EVER!
HIC- HIC- HIC- HIC-
WELL, I ONLY KNOW ONE MORE CURE- IT'S A LIL' ROUGH, BUT---
NONO! IF YOU SAY IT'S A LIL' ROUGH- IT'S OUT!
JUST LET HER TRY THIS LAST TIME- IT MIGHT WORK!
HIC- HIC- HIC-
OH! YOU'RE GOING TO HYPNOTIZE HIM OUT OF THEM, HUH?
IF THIS CURE FAILS I'LL DO WORSEN THAT- NOW HOLD IT- RELAX AND CLOSE YOUR EYES-
HIC- HIC- HIC HIC-
THIS SURPRISE SLAP ON THE BACK IS THE LAST RESORT WHEN ALL OTHER CURES FAIL!
SLAP
WELL, I CURED HIS HICCOUGHS, DIDN'T I?
YES! BUT IF THAT'S A CURE, I'LL TAKE VANILLA!
© 1936, King Features Syndicate, Inc., Great Britain rights reserved.
LUCKY BUCKS PLAY MONEY 2
LUCKY BUCKS PLAY MONEY 2
LUCKY BUCKS PLAY MONEY 2

BETTY BOOP
BY MAX FLEISCHER
Registered U. S. Patent Office
OW! WHAT'S THAT RACKET- CUT!
OH, OH! AUNT TILLIE AND BUBBY ARE AT IT AGAIN!
BA-A WA-A BAW.
SPANKED YOU? WELL, YOU MUST HAVE DONE SOMETHING AND DESERVED IT!
BA-A- I DIDN'T DO NOTHIN'- I ONLY PUT A LIL' SAND IN HER MAKE-UP CREAM!
NO! JUST FOR THAT, I WON'T PLAY IN HER OLD PICTURE!
DON'T BE SILLY- YOU WANT TO HELP MAKE HER DEBUT AS A STAR A SUCCESS!
NO! NO! NO! NO! NO!
DON'T BE LIKE THAT- WHY, THIS IS AUNT TILLIE'S FIRST STARRING VEHICLE!
AND A LOT DEPENDS ON YOU, BUBBY!
NO! NAW! NUH! NO!!
--- AND YOUR BIG SCENE IS WHEN YOU HIT AUNT TILLIE WITH A PIE!
YEAH! A CUSTARD PIE- YOU'RE TO SOCK HER RIGHT ON THE NOGGIN-HA-HA AND LISTEN--
SOLD!
THEY ALL WANT TO WISH YOU LUCK IN YOUR FIRST STARRING PART!
YES, AUNT TILLIE, I'M GIVING YOU THIS LIL' HINDOO CHARM FOR LUCK!
AND I'M DONATIN' THIS LIL' OLD RABBIT'S FOOT!
AND THIS FOUR-LEAF CLOVER -ER-
MY PUH BLIC I THANK YUH. PUH-LENTY YOWZAH!
CAMERA! NOW TAKE GOOD AIM- DON'T MISS HER IF YOU CAN!
DON'T WORRY, YOU WON'T NEED A RETAKE ON THIS SCENE!
CLANK!
DID SHE FALL OR WAS SHE PUSHED?
MY! WHO BAKED THAT PIE?
PIE, ME EYE- IT WAS THE HORSE-SHOE THAT WAS IN IT!
BUT WHAT WAS THE IDEA OF PUTTING A HORSE-SHOE IN THE PIE?
OH! THAT WAS TO WISH HER LUCK!
7-19
LUCKY BUCKS PLAY MONEY
2
LUCKY BUCKS PLAY MONEY
2
LUCKY BUCKS PLAY MONEY
2

BETTY BOOP
BY
MAX FLEISCHER
Registered U.S. Patent Office
YES, AUNT TILLIE, THE SCENES ARE LAID A-WAY BACK IN THE "90's"
OH! A COSTUME PICTURE, HUH?
IN A WAY, YES - YOU PLAY A BATHING BEAUTY OF THAT PERIOD!
WELL, IF I DO SAY IT, MYSELF - I AINT GOT THE WORST FIGGER IN THE WORLD
AT'S WHAT I SAID - I PLAY THE LIFE-GUARD IN YOUR PICTURE, TILLIE!
YEAH? WHERE'S YOUR WATER-WINGS?
WHY DON'T YOU BEHAVE?
WHERE'S THE HELMET THAT GOES WITH THAT DEEP-SEA DIVING-SUIT?
THIS AIN'T A FASHION SHORT - IT'S A COMEDY OF THE "90's"
YES, THIS IS THE STYLE THEY WORE IN THE "90's"
?
COME ON, ALL SET FOR THE COMEDY, RESCUE SCENE!
HA-HA! YOU LOOK LIKE SOMETHING THE CAT DRAGGED IN - HA-HA!
LISTEN "PANTIE LEGS" - YOU'RE NO BARGAIN, Y'SELF!
I HOPE HUNKY DORY IS A GOOD SWIMMER!
THAT'S IT, HUNKY - NOW YOU RESCUE TILLIE - OKAY! CAMERA!
HALP!
HA-HAR! SWELL! VERY REALISTIC - PERFECT COMEDY HA HA!
HALP! HALP! HALP!
? ?
?
?
GLUG-GLUB-GLUG-
GLUB GLUG GLUB GLUG
HELP!
HALP!
GREAT STUFF! HA-HA! THAT WAS THE FUNNIEST RESCUE SCENE I EVER SAW!
IT WAS VERY FUNNY, BUT--
OH! YEAH?
© 1936, King Features Syndicate, Inc., Great Britain rights reserved.
?
?
WELL, SILLY, YOU'LL NEED SOMEBODY TO RESCUE YOU AS SOON AS I GET MY STRENGTH BACK!
7-26
LUCKY BUCKS
PLAY MONEY
2
BUCK
LUCKY BUCKS
PLAY MONEY
2
BUCK
LUCKY BUCKS
PLAY MONEY
2
BUCK

BETTY BOOP
BY MAX FLEISCHER
Registered U. S. Patent Office
NO PART! NOT EVEN A "BIT"- GUESS I'M ALL WASHED UP AS A COMEDY MOVIE STAR!
DON'T BE SILLY, AUNT TILLIE - ALL YOU NEED IS AN AGENT!
AGENT, ME EYE - WHAT D'YE TAKE ME FOR A BOOK OR SUMPIN'?
NO, NO! AN AGENT TO SECURE YOU PARTS AT THE DIFFERENT STUDIOS!
BEG PARDON - DID I HEAR THE WORD AGENT - OR AM I TOO LOUD?
PS-ST! HOW ABOUT HUNKY DORY?
WELL, IT WON'T HURT TO TRY HIM!
IT'S VERY SIMPLE - ALL YOU HAVE TO DO IS CONTACT THE CASTING DIRECTORS AND - - -
GET IT - YOU'RE NOW MY AGENT - HAVE YOU HAD ANY EXPERIENCE AS AN AGENT, HUNKY?
PLENTY! BOOKS, INSURANCE 'N'EVERYTHIN'
HOPE YOU GET LOTS OF PARTS LINED UP FOR ME--
DON'T WORRY - YOU'LL HAVE MORE PARTS THAN A SWISS WATCH!
YEP! I'VE GOT YOU ALL SIGNED UP FOR FIVE - COUNT 'EM - STAR PARTS!
GREAT! HUNKY, YOU'RE SOME AGENT!
SUCCESS! I'M MADE!
LATER
O-OH! IT MUST BE THE DIRECTORS WITH THE SCRIPTS!
R-R-ING
YEZZA! I'D HAVE SIGNED YOU FOR MORE, BUT I RAN OUT OF STUDIOS!
WHAT ?
WELL OF ALL TH'- - - -
GANGWAY! GANGWAY!
WHAT! YOU TURNED DOWN ALL FIVE PICTURES AFTER HUNKY SIGNING YOU UP FOR THEM!
I HAD TO AND THEY'RE GOING TO SUE
HE SIGNED ME FOR FIVE PICTURES WITH FIVE DIFFERENT STUDIOS TO START AT THE SAME TIME AND I AIN'T QUINTUPLETS!
© 1936, King Features Syndicate, Inc., Great Britain rights reserved.
LUCKY BUCKS PLAY MONEY 2 BUCK
LUCKY BUCKS PLAY MONEY 2 BUCK
LUCKY BUCKS PLAY MONEY 2 BUCK

BETTY BOOP
BY
MAX FLEISCHER
Registered U S Petent Office
YES, AUNT TILLIE - HERE'S THE SCRIPT OF THE MELO-DRAMA YOU PLAY NEXT!
WELL, I HOPE IT AIN'T TOO MELLOW!
IT'S A SWELL PLAY-COME ON, HUNKY DORY CAN HELP YOU REHEARSE IT!
LET'S REHEARSE THE LOVE SCENES FIRST?
WHY DON'T YOU BEHAVE?
NOW YOU'RE LIL' NELL, THE HEROINE AND HUNKY, YOU PLAY THE VILLAIN!
MAYBE I CAN'T PLAY IT GOOD, BUT I CAN PLAY IT LOUD!
S'MATTER, "PUTTSIE" C'MON AND PLAY!
GIMME THEM PAPERS, LIL' NELL, OR ELSE-
HEH, HEH! NOW I HAVE YUH IN ME POWER - SO WHAT?
AW! DON'T BE LIKE THAT - S'MATTER WITH YOU?
THAT'S IT! PUT LOTS OF FEELING INTO THE LINES -
SPARE MUH! WON'T NOBODY SAVE MUH?
S'SCRAM-OUT INTO THE CROOL WOILD YOU GO AN'--
WHAT TH'---
BOP!
BUBBY! WHAT DO YOU MEAN BY HITTING HUNKY WITH THAT VASE?
NO, NO! DON'T CENSURE THE LITTLE DARLING FOR SUCH A GALLANT GESTURE!
WHAT D'YE MEAN - GALLANT GESTURE?
THE LITTLE DEAR DID IT, THINKING HE WAS SAVING ME FROM THE BAD MANS!
SAVIN' YOU, ME EYE--!
?
WHAT?
'AT'S WHAT I SAID - I DID IT 'CAUSE HIS LOUD MOUTH WAS SCARIN' MY PUP!
HOT? BUT WHY NOT PUTA DA ICE ONA DA HEAD?
'CAUSE THAT AIN'T WHERE SHE SPANKED ME, SILLY!
8-9

BETTY BOOP
BY
MAX FLEISCHER
Registered U.S. Patent Office
NOW WE'LL HAVE A LONG REHEARSAL - YOU MUST BE GOOD TO GET THIS BIG PART!
YOU'RE TELLIN' ME - I'M SO-O NERVOUS I GOT TO HAVE ABSOLUTE QUIET OR ELSE -
YOU SAY EVEN THE TICKING OF THE CLOCK ANNOYS YOU?
AND HOW - IN THE STATE I'M IN IT SOUNDS LIKE A TAP DANCER ON A TIN ROOF!
WHY, THE SLIGHTEST NOISE MAKES ME AS JUMPY AS A FLEA ON A HOT ROCK!
DON'T BE SILLY, AUNT TILLIE - PULL YOURSELF TOGETHER!
WAHOO! YEOW!! GANGWAY!
EEK!!
BUBBY! NOT SO LOUD!
WHY, MY NERVES ARE AS FRAYED AS THE ELBOWS OF A HOBO'S COAT!
AUNT TILLIE HAS TO REHEARSE THIS BIG PART AND SHE WON'T BE ABLE TO IF YOU KEEP MAKING NOISE!
CAN I DEPEND ON THAT?
NOW EVERYTHING IS NICE AND QUIET - LETS START---
WHAT D'YE MEAN - QUIET?
TA-TA-UMPAH-UMPAH TOOT! TOOT!
PLAY THAT ON YOUR DANGONE BAZOOS!
HM-M! GUESS WE'LL HAVE TO LOOK FOR A MORE QUIET PLACE!
OW!
BUY OL' CLO'S OL' CLO'S
GET YOUR CAR, BETTY - I'LL FIND A QUIET SPOT!
© 1936, King Features Syndicate, Inc., World rights reserved
CLANG CLANG
TOOT TOOT
SICK, ME EYE - JUST DRIVE TO A HOSPITAL - THAT'S ALL!
WEE-E-E
P.D.
HEY! DON'T YOU KNOW THIS IS A QUIET ZONE?
THAT'S WHY I CAME HERE TO REHEARSE, SILLY!
QUIET ZONE
8-16
LUCKY BUCKS
PLAY MONEY
2
BUCK

BETTY BOOP
-BY-
MAX FLEISCHER
YES, AUNT TILLIE GETS THE LEADING COMEDY ROLE. THAT IS, IF –
OH! THERE'S A CATCH IN IT, HUH?
IF WHAT, SILLY?
IF YOU REDUCE ABOUT 20 LBS.– HERE'S A STRICT DIET FROM THE DOCTOR!
MUST I TAKE IT BEFORE OR AFTER MEALS?
WHY DON'T YOU BEHAVE?
IT'S WORTH REDUCING FOR– IT'S A FAT PART!
YEAH? THEN WHY DO I HAVE TO BE THIN TO PLAY IT?
WEEK LATER
SHE SAID SHE'S HAD NOTHING BUT THE STRICT DIET--
THAT IS OUTSIDE OF MY REGULAR MEALS!
THIS WAY FOR THE SCALES!
?
OW! WHY, YOU GAIN INSTEAD OF LOSE!
HM-M! GUESS I'M ONE OF THOSE "POOR LOSERS" YOU HEAR ABOUT!
SHORTS? I THOUGHT THIS WAS A FEATURE PICTURE?
I MEAN "SHORTS" FOR RUNNING– YOU'VE GOT TO REDUCE!
YOU KNOW– ROAD-WORK LIKE AN ATHLETE DOES!
RUNNIN' OFF MY WEIGHT SEEMS SO SILLY!
THEY SAY IT'S THE BEST WAY TO REDUCE, AUNT TILLIE!
THE FIRST TEN MILES ARE THE HARDEST!
H 5671
NOT SO FAST– I'M NO "BREVITY"!
KEEP IT UP– YOU'RE DOING FINE!
HEY! WHERE'S THE FIRE?
HA-HA! SO LONG– IT'S ONLY ABOUT TWO-HOURS' WALK TO THE NEXT TOWN– IF YOU RUN!
OH! IT'S FIVE MILES!
YES, THAT'S ENOUGH RUN FOR THE FIRST DAY– WE'LL PARK HERE AND WAIT FOR HER!
Z-Z-Z Z-Z-
WELL, OF ALL THE--
© 1936, King Features Syndicate, Inc., World rights reserved
PLAY MONEY
PLAY MONEY
PLAY MONEY

BETTY BOOP
-BY-
MAX FLEISCHER
Registered U. S. Patent Office
YES, YES, RIGHT AWAY----OH, AUNT TILLIE, THEY WANT BUBBY TO PLAY OPPOSITE THE CHILD STAR, "CURLY LOCKS"!
WELL, BEING OPPOSITE TO ANYTHING IS THAT KID'S DISH!
HE'S NOT UNDER THE BED! YOO-HOO-O!! BUB-BEE!
I'LL GET HIM- I KNOW WHERE HIS HIDEOUT IS!
NO CASTOR OIL! THEY WANT YOU TO PLAY "WITH CURLY LOCKS"
LET GO! I DON'T PLAY WITH GIRLS-I'M NO SISSIE!
BUT, BUBBY- YOU'RE TO PLAY WITH HER IN A BIG PICTURE!
HE SAYS HE'S NOT BEING TEMPERAMENTAL- IT'S JUST PLAIN TEMPER!
WHY DON'T YOU BEHAVE?
BUBBY- THERE'LL BE A BIG ELEPHANT IN THE PICTURE AND---
WHAT D'YE MEAN BY THAT LAST CRACK- "-YOU DIDN'T KNOW I WAS IN IT"?
YOU MUSTN'T CALL YOUR AUNT TILLIE AN ELEPHANT, BUBBY!
HE'S JUST A LITTLE SHY!
YEAH! SHY A LOT OF THINGS HE OUGHT TO BE!
OH! HE'LL BE OKAY WHEN HE SEES "CURLY LOCKS"!
SHE BETTER BE GOOD!
I'LL SAY SHE IS- THERE SHE COMES NOW-OH! CURLY DEAR!
NOW LEAVE THEM ALONE SO THEY'LL GET ACQUAINTED, THEN THEY WON'T ACT STRANGE IN THE SCENES!
-ER- 'LO!
OH! 'LO, LIL' GIRL!
WHAT!! I'M A LIL' BOY!
LIL' BOYS DON'T WEAR DRESSES-
-THEY WEAR PANTS!
OH, YEAH?
WELL, WHO SAID THEY DIDN'T?
?
© 1936, King Features Syndicate, Inc., World rights reserved.
PLAY MONEY
2
BUCK

BETTY BOOP
BY MAX FLEISCHER
Registered U. S. Patent Office.
'C'MON, MISTER VAN TWINKLE, 'N' PLAY COWBOY- YOU BE THE COW 'N'--
NO, BUBBY, WE HAVE AN IMPORTANT REHEARSAL TO DO!
BE THE COW - YOU'RE VERY FLATTERING, I MUST SAY
YEAH, BUT NOT TO THE COW!
NOW, VAN, SHALL WE REHEARSE THE -ER- LOVE SCENES FIRST?
-ER-BY ALL MEANS, BETTY!
BANG! BANG! RIDE 'EM, COWBOY- YIP-PEE! WOW!!
OW! STOP IT, BUBBY. HOW DO YOU THINK WE CAN REHEARSE WITH THAT RACKET?
?
MISTER VAN TWINKLE MUST HAVE ABSOLUTE QUIET!
HE'LL HAVE IT IF I HAVE TO HOLLER MY HEAD OFF TO GET IT FOR HIM!
PLAY WITH HIM IN THE BACK YARD - ANY PLACE WHERE HE WON'T ANNOY MISTER VAN TWINKLE!
'C'MON, BUBBY, DON'T YOU KNOW LITTLE BOYS SHOULD BE SEEN, NOT HEARD?
WHY DON'T YOU BEHAVE?
DON'T WORRY, VAN, AUNT TILLIE WILL KEEP HIM QUIET!
BUT WHO'S GOING TO KEEP HER QUIET?
OUT! NOW IT'S MY TURN TO BAT!
OBOY! YOU'RE SOME PLAYER!
BAM
'C'MON, PUT IT OVER AND I'LL KNOCK IT INTO THE NEXT COUNTY!
HERE'S ONE THAT WILL HAVE YOU SWINGIN' LIKE A GATE!
BABE RUTH IN HIS PALMY DAYS DIDN'T HAVE NOTHING ON THAT SOCK!
BAM
WOW! WHAT A WALLOP! IT'S A HOMER!
OH, OH!
CRASH
BUB-BEE! AUNT TIL-LEE!!
GOOD BYE- M!!
SH-H-!
© 1936, King Features Syndicate, Inc., World rights reserved.

BETTY BOOP
BY MAX FLEISCHER
Registered U.S. Patent Office
THAT'S VAN TWINKLE CALLING. SO PLEASE KEEP BUBBY QUIET!
HE'LL BE QUIET 'CAUSE HE'S PRACTISIN FOR THE BOY SCOUT ENCAMPMENT!
R-R-ING.
GREETINGS, VAN- ARE YOU FEELING BETTER?
YES, BUT MY NERVES ARE A BIT JUMPY!
DON'T WORRY- EVERYTHING WILL BE QUIET WHILE WE REHEARSE -ER-???
WHAT TH'--
TOOT-TOOT-TA-TA TATATA TA-A-
OW!
CALM YOURSELF, VAN. I'LL STOP THAT TOOTING!
TA-TA-TATATA-TA-TA-TATATA-TA-A-
STOP IT, BOBBY. YOU MUST DO YOUR BUGLE PRACTICE IN THE DAYTIME!
TA-TA-TATATA-TA-TA TA-A-A-
BUGLE CALLS
WE JUST MUST HAVE QUIET, THAT'S ALL!
THE ONLY TIME THIS KID IS QUIET IS WHEN HE'S ASLEEP AND THAT'S WHERE HE'S GOIN'!
AW! WHY DON'T YOU BEHAVE?
IT WAS BUBBY PRACTISING HIS BUGLE CALLS. AUNT TILLIE WILL PUT HIM TO SLEEP!
CAN I DEPEND ON THAT?
?
OW!
OH! HE'S THE DARIN' YOUNG MAN ON THE FLYIN' TRAPEZE-
-HE FLEW THROUGH THE AIR WITH THE GREATEST OF EASE--
Z-Z-Z
BUT CAN'T YOU ROCK HIM TO SLEEP WITHOUT THAT-ER-SINGING?
NO! HE WON'T GO TO SLEEP UNLESS I SING!
© 1936, King Features Syndicate, Inc., World rights reserved
GIVE THE KID BACK HIS BUGLE PLEASE!
? ?
LUCKY BUCKS PLAY MONEY 2
LUCKY BUCKS PLAY MONEY 2
LUCKY BUCKS PLAY MONEY 2

BETTY BOOP
-BY-
MAX FLEISCHER
Registered U. S. Patent Office.
AUNT TILLIE, YOU MUST REHEARSE THIS LOVE SCENE TILL YOU'RE PERFECT - IT'S THE BIG SHOT OF THE PICTURE!
YOU'RE TELLIN' ME - I'M ALL OF A FLITTER ABOUT IT!
CLAM Y'SELF, SWEET!
WELL, THERE'S NOTHING TO MAKE YOU NERVOUS - EVERYTHING IS NICE AND QUIET AND - ---???
YEAH! SO QUIET YOU COULD HEAR A ROLLIN-PIN DROP! OW!
TA-TA-TA-TA-
BUBBY! DO YOU HEAR? STOP IT!!
TATA-TATA-TA-A-TATA
IF YOU MUST PRACTICE YOUR BOY SCOUT BUGLE CALLS - PLEASE DO IT OUTSIDE!
OH! AWRI'! AWRI'!
THERE - NOW HE'S TAKING HIS TOOTING OUTSIDE!
CAN I DEPEND ON THAT?
YOU CAN DEPEND ON THAT KID FOR NOISE - ALWAYS
OW! LET'S REHEARSE IN A BOILER FACTORY. IT'LL BE QUIETER!
OH! THAT IS VERY ANNOYING!
TA TA-TA-TA
PULL Y'SELF TOGETHER, TILLIE, I'LL STOP HIM!
SLUP, SLUP - WANT A BITE OF LEMON, BUBBY?
TATA. TATA-TATA. TA-TA TOOT SLUP-SLUP-
?
TEE HEE!
HAR-HA!
SLUP SLUP SLUP
TATA-TATA-TOOT-SLUP-TOOT-SLUP-SLUP....
TEE HEE! THAT LEMON STOPPED HIM!
DERN TOOTIN THE TOOTIN IS OVER!
© 1936, King Features Syndicate, Inc. World rights reserved
THAT LEMON IDEA WAS VERY CLEVER, HUNKY!
HUNKY HAS MORE TRICKS UP HIS SLEEVE THAN A CANDIDATE HAS PROMISES!
'S JUST AN OLD KID DAYS CUSTOM WE WORKED ON STREET BANDS!
?
LOOK! THEY MADE ME DRUMMER BOY 'STEAD OF BUGLER!
?
DUB-RUBA-DUB-DUB RUBA-DUB-
LUCKY BUCKS PLAY MONEY 2 2
LUCKY BUCKS PLAY MONEY 2 2
LUCKY BUCKS PLAY MONEY 2 2

BETTY BOOP
-BY-
MAX FLEISCHER
Registered U S Patent Office
YEAH, BUT AUNT TILLIE MUST SHOW RARE DRAMATIC ABILITY TO GET THE PART—YOU COACH HER!
RARE? WITH MY NERVES IT'LL BE RAW!
?
BUBBY, YOU JUST CAN'T PRACTISE YOUR BOY SCOUT BUGLE CALLS HERE
OW! HE WOULD START HIS TOOTIN' AT A TIME LIKE THIS
TATA-TATA-TA-A-
OH, DEAR, I'M ON MY NERVES SO OVER THIS BIG PART. THAT THE LEAST NOISE GIVES ME THE JITTERS!
THERE, THERE, CALM YOURSELF!
PS-ST! PULL YOURSELF TOGETHER TILLIE - I'LL TAKE CARE OF BUBBY!
CLICK CLICK
-AND I'VE JUST GOT TO HAVE ABSOLUTE QUIET IF I EXPECT TO LEARN THIS PART RIGHT!
VERY TRUE AND YOU'LL HAVE IT NOW-HUNKY WILL KEEP BUBBY AMUSED OUTSIDE!
BUT LISTEN-EVERYTHING IS QUIET NOW!
YES - ALL BUT MY NERVES - THEY'RE STILL JITTERY!
HUNKY WILL KEEP BUBBY INTERESTED TEACHING HIM BOY SCOUT PRACTICES!
I HOPE HE DEMONSTRATES HIKING TO HIM!
FINE! NOW YOU'RE CALM-LET'S START ON THE SCRIPT!
OKAY! LET'S GO!
?
OH! NOW HE'S PLAYIN' A BUGLE AND A DRUM, TOO!
TOOT-TOOT-TATA-TATA-TA-A-RUBA-DUB-DUB-DUB-
OW! A BUGLER AIN'T BAD ENOUGH-HE HAS TO LEARN TO BE A "ONE-MAN BAND"!
I CAN'T UNDERSTAND THIS!
TATA-TATA-RUBA-DUB-DUB-
?
WELL, I'LL BE-
TA-TA-TA-
RUBA-DUB-DUB-
SOCK
TATA-TATA-TA-A-
RUBA-DUB-DUB-

BETTY BOOP
BY MAX FLEISCHER
Registered U. S. Patent Office.
OH! IT WAS THE MOTHER OF "KUTIE KIDD" THE YOUNG MOVIE STAR-THEY'RE CALLING TO SEE BROTHER BUBBY-FIND HIM, QUICK!
OH, YEAH? YOU'D BETTER "CALL ALL CARS"!
CLICK
NOT HIDING HERE-WE MUST FIND HIM-WE CAN'T MISS THIS BIG CHANCE OF PLAYING OPPOSITE "KUTIE KIDD"!
WELL, I'M LOOKING EVERY PLACE I CAN THINK OF!
AND IT DOESN'T LOOK LIKE HE'S BEEN UP HERE IN THE ATTIC!
THAT'S EASILY SEEN--IT'S TOO CLEAN-LOOKING!
FOR THE LAST TIME-WHERE IS BUBBY HIDING?
WE AIN'T HIDIN' HIM-YOU CAN SEARCH US!
AND EVEN CASEY, THE COP, AIN'T SEEN HIM!
HE MUST BE HIDING HERE SOME PLACE-LOOK IN THE YARD AGAIN!
I NEVER SAW A CHILD THAT HATED GETTING CLEANED UP LIKE HE DOES-YOO-HOO! BUBBY!
HE THINKS A BATH-TUB SHOULD BE USED ONLY TO SAIL BOATS IN!
FINDING A NEEDLE IN A HAYSTACK WOULD BE A PUSH-OVER ALONG SIDE OF THAT KID-NOW I'VE GOT GO GET CLEANED UP!
OH, DEAR! AND HERE THEY COME!
YES, I HEARD YOUR YOUNG BROTHER BUBBY WAS JUST THE TYPE TO PLAY OPPOSITE "KUTIE"!
OPPOSITE IS RIGHT-HE ALWAYS DOES JUST THE OPPOSITE!
COURSE, I'D HAVE TO SEE HIM TO MAKE SURE!
I'M SURE BUBBY IS JUST THE TYPE!
WHAT-NO BUBBY?
OH! ISN'T HE CUTE? AND SO NEAT AND CLEAN-LOOKING!
HOW DEE YUH DO-
LUCKY BUCKS PLAY MONEY
LUCKY BUCKS PLAY MONEY
LUCKY BUCKS PLAY MONEY

BETTY BOOP
BY MAX FLEISCHER
Registered U. S. Patent Office
BUBBY IS ALL RIGHT- HE'S PLAYING BOY SCOUT!
OW! WELL, OF ALL THE--
HE WAS USING YOUR NEW DRESS FOR A TENT?
-AND NOT ONLY THAT- BUT HE WAS USING MY NEW CORSETS FOR A FORT!
AW! A BOY SCOUT GOTTA HAVE A TENT
OUR CAPTAIN SAID WE MUST PRACTISE BOY-SCOUTING AT HOME- I GOTTA LEARN LOTS OF THINGS!
I'M BUSY- SO AUNT TILLIE WILL HELP YOU TO LEARN THEM!
I KNOW MORE ABOUT BOY-SCOUTIN' THEN THE OLD BOY, HIMSELF!
CAN AUNT TILLIE MAKE A FIRE BY RUBBING WOOD TOGETHER?
SURELY- SHE KNOWS ALL ABOUT INDIAN LORE!
WHY, I COULD MAKE OLD SITTIN BULL SIT UP AND TAKE NOTICE
OBOY! IF YOU CAN TEACH ME HOW TO MAKE A FIRE I'LL BE A FULL-FLEDGED BOY SCOUT!
YEAH? WELL, CONSIDER YOURSELF A BOY SCOUT RIGHT NOW!
HERE'S THE PIECES OF WOOD!
NOW GET ME A PIECE OF CORD AND I'LL SHOW YOU HOW SIMPLE IT IS TO MAKE A FIRE WITHOUT MATCHES!
SEE? IT'S THE FRICTION THAT DOES IT- NOW IF YOU WAS MILES FROM HABITATION WITHOUT A MATCH-
HABITATION? I NEVER HEARD OF THAT TOWN!
IN FACT, THE INDIANS DIDN'T HAVE MATCHES SO THEY HAD TO KNOW HOW TO MAKE A FIRE LIKE THIS!
HURRY! LUNCH IS READY!
OH, YEAH? LIKE WHAT?
WELL, IT'S A GOOD TRICK, IF I DON'T DO IT!
?
TSK! TSK!
© 1936, King Features Syndicate, Inc., World rights reserved
HURRY! DINNER IS READY!
HOO-HUM-M!
MUCH LATER!
THAT'S WHAT I SAID-HAVE YOU GOT A MATCH!
NO! BUT I'LL GIVE YOU A LIGHT!
?
LUCKY BUCKS
PLAY MONEY
2
LUCKY BUCKS
PLAY MONEY
2
LUCKY BUCKS
PLAY MONEY
2

BETTY BOOP
BY
MAX FLEISCHER
Registered U. S. Patent Office
OH! THEY'RE FOR YOUR BIRTHDAY, AUNT TILLIE - FROM HUNKY DORY -
SO THE LIL' HALF-PINT DID REMEMBER ME, HUH?
HM-M! NO! THEY'RE FROM A MISTER DEWBERRY!
DIZZY DEWBERRY - THE DARLING - SNIFF! AIN'T THEY "GORJAH"?
I WOULDN'T LET A FEW FLOWERS INFLUENCE ME!
YEAH? THAT'S MORE'N WHAT THAT SHRIMP HUNKY DORY SENT.
YOUR RIVAL HAS SURE PUT YOU ON THE SPOT WITH THIS BOUQUET - YOU KNOW HOW SHE LOVES FLOWERS?
GULP! SHE LOVES "T" BONE STEAKS, TOO!
FLOWERS ARE THE SUREST WAY TO HER HEART!
WELL, I'LL HIE MYSELF TO THE HILLS 'N' DALES WHERE NATURE WILL PROVIDE A "BOOKAY" FIT FOR A QUEEN!
SUNFLOWERS, BLUEBELLS, DAFFODILS AND DAISIES - OL' DAME NATURE'S PRODUCT OF POSIES WILL MAKE THAT MUG'S HOTHOUSE "BOOKAY" LOOK LIKE A SPRAY OF TIMOTHY HAY!
IT'S HUNKY DORY WITH A GLORIOUS BUNCH OF WILD FLOWERS - PICKED BY HIS OWN HAND!
SUCH BEAUTIFUL SENTIMENT!
AND IT SHOWS HIS POETIC NATURE - IT'S A BEAUTIFUL GESTURE!
AH! ME - A PRICELESS GIFT - PRICELESS!
AH! WILD FLOWERS NATURE'S MOST BEAUTIFUL GIFT---
YASSUH! THE BEAUTY OF THE GLENS 'N' DELLS - THE HILLS 'N' THE MEADOWS 'N'---
WELL, OF ALL THE ~~
OLD KID NATURE IS PRETTY GOOD, BUT SHE CAN'T GROW ANYTHIN' AS BEAUTIFUL AS A TEN-BUCK NOTE
'AT'S WHAT I SAID $10 WORTH OF YOUR BEST FLOWERS!
PEACE OFFERING, HUH?
© 1936, King Features Syndicate, Inc., World rights reserved.
LUCKY BUCKS PLAY MONEY 2
LUCKY BUCKS PLAY MONEY 2
LUCKY BUCKS PLAY MONEY 2

BETTY BOOP
-BY-
MAX FLEISCHER
Registered U S Patent Office
LOOK! A BOOKAY OF POSIES FROM "DIZZY" DEWBERRY!
AGAIN? TALK ABOUT "SAYING IT WITH FLOWERS" HE REALLY STUTTERS!
IT'LL SAVE US FROM BUYING FLOWERS FOR THE TABLE!
SNIFF! IF THERE'S ONE THING I LOVE MORE'N FLOWERS - IT'S FLOWERS!
THAT RIVAL OF MINE MUST BE A FLORIST
AND TO THINK THAT EGG, HUNKY DORY, NEVER GAVE ME ANYTHIN' BUT A PAIN IN THE NECK!
HM-M! HOW AM I GONNA COMPETE WITH THAT POSY-GIVING MUG WITH ONLY TWO-BITS?
AH! I HAVE IT!! THE HILLS 'N' DALES, THE FIELDS 'N' MEADOWS, OL' DAME NATURE'S FLOWER GARDENS — FREE! GRATIS 'N' ~
HERE WE ARE - WITH FLOWERS OF EVERY HUE - THERE FOR THE PICKIN'!
MILK
GRADE A TO Z
I'LL MAKE THAT BIG MUG'S "HOTHOUSE BOOKAY" LOOK LIKE A SPRIG OF TUMBLE WEEDS!
THE FLOWERS THAT BLOOM IN THE SPRING TRA-LA
THE DARLING! WILD FLOWERS - DAME NATURE'S GREATEST GIFT!
SUCH BEAUTIFUL SENTIMENT!
OH! DAISIES, BUTTERCUPS, DAFFODILS GOLDEN ROD AND - - -
AH! DAFFY DILS 'N' GOLDEN ROD WITH THE GLINT OF VIRGIN GOLD IN ITS GOLDEN-HUED BLOSSOMS
WILD FLOWERS FOR MY LIL' "WILD FLOWER"!
YOU SWEETIE - PICKED BY YOUR OWN HANDS - SUCH SENTIMENT!
© King Features Syndicate, Inc. World rights reserved
WILD FLOWERS! HUNKY SURE HAS A POETIC NATURE!
SNIFF!! I'LL SAY — HE'S GOT NOTHIN' ELSE BUT!
NEXT DAY!
GETTING "HAY FEVER" AND "POISON OAK" ARE VERY ANNOYING, BUT - -
IT'S THE ONLY TIME THAT WEASEL EVER GAVE ME ANYTHIN' - WOW! AND HE SURE GAVE ME PLENTY!
AH-CHOO AH-CHOO
11-7

BETTY BOOP
-BY-
MAX FLEISCHER
Registered U. S. Patent Office
LOOKIT THE CUTE LIL' POOCH "DIZZY" DEWBERRY GAVE ME!
WOOF WUF
WHAT A MAN - CANDY, FLOWERS, NOW A PUP!
"DIZZY" IS SMART- HE KNOWS YOU LOVE DOGS, AUNT TILLIE!
I CAN'T LET THAT RIVAL OF MINE BEAT ME OUT WITH A POOCH
LOOK! HE CAN DO TRICKS AND EVERYTHING- CHUMP, FRITZ!
OH, YEAH? WELL, WHAT DID THAT EGG, HUNKY DORY, EVER GIVE ME?
YASSUH! IT BEHOOVES ME TO PRESENT TILLIE WITH A POOCH OR I'M SUNK!
THAT'S THE PRICE, BROTHER, $50 A PIECE!
WHY, I COULD BUY A HORSE FOR THAT!
$50 AND ME HOLDING TWO BUCKS- LOOKS LIKE "DIZZY" DEWBERRY HAS ELIMINATED ME FROM THE TOURNAMENT!
TALK ABOUT PUPPY LOVE IF I ONLY HAD A PUP TO MATCH THAT RIVAL'S GIFT I'D STILL BE "BOY-FRIEND NO. 1" - BUT NO DICE!
WELL, I'LL GO IN AND DEMAND OF HER TO DECIDE BETWEEN US AND THEN BUST OUT CRYIN'!
WELL, I'LL SAY THAT'S AWFULLY SWEET OF YOU, HUNKY!
O BOY! SWEET IS NO NAME FOR IT!
ER- BEG PARDON!
I ALWAYS WANTED A LIL' "SCOTTIE"- HOW DID YOU KNOW, YOU DARLING?
I'M GLAD YOU APPRECIATE HUNKY'S THOUGHTFUL GIFT!
I'LL NEVER DOUBT YOU AGAIN- MY GREAT, BIG GENEROUS, THOUGHTFUL BOY!
GR-R-
SMACK
© 1936, King Features Syndicate, Inc., World rights reserved
YOUR BEST "T"-BONE STEAK- FOR THE BEST DAWGONE DOG IN THE WORLD!
DID HE SAVE YOUR LIFE, OR SUMPIN'?
LUCKY BUCKS
PLAY MONEY
LUCKY BUCKS
PLAY MONEY
LUCKY BUCKS
PLAY MONEY

BETTY BOOP
-BY-
MAX FLEISCHER
Registered U. S. Patent Office
HOW CAN I COMPETE WITH THAT NEW RIVAL, "DIZZY" DEWBERRY, THE WAY HE'S SHOWERIN' HER WITH GIFTS?
WELL, YOU CAN'T BLAME AUNT TILLIE - ALL GIRLS ARE FLATTERED BY GIFTS!
LOOKIT THE BEAUTIFUL PEARL RING DIZZY GAVE ME!
MY! WHAT A BIG ONE - IS IT REAL?
BAH! PROBABLY A PHONY LIKE HIMSELF!
THERE GOES POOR HUNKY ALL BROKEN UP!
HE'S BEEN BROKE EVER SINCE I MET HIM - MAYBE THIS'LL MAKE HIM SNAP OUT OF IT!
FLOWERS, THEATRE TICKETS, CANDY - NOW JEWELRY - IT MAY BE A YACHT OR SUMPIN' NEXT!
OW! WHAT COMPETITION - THE BIG 'UMPCHAY IS SURE MAKIN' ME LOOK LIKE AN AWFUL MUG!
THE BATTLE OF GIFTS, HUH? WELL, I CAN'T LET THAT BIG CLOWN TOP ME!
JEWELE
YES, SIR - THAT RARE PEARL NECKLACE ONCE BELONGED TO PRINCESS IFFINDOFFER!
WELL, SECOND-HAND OR NOT, IT LOOKS OKAY TO ME - WRAP IT UP!
YOU SAY IT'S A DELIVERY-BOY FROM A SWANKY JEWELER?
YEAH! I'LL BET IT'S A GIFT FROM HUNKY!
R-R-ING!
OH! ISN'T THAT SWEET OF HUNKY --ER---???
A PEARL NECKLACE? ---WHAT!! TAKE IT BACK! THAT'S WHAT I SAID - I WON'T ACCEPT IT!
NOW IS THAT A NICE WAY TO TREAT HUNKY'S GIFT? OF COURSE, YOU SHOULD ACCEPT IT!
ACCEPT IT, ME EYE -
THE LIL' CRACKPOT SENT IT C.O.D.!
© 1936, King Features Syndicate, Inc., World rights reserved
LUCKY BUCKS
PLAY MONEY
2
LUCKY BUCKS
PLAY MONEY
2
LUCKY BUCKS
PLAY MONEY
2

BETTY BOOP
BY
MAX FLEISCHER
Registered U. S. Patent Office.
R-R-ING!
THAT'S "DIZZY" DEWBERRY NOW - I KNOW YOU'LL LOVE TO MEET HIM!
DON'T BE JEALOUS HUNKY, HE'S JUST A PASSING FANCY!
WELL, HE BETTER NOT MAKE ANY PASSES AT ME
AND NOW, DIZZY, DEAR, MEET MR. HUNKY DORY!
GET UP OFF YOUR KNEES - STAND UP WHEN A LADY INTRODUCES YUH!
I MAY BE A LIL' SHORT, BUT YOU'RE A LIL' SHORT, YOURSELF, SILLY, IN THE BROW
?
?
OH! A WISE-CRACKER, HUH? WELL, THAT NOGGIN' SUITS ME OKAY, SHORT PANTS!
I'VE SEEN BETTER ON TOTEM POLES!
NOW IS THAT NICE?
ANOTHER CRACK OUT OF YOU, HALF PINT, AND I'LL SLAP YOU BOWLEGGED!
WHY DON'T YOU BEHAVE?
OH, YEAH? HOLD ME - HOLD ME!
PS-ST! C'MON OUT-SIDE, "BOOTNOSE" - I DON'T WANT TO MESS UP THE FURNITURE!
OW! STOP 'EM!
LE'S GO! S'GOOD IDEA - YOU'LL HAVE MORE ROOM TO FALL DOWN!
B-BUT L-LISTEN, D-DIZZY, I WAS ONLY FAKIN' IN FRONT OF TILLIE - CAN'T YOU TAKE A JOKE?
I'LL SAY I CAN - WATCH ME TAKE YOU!
POW!
?
P-POOR LIL' HUNKY - THAT BIG BRUTE, "DIZZY," WILL TAKE HIM APART AND IT'S ALL MY FAULT, BOO-HOO!
HERE, CALM YOURSELF - REMEMBER HUNKY IS A GOOD RUNNER!
AHEM! JUST A SAMPLE OF HOW I HANDLE MY RIVALS!
HUNKY, DEAR - MY HERO!
?
© 1936, King Features Syndicate, Inc., World rights reserved
YES, HERE'S THE PRICE OF NEW GLOVES, BATS 'N' BALLS AND AN EXTRA BUCK FOR THE KID WHO HIT THAT FOUL TIP!
WHAT! NO BASE-BALL SUITS?
LUCKY BUCKS
PLAY MONEY
2 BUCK
PLAY MONEY
PLAY MONEY

BETTY BOOP
-BY-
MAX FLEISCHER
Registered U S Patent Office
...AND YOU'RE BRINGING YOUR LITTLE SON, PHILBERT, ALONG? OH! BUBBY WILL JUST LOVE THAT, MRS. HYATT."
PHILBERT? I AIN'T PLAYIN' WITH NO SISSY WITH A NAME LIKE THAT!
OH, YEAH? I S'POSE HE'LL WANT TO PLAY "TIDDLE-DY-WINKS" OR SUMPIN'!
WELL, YOU CAN TEACH HIM HOW TO PLAY SOME OF YOUR GAMES!
PHILBERT JUST ADORES GAMES!
BUBBY! NOW TAKE PHILBERT OUT AND TEACH HIM SOME GAMES!
GREETINGS AND SALUTATIONS, OLD BEAN!
I LIKE HIM TO TAKE HIS RECREATION IN THE OPEN!
YES, BUBBY JUST DETESTS INDOOR GAMES!
I'LL SAY I'LL SHOW YOU SOME GAMES!
THAT'S SPORTING OF YOU, OLD CHAP!
LET'S YOU AND ME RASSLE FIRST!
FINE! SHALL IT BE "GRECO-ROMAN" OR "CATCH-AS CATCH-CAN"? I'LL REMOVE MY GLASSES-
SEE, PHILBERT, THIS IS CALLED A "FLYIN' TACKLE" AND--ER--
"I THINK THIS "AIR-PLANE SPIN" IS MORE EFFECTIVE BUBBY----
-FOLLOWED UP WITH AN "AUSTRALIAN BODY SLAM"- OR AM I TOO LOUD?
OOF!
BUT I THOUGHT IT WAS TO BE BEST TWO OUT OF THREE?
-ER-NO, I JUST THOUGHT WE OUGHTA DO SOME BOXIN'!
COME ON- LEAD YOUR RIGHT!
OH! ONE SHOULD NEVER LEAD WITH ONE'S RIGHT FOR ONE'S CHIN!
HOW'S THAT?
TSK! TSK! YOUR JUDGEMENT OF DISTANCE AND TIMING ARE VERY BAD-
SEE! YOU LEFT YOURSELF WIDE OPEN FOR A RIGHT CROSS!
BOP
WELL, AREN'T THERE ANY OTHER GAMES YOU KNOW, BUBBY?
YES, ONE MORE- COME INTO THE HOUSE!
12-12
© 1936 King Features Syndicate, Inc. World rights reserved.
MY! MY! CHECKERS!!!
IT WAS BUBBY'S SUGGESTION!

BETTY BOOP
-BY-
MAX FLEISCHER
Registered U S Patent Office
I'VE LOOKED FROM CELLAR TO ATTIC FOR HIM-THAT KID IS HARDER TO FIND THAN A TAXI ON A RAINY DAY!
THERE HE GOES! CATCH HIM - QUICK!
THAT'S WHAT I SAID-YOU'D HAVE TO RUN FASTER THAN "OWENS" TO GET AWAY FROM ME!
PUFF! PUFF! YOU'RE TELLIN' ME!
THANK GOODNESS, HE DIDN'T GET AWAY FROM YOU!
WELL, IT WASN'T BECAUSE HE WASN'T TRYING - I HAD TO CHASE HIM TWENTY BLOCKS!
OW!
STOP SPLASHING! I SHOULD WEAR A DEEP-SEA DIVING-SUIT WHEN I GIVE YOU A BATH!
STOP HIM BEFORE HE MESSES UP THE WHOLE HOUSE!
BUT YOU MUST LET AUNT TILLIE DRY YOU OFF!
OW! SHE'S TRYIN' TO RUB THE SKIN OFF ME!
BUT YOU MUST LOOK NICE WHEN MRS. SWANKY CALLS THIS AFTERNOON!
THIS IS THE ONLY OUTFIT HE HAS, CLEAN.
PHEW! FIXING UP THAT KID IS MORE WORK THAN GETTING A "DEB" READY FOR A COMING-OUT PARTY!
WELL, I WANT HIM TO LOOK NICE AND PRETTY!
NOW CAN I GO OUT AND PLAY A LITTLE?
YES, BUT DON'T GET DIRTY-REMEMBER MRS. SWANKY IS CALLING.
AND ALSO REMEMBER THAT'S THE ONLY CLEAN OUTFIT YOU HAVE!
ENDS BACK! 24-68-124-32-105--
?
I'M SO ANXIOUS TO SEE YOUR LITTLE BROTHER!
AUNT TILLIE IS CALLING HIM IN NOW!
BUBBY! HERE HE COMES-
12-19
WHAT TH'---
?
HELLO! GEE! I JUST MADE A TOUCH-DOWN!

BETTY BOOP
BY
MAX FLEISCHER
Registered U. S. Patent Office.
HERE'S THE TONIC THE DOCTOR ORDERED FOR BUBBY - YOU MUST SHAKE WELL BEFORE USING OR SHAKE HIM WELL AFTER USING!
AND HE'S TO TAKE IT IN A LITTLE WATER!
OH, YEAH? WELL, I AIN'T GETTIN' IN NO TUB TO TAKE NO MEDICINE
YOU MUST TAKE IT - IT'S THE DOCTOR'S ORDERS, BUBBY!
SO YOU WON'T TAKE IT, HUH?
NO! I CAN'T TAKE IT!
HAVE YOU GOT HIM, AUNT TILLIE?
YES, PHEW! I'LL NEED A DOSE OF THE TONIC, MYSELF, AFTER ALL THIS EXCITEMENT!
WAW
BAW
THAT'S A GOOD BOY - TAKE YOUR TONIC!
NO! I KNOW IT TASTES AWFUL!
DON'T BE SILLY - IT TASTES LIKE CANDY - LOOK I'LL TAKE A DOSE FIRST!
THAT'S WHAT YOU TOLD ME ABOUT CASTOR OIL!
SEE! AUNT TILLIE TAKE IT!
SLUP! UGH! UM-M! OH! IT TASTES SO NICE!
UM-M! SEE! AUNT TILLIE LOVES IT!
WELL, THEN, LET HER HAVE IT!
JUST ONE LIL' SPOONFUL IT'LL MAKE YOU A BIG, STRONG BOY AND --
YES, THEN YOU'LL MAKE THE FOOTBALL TEAM, SURE!
SLUP! UGH! SEE! AUNT TILLIE IS TAKING ANOTHER DOSE UM-M! NICE!
NO! NO! NO! NO! NO!
ALLRIGHT! LOOK! I'LL TAKE ANOTHER DOSE! SLUP!
AND IF YOU TAKE IT I'LL BUY YOU A NEW FOOTBALL!
BAW! WAW! NO!
THINK OF THAT - FOR JUST TAKING ONE DOSE YOU GET A NEW FOOTBALL?
AND A NEW FOOTBALL SUIT, TOO!
AND WILL YOU BUY ME A FOOTBALL "HEAD-GEAR" TOO?
YES! YES! YES! YES! YES!
ALLRIGHT! I'LL TAKE IT!
OW! IT'S EMPTY!
?
YEAH? OH! AIN'T THAT TOO BAD?
12-27
© 1936, King Features Syndicate, Inc., World rights reserved
LUCKY BUCKS PLAY MONEY 2
LUCKY BUCKS PLAY MONEY 2
LUCKY BUCKS PLAY MONEY 2

BETTY BOOP
by MAX FLEISCHER
Registered U S Patent Office
BROADCAST STATION? YOU SAY YOU WANT AUNT TILLIE FOR AN AUDITION?
A RADIO QUEEN!! AT LAST I'VE MADE THE AIR!
AFTER THEY HEAR YOU - YOU'LL GET IT, TOO!
YOUR VOICE MUST PASS THE AUDITION TEST FIRST, YOU KNOW?
IF I DO SAY IT, MYSELF, I SING PRETTY GOOD!
WELL, NOT GOOD, BUT LOUD!
I'VE MADE ARRANGEMENTS FOR "PROFESSOR YODELHOLLER" TO TRAIN YOUR VOICE AND - - -
WHAT! D'YE THINK IT'S THAT WILD?
SO DISS AUNT TILLIE - HAS SHE HAD IT ANY VOICE-TRAININ' YET?
NO. IT'S AN UNTRAINED VOICE, PROFESSOR, BUT - -
THE MAKIN'S IS THERE AND - -
O SOLE MIO - -
ACH! NO, NO 'I SAID SING IT - DISS AIN'T IT A HOG-CALLIN' CONTEST -
?
YES, I WANT TO STUDY - D'YE THINK I OUGHTA GO TO ITALY?
ACH! FARDDER YET DEN DOT!
NOW IS THAT NICE?
OH! A WISE-CRACKER, HUH? WELL, LISTEN, "MOON-FACE", CAN YOU HELP MY VOICE OR NOT?
ACH! DOT'S BEYOND HELP - I'M A MOOSISHUN NOT A MAGISHUN YET!
JUST GIVE HER ANOTHER CHANCE PROF.!
O SOLE MIO -
HOW'S THAT? SHE CAN BEAT ANY-BODY IN THE WORLD!
PRETTY GOOD, BUT -
VOICE! ACH! I'VE HEARD BETTER MITT A BULL-FRUGG!
THERE! THAT SHOWS MY VOICE HAS APPEAL OR SUMPIN'
?
AUNT TILLIE! SING AGAIN, WILL HUH?
THE LITTLE DARLINGS - I'M GLAD THERE'S SOMEBODY WHO LIKES MY SINGIN'
LIKE YOUR SINGIN', ME EYE -
I BET 'EM ALL THAT YOU COULD HOLLER LOUDER THAN JOE, THE FISH-PEDDLER!
© 1937, King Features Syndicate, Inc. World rights reserved.
1-16

BETTY BOOP
BY
MAX FLEISCHER
Registered U S Petent Office
Y'SAY THIS NEW BOY FRIEND, MR. FINICKY, ADMIRES A GOOD COOK?
YES, I'M BAKING A CAKE FOR HIM - I WANT TO MAKE A GOOD IMPRESSION ON HIM!
IT LOOKS LIKE A CAKE - SMELLS LIKE A CAKE. NOW IF IT ONLY TASTES LIKE A --
THAT'S WHAT I'M WORRIED ABOUT - HE'S SO FUSSY!
BUT WE'RE BOTH ON A STRICT DIET - HOW ARE WE TO KNOW IF IT TASTES ALL RIGHT?
I'VE GOT IT! TEST IT ON BUBBY!
THANK YOU SO-O-MUCH!
WELL, AUNT TILLIE, WE'LL SOON KNOW IF IT'S GOOD!
YES - OR GOOD FOR NOTHING!
HOW'S ABOUT ANOTHER PIECE, SIS?
WHY, YOU FLATTER ME AND MY BAKING, BUBBY!
OH! A LIL' CAKE-EATER, HUH?
SURE, IT MUST BE GOOD WHEN THAT FUSSY KID COMES BACK FOR MORE!
I HOPE SO - 'CAUSE MR. FINICKY ADMIRES A GOOD COOK!
MAY I HAVE ANOTHER PIECE, SIS?
NOW THIS IS THE LAST - I MUST SAVE THE REST FOR MR. FINICKY!
YOU CAN'T EAT YOUR CAKE AND HAVE IT, TOO!
I'LL MAKE A BIG HIT WITH MR. FINICKY IF IT IS A GOOD CAKE!
YOU MAY BE SURE OF IT - KIDS ARE THE BEST JUDGES EVER!
NOW DON'T FIGHT OVER IT — YOU'LL ALL GET SOME!
OH, MY! I DIDN'T IMAGINE IT WAS THAT GOOD - LISTEN TO THEM FIGHTING OVER IT!
YES, SIR - THAT MAKES IT UNANIMOUS!
WHAT! ME EAT IT? DON'T BE SILLY. BUT THE PUPS SEEM TO LIKE IT!
1-30

BETTY BOOP
BY MAX FLEISCHER
Registered U S Patent Office
YEAH! THE "SCOOTER DERBY" IS THIS AFTERNOON- WHY DON'T YOU BUILD A SCOOTER AND ENTER?
OBOY! MAYBE I'LL DO THAT!
-'N' I CAN BUY THE PARTS CHEAP- JUST FOUR WHEELS 'N'--
NO, NO! YOU'RE TOO YOUNG TO RACE IN A "SCOOTER DERBY" AND BESIDES-
SCOOT ALONG AND GET ME THE CLOTHES-PINS!
YOU CAN THINK OF MORE SILLY THINGS TO DO THAN A POLITICIAN-
-OR WHY DON'T YOU GET SOME OF YOUR PALS AND PLAY INDIAN?
AW! CAUSE THEY'RE ALL IN THE "SCOOTER DERBY"!
BUBBY'S BEEN SITTING THERE IN DEEP THOUGHT FOR AN HOUR!
AND WHEN THAT LAD IS STILL FOR A SPLIT SECOND- LOOKOUT!
YES, SIR! AND THIS WILL MAKE A SWELL BODY!
NOW WHAT WOULD ANYBODY WANT TO CUT OFF A PIECE OF CLOTHES-LINE FOR, WHY--
AND YOU SAY BUBBY AGREED TO WATCH YOUR DOLL-BUGGY TILL YOU CAME BACK?
HIM MINDING A DOLL-BUGGY? THAT SOUNDS FISHY!
WHEN I CAME BACK THE WHEELS WERE GONE 'N' SO WAS HE!
NOW, THERE'S SOMETHING VERY ODD ABOUT ALL THESE THINGS MISSING!
YOU'RE TELLIN' ME - LET'S FIND BUBBY!
BUBBY IN THE "SCOOTER DERBY"- WITH WHAT?
THAT'S WHAT I'D LIKE TO KNOW!
GET ON THE MARK THERE. BUBBY- GO!!
2-6
COME BACK WITH THEM WHEELS 'N' CLOTHES-LINE 'N' BOX-
DO YOU HEAR, BUBBY? STOP THIS INSTANT! STOP-
WOW! BUBBY WINS!
3

BETTY BOOP
-BY-
MAX FLEISCHER
Registered U S Petent Office
YES, HUNKY DORY IS BACK TO ASK FOR YOUR HAND AGAIN!
WELL, THE LIL' SQUIRT WILL GET MY FOOT!
OH! AUNT TILLIE, I WOULDN'T BE THAT CRUDE!
I'VE GOT TO BE — THAT "YES MAN" WON'T TAKE "NO" FOR AN ANSWER!
HE'S MAD ABOUT YOU. YOU COULD DO A LOT WORSE THAN MARRY HUNKY!
NOT MUCH WORSE! WHY MY FUTUEE WOULD BE ALL BEHIND ME WITH THAT HALF-PINT!
REMEMBER, HE'S MADLY IN LOVE WITH YOU, SO PLEASE BREAK IT GENTLY!
I'LL BREAK SOMETHIN' GENTLY OVER HIS DUMB HEAD IF HE COMES BACK AGAIN!
-AND IN THE FIFTH PLACE - YOU'RE TOO LAZY TO WORK - SO HOW COULD YOU SUPPORT A FAMILY?
-ER-WELL, HOW MANY ARE IN YOUR FAMILY?
-AND NOT ONLY THAT, BUT I WOULDN'T MARRY YOU IF YOU WERE THE LAST MAN ON EARTH---
AM I TO TAKE THIS AS A REFUSAL?
LOOK AT HIM - THE POOR BOY IS TAKING IT TERRIBLY HARD!
HM-M! MY STARS! I DIDN'T THINK HE'D TAKE IT THAT HARD!
HE'S WHAT?
HE'S GONE TOWARDS THE RIVER!! QUICK! STOP HIM!
OH! HE'S OUT OF SIGHT! YOO-HOO!! HUNKY! COME BACK!
OW! DON'T DO IT, HUNKY, DEAR — I'LL SAY "YES"!
WELL, OF ALL TH'---
YEAH! I'VE CAUGHT SIX SINCE YOU'VE BEEN GONE!
LOOK! I'VE GOT A BITE SO QUICK!
2-20
©1937, King Features Syndicate, Inc. World rights reserved.
THAT'S WHAT I SAID - WHAT D'YE MEAN BY FOOLING ME LIKE THAT YOU --
?

BETTY BOOP
-BY-
MAX FLEISCHER
Registered U S Patent Office
HO-HUM-M! OH! HOW I HATE TO WAKE UP IN THE MORNING!
YOU'LL WAKE UP LIKE A "LONG SHOT SLEEPER" WHEN THE CHECKS ARE DOWN - AFTER YOU SEE THE MORNING PAPERS!
DON WAHN, THE WORLD'S GREATEST HEART FLUTTERER, SEEKING A LEADING LADY - WELL HERE'S WHERE I HELP HIM TO FIND ONE!
DAILY O BLAH
STAR ARRIVES
DON WAHN SIGNS WITH P.D.Q. SEEKS LEADING LADY
WHAT! NO BREAKFAST?
NO! AUNT TILLIE, WHY SPEAK OF FOOD AT A TIME LIKE THIS!
-AND 'PHONE THE STUDIO HAIR-DRESSER THAT I WANT HER WHOLE STAFF RIGHT AWAY!
I MUST LOOK MY BEST WHEN HE SEES ME, 'CAUSE I'LL HAVE MORE COMPETITION THAN THERE IS IN AN OLYMPIC MEET!
THEY SAY BEAUTY IS ONLY SKIN DEEP! OUCH! FEELS LIKE YOU'RE TRYING TO VERIFY THE RUMOR!
WE'LL GET READY FOR YOUR FACIAL NEXT!
OO-LALA! YOU ARE TOO, TOO, BEAUTIFUL!
IT WAS AN AWFUL STRAIN, BUT IT'LL BE WORTH IT IF I GET THAT ROLE WITH DON WAHN!
YOU SAY THEY'VE JUST RESCUED HIM FROM AN ARMY OF LEADING LADIES!
YES, THEY'VE GOT HIM PARKED IN THE CHIEF'S OFFICE!
STUDIO
DON, MEET BETTY BOOP, A CANDIDATE FOR THAT LEADING LADY ROLE!
IS SHE BLONDE OR BRUNETTE?
OH! DARK GLASSES!
2-27
-AND AFTER ALL MY TROUBLE TO GET BEAUTIFIED - HE'S WEARING DARK GLASSES!
KLIEG LIGHTS! EYE STRAIN! THE DOCTOR'S ORDERS - MUST PROTECT HIS EYES --
TELL HIM IT'S ALLRIGHT - I'M SUPPOSED TO BE EASY ON THE EYES!
WOW! YOU'RE TELLIN' ME!
?

BETTY BOOP
-BY-
MAX FLEISCHER
Registered U S Petent Office
YOU SAY YOU'RE CALLING THIS AFTERNOON? OH! MISTER DON WAHN— THAT'S SO SWEET OF YOU!
YOO-HOO! AUNT TILLIE—DON WAHN, THE BIG MOVIE STAR, IS CALLING—OH! I'M SO THRILLED—GET THE MOP AND---
THE PLACE IS A MESS—HURRY, WE MUST CLEAN IT UP—YOU KNOW IT'S THE MAID'S DAY OFF!
IT WOULD BE—WHY ALL THE FUSS? IS HE CALLING TO SEE YOU OR THE PLACE?
LOVE STORIES
HURRY, BUBBY, YOU MUST PUT AWAY ALL YOUR TOYS—MR. DON WAHN IS PAYING US A VISIT!
OH, YEAH? AND I'LL BET THAT'S ALL THE BIG UMPCHAY EVER PAYS!
TO THINK THE GREAT DON WAHN IS CALLING ON ME FIRST—IT PUTS A BIG FEATHER IN MY CAP!
YES, AND A BIG VACUUM-CLEANER IN YOUR HAND!
AUNT TILLIE, THIS WILL BE THE BIGGEST THRILL OF MY LIFE—ENTERTAINING THE GREAT DON WAHN!
IF YOU CALL THIS ENTERTAINING I'LL TAKE VANILLA!
I WANT TO MAKE A GOOD IMPRESSION—SHOW HIM THAT I KEEP MY PLACE IN GOOD TASTE!
BUT WHY TEAR THE PLACE APART TO DO IT?
THIS CHAIR HERE—NOW WHERE WILL WE PUT THE PIANO?
UMPH! WHAT D'YE MEAN, WE? IF YOU DON'T DEC DE QUICK THE PIANO WILL!
WELL IT'S ALL SPICK AND SPAN AT LAST—PHEW! AM I GLAD IT'S FINISHED? IT ALL BUT FINISHED ME!
HO-HUM-M! ME TOO! IT WAS SOME JOB!
Z-Z Z-Z BZ-Z
BETTY! MISTER DON WAHN IS HERE—ER-- -ER---
3·6
B-BUT-BUT--
NO, NO! DON'T DISTURB HER. SHE LOOKS ALL FAGGED OUT—JUST TELL HER THAT I CALLED!

BETTY BOOP
-BY-
MAX FLEISCHER
Registered U S Patent Office
HERE HE IS, HIDING UNDER THE COVERS- D'YE HEAR! COME OUT OR I'LL GO IN AFTER YOU!
HOW HE HATES TO GET DRESSED UP AND I WANT HIM TO LOOK NICE WHEN DON WAHN CALLS!
HONEST, IS DON WAHN, THE BIG MOVIE STAR GONNA BE HERE?
YES, IN PERSON-WHY YOU SHOULD BE THRILLED, BUBBY!
OH! I'M SURE HE'LL GIVE YOU HIS AUTOGRAPH AND THEY ARE VERY RARE TOO!
GOSH! BET THEY'RE ALMOST AS RARE AS BABE RUTH'S OR DIZZY DEAN'S, HUH?
YES, DON, BUBBY WANTS YOUR AUTOGRAPH FOR HIS COLLECTION!
AH! A COLLECTOR WHO KNOWS HIS AUTOGRAPHS!
SO NICE OF YOU, DON, I KNOW YOU SELDOM GIVE YOUR AUTOGRAPH!
THAT'S WHAT MAKES THEM SO RARE AND SOUGHT AFTER BY COLLECTORS!
THANKS A MILLION!
WOW! AN AUTOGRAPH OF DON WAHN, THE BIG MOVIE STAR!
OBOY! THAT'S JUST WHAT WE NEED!
MY PALS HERE WANT AN AUTOGRAPH OF YOURS TOO MISTER DON WAHN!
OH! BUBBY, YOU MUST'N'T---
TUT, TUT, BETTY- OF COURSE I WILL-I FEEL FLATTERED!
MY FANS! THEY'RE A PART OF MY ADORING PUBLIC-WHY SHOULD I-THEIR IDOL-REFUSE THEM!
LOOK! WHAT HAPPINESS IT GIVES THEM HAVING ONE OF YOUR RARE AUTOGRAPHS
YES, SIR, YOU SURE DID US SOME FAVOR, MISTER!
IT'S A PRICELESS POSSESSION. ONE THEY WILL CHERISH FOR LIFE!
YEAH! THEY'LL TREASURE IT-THE AUTOGRAPH OF THEIR IDOL-THEIR HERO-
THEIR HERO ME EYE-TAKE A GANDER OUT THE WINDOW!
?
?
WE'RE ROOTIN FOR YOU TO WIN YOUR NEXT FIGHT KAYO!
YEAH 'KAYO'- WE'LL TRADE AN AUTOGRAPH OF DON WAHN, THE BIG MOVIE STAR, FOR ONE OF YOURS!
AH OUGHTA CHARGE YO ALL TWO OB DEM FO ONE OB MINE!
TRADE EM- WE KIN GET TWO BITS APIECE FO' DEM DON WAHNS'!
KAYO BAM

BETTY BOOP
BY
MAX FLEISCHER
Registered U S Patent Office
HO-HUM! OH! HOW I HATE TO WAKE UP IN THE MORNING!
YEAH! WELL, YOU'LL WAKE UP WHEN YOU READ WHAT THE COLUMNISTS HAVE WRITTEN ABOUT THE NEW ROMANCE OF DON WAHN!
THE FICKLE-HEARTED TWO-TIMER! YES, GIVE ME EVERY ONE OF HIS PHOTOS AND I'LL BURN UP ALL HIS LETTERS TOO!
IF IT WAS ME I'D BURN HIM UP, TOO BUT PLENTY!
HIS DAILY ORCHIDS, BAH! I DON'T WANT ANYTHING AROUND THAT'LL REMIND ME OF HIM!
YUM-M! DON'T WORRY, BETTY, I'LL GET RID OF HIS CANDY FOR YOU!
THAT'S WHAT I SAID - TURN IT OFF! I DON'T WANT TO EVEN HEAR HIS VOICE!
...AN ELECTRIC TRANSCRIPTION OF A SCENE FROM "GREAT LOVER" STARRING DON WAHN..
FASTER! YOU MUST GET ME AWAY FROM THE SIGHT AND SOUND OF HIM, OH!
CALLING ALL FANS - DON'T MISS SEEING DON WAHN IN "GREAT LOVER"--
YOU SHOULD HAVE WORN EAR MUFFS AND DARK GLASSES!
COLOSSAL! DON WAHN IN GREAT LOVER
NOW PLAYING DON WAHN IN THE "GREAT LOVER"!
HURRY! TO GET OUT OF THE SIGHT OF HIM WE MUST GET OUT IN THE COUNTRY!
WHAT COUNTRY?
DON WAHN
BUT YOU MUST DRIVE UNTIL I GET AWAY FROM EVEN THE SIGHT OF HIM!
HM-M! WHY NOT TRY CLOSING YOUR EYES?
DON WAHN DON'T MISS IT!
SEE DON WAHN IN GREAT LOVER
DON WAHN IN "GREAT LO
DON WAHN IN GREAT LOVER
AH! THE SOOTHING PASTORAL SCENES - UNSPOILED BY ANY REMINDER OF THAT FICKLE DON WAHN!
SEE YOU! LOOK! THAT TWO TIMER IS EVERY-WHERE, EVEN IN THE AIR!
PHEW! WELL IT WAS A LONG, HARD TRIP BUT WE FINALLY GOT AWAY FROM ANY SIGHT OR SOUND OF HIM!
IT WAS WORTH ALL THE TROUBLE LOOK AT THIS BEAUTIFUL SPOT ISOLATED FROM HIM 'N EVERYTHIN'.
WHAT D'YE MEAN, ISOLATED?
OKAY! CAMERA!
OH! A MOVIE COMPANY ON LOCATION!
©1937, King Features Syndicate, Inc. World rights reserved.
3-27
?
DON!
BETTY! OH, THIS IS SO SWEET OF YOU TO VISIT ME ON LOCATION - I NEVER DREAMED YOU CARED SO MUCH!

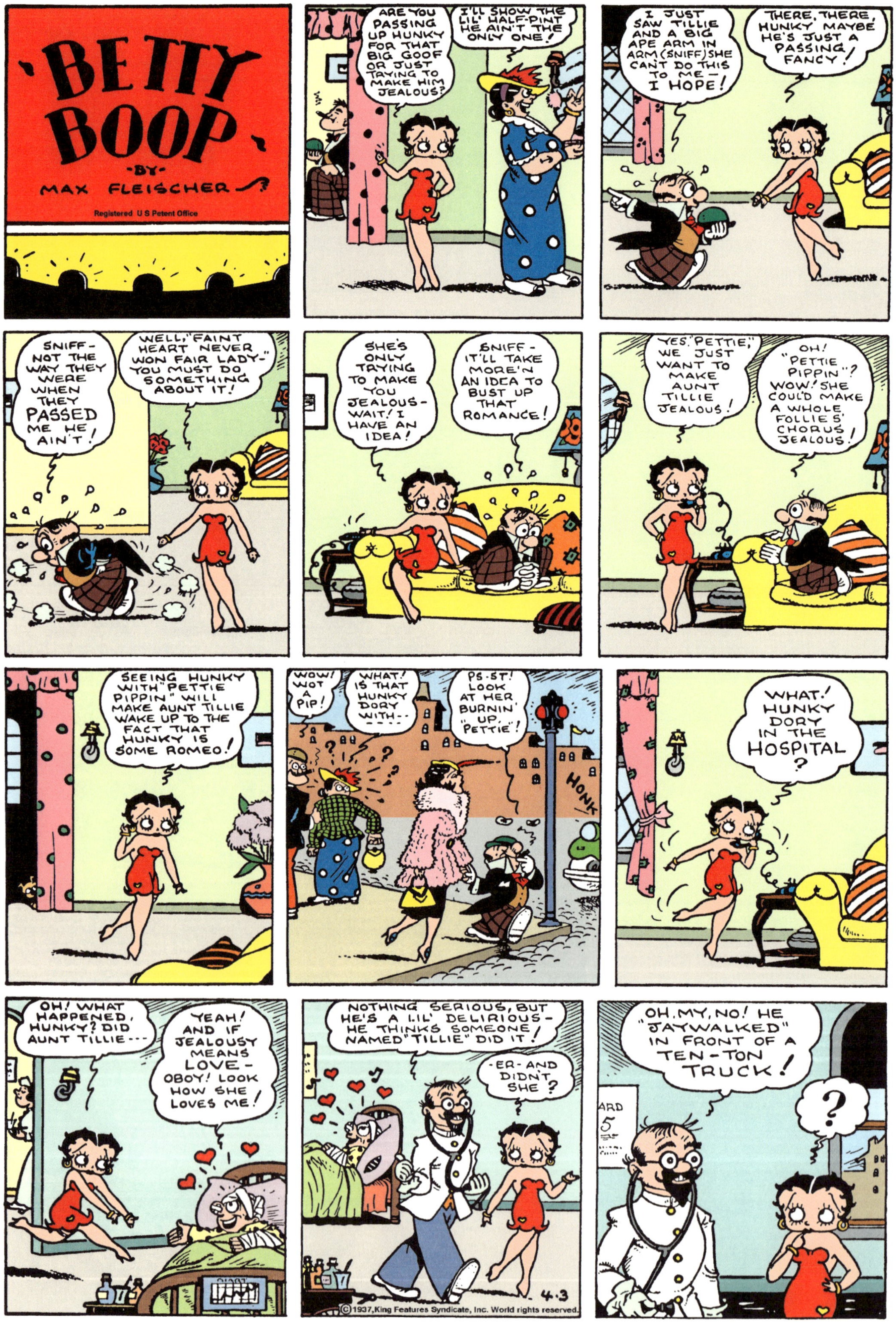
BETTY BOOP
-BY-
MAX FLEISCHER
Registered U S Patent Office
ARE YOU PASSING UP HUNKY FOR THAT BIG GOOF OR JUST TRYING TO MAKE HIM JEALOUS?
I'LL SHOW THE LIL' HALF-PINT HE AIN'T THE ONLY ONE!
I JUST SAW TILLIE AND A BIG APE ARM IN ARM (SNIFF) SHE CAN'T DO THIS TO ME — I HOPE!
THERE, THERE, HUNKY MAYBE HE'S JUST A PASSING FANCY!
SNIFF - NOT THE WAY THEY WERE WHEN THEY PASSED ME HE AIN'T!
WELL, "FAINT HEART NEVER WON FAIR LADY" - YOU MUST DO SOMETHING ABOUT IT!
SHE'S ONLY TRYING TO MAKE YOU JEALOUS - WAIT! I HAVE AN IDEA!
SNIFF - IT'LL TAKE MORE'N AN IDEA TO BUST UP THAT ROMANCE!
YES, "PETTIE," WE JUST WANT TO MAKE AUNT TILLIE JEALOUS!
OH! "PETTIE PIPPIN"? WOW! SHE COULD MAKE A WHOLE FOLLIES' CHORUS JEALOUS!
SEEING HUNKY WITH "PETTIE PIPPIN" WILL MAKE AUNT TILLIE WAKE UP TO THE FACT THAT HUNKY IS SOME ROMEO!
WOW! WOT A PIP!
WHAT! IS THAT HUNKY DORY WITH - - - -
PS-ST! LOOK AT HER BURNIN' UP, "PETTIE"!
HONK
WHAT! HUNKY DORY IN THE HOSPITAL?
OH! WHAT HAPPENED, HUNKY? DID AUNT TILLIE - - -
YEAH! AND IF JEALOUSY MEANS LOVE - OBOY! LOOK HOW SHE LOVES ME!
NOTHING SERIOUS, BUT HE'S A LIL' DELIRIOUS - HE THINKS SOMEONE NAMED "TILLIE" DID IT!
-ER- AND DIDN'T SHE?
4-3
© 1937, King Features Syndicate, Inc. World rights reserved.
OH, MY, NO! HE "JAYWALKED" IN FRONT OF A TEN-TON TRUCK!
?

BETTY BOOP
BY MAX FLEISCHER
Registered U S Petent Office
YES WHEN YOUR BOY FRIEND DON WAHN CALLS HE'LL FIND EVERY-THING IN ITS PLACE!
NOW IF YOU AND BUBBY WILL STAY IN YOURS EVERYTHING WILL BE FINE!
ALL THIS FUSS - MY STARS, WHEN IS THIS ROMEO EVER GOING TO PROPOSE?
YOU AND BUBBY NEVER GIVE HIM A CHANCE WITH YOUR BUTTING IN!
WELL, YOU WON'T BE BOTHERED BY BUBBY - HE'S GOING TO BED RIGHT NOW!
IT WOULDN'T BE A BAD IDEA IF YOU DID TOO - OH! HERE'S DON!
R-R-ING
YES DON I'M GOING TO BE ALONE I HOPE!
SWELL 'CAUSE I HAVE SOME-THING VERY IMPORTANT TO ASK YOU BETTY!
NO, MA'AM - DEY WOULDN'T GIB ME DE MESSAGE DEY WANTS TO TALK TO YO' PUSSUNLY!
THEY WOULD! EXCUSE ME, PLEASE DON!
DON'T WORRY DON, THERE WON'T BE ANY MORE INTERRUPTIONS - I TOOK THE RECEIVER OFF THE HOOK!
HOPE YOU'RE RIGHT, 'CAUSE I - ER
NOPE! BUBBY WON'T GO TO SLEEP - HE SAID YOU FORGOT TO KISS HIM "GOOD NIGHT"!
GR-R - HOW I'D LIKE TO SAY GOOD NIGHT TO THAT PEST!
OH! I'M SORRY!
PARDON THE INTERRUPTIONS DON, BUT BUBBY IS SUCH A SENTIMENTAL LITTLE THING!
SO AM I IF YOU'D ONLY GIVE ME A CHANCE!
NOW WHAT DID YOU WANT TO ASK ME DON?
-ER IT'S SOMETHING I'VE WANTED TO ASK YOU A LONG TIME - ER
'S'NO USE - HE WANTS YOU TO SING HIM TO SLEEP - HE SAYS MY SINGING KEEPS HIM AWAKE!
SORRY DON BUT I WON'T BE LONG!
4 10
©1937, King Features Syndicate, Inc. World rights reserved.
HE'S FINALLY GONE TO SLEEP! OH! YOU GOING? BUT I THOUGHT YOU HAD SOMETHING IMPORTANT TO SAY TO ME!
I HAVE! GOOD NIGHT!

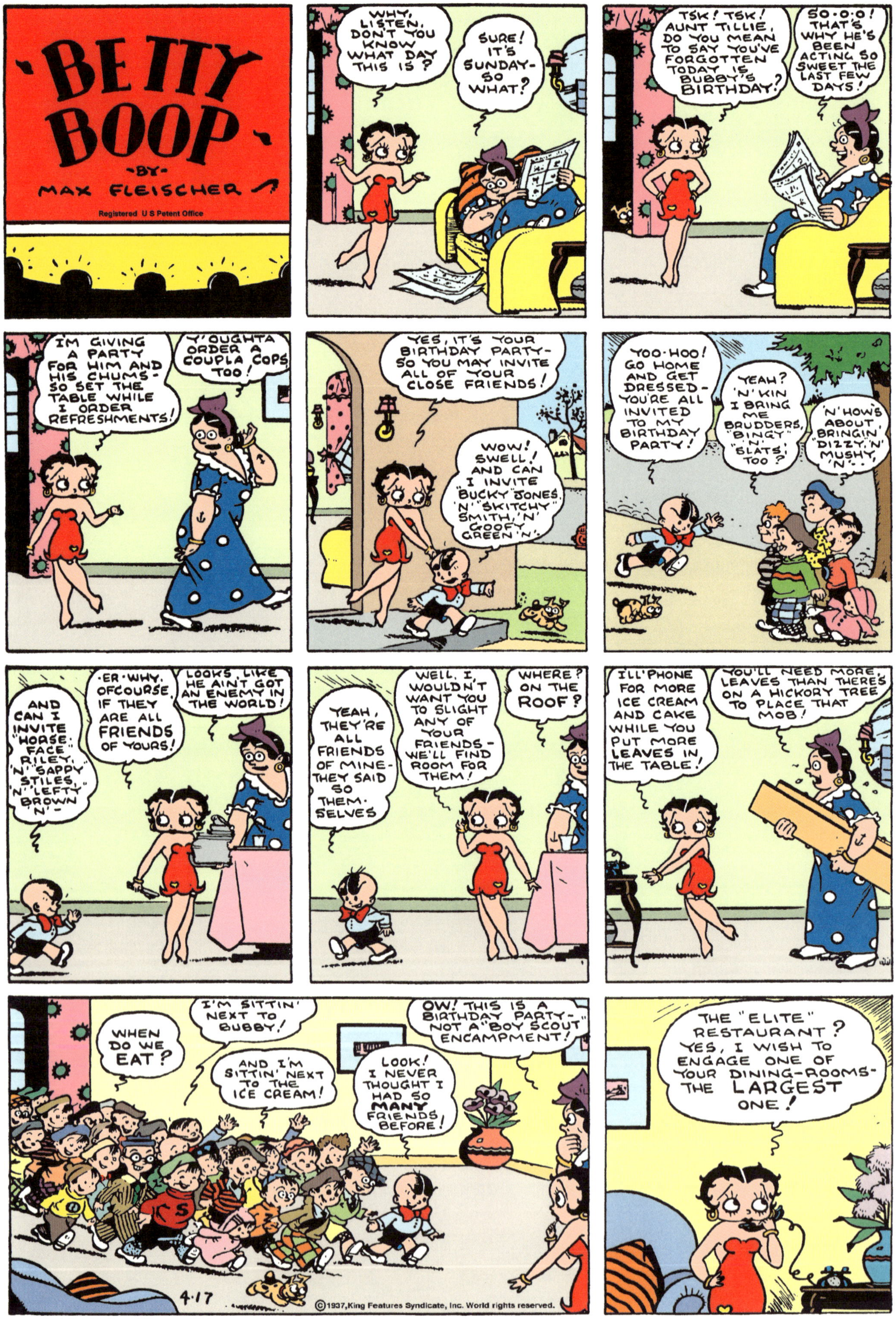
BETTY BOOP
-BY-
MAX FLEISCHER
Registered U S Patent Office
WHY, LISTEN, DON'T YOU KNOW WHAT DAY THIS IS?
SURE! IT'S SUNDAY-SO WHAT?
TSK! TSK! AUNT TILLIE, DO YOU MEAN TO SAY YOU'VE FORGOTTEN TODAY IS BUBBY'S BIRTHDAY?
SO-O-O! THAT'S WHY HE'S BEEN ACTING SO SWEET THE LAST FEW DAYS!
I'M GIVING A PARTY FOR HIM AND HIS CHUMS-SO SET THE TABLE WHILE I ORDER REFRESHMENTS!
Y'OUGHTA ORDER A COUPLA COPS TOO!
YES, IT'S YOUR BIRTHDAY PARTY-SO YOU MAY INVITE ALL OF YOUR CLOSE FRIENDS!
WOW! SWELL! AND CAN I INVITE "BUCKY" JONES 'N' "SKITCHY" SMITH, 'N' GOOFY GREEN 'N'-
YOO-HOO! GO HOME AND GET DRESSED-YOU'RE ALL INVITED TO MY BIRTHDAY PARTY!
YEAH? 'N' KIN I BRING ME BRUDDERS, "BINGY" 'N' "SLATS," TOO?
'N' HOW'S ABOUT BRINGIN' "DIZZY" 'N' MUSHY 'N'-
AND CAN I INVITE "HORSE-FACE" RILEY, 'N' "SAPPY" STILES 'N' "LEFTY" BROWN 'N'-
-ER-WHY, OFCOURSE, IF THEY ARE ALL FRIENDS OF YOURS!
LOOKS LIKE HE AIN'T GOT AN ENEMY IN THE WORLD!
YEAH, THEY'RE ALL FRIENDS OF MINE-THEY SAID SO THEM-SELVES
WELL, I WOULDN'T WANT YOU TO SLIGHT ANY OF YOUR FRIENDS-WE'LL FIND ROOM FOR THEM!
WHERE? ON THE ROOF?
I'LL PHONE FOR MORE ICE CREAM AND CAKE WHILE YOU PUT MORE LEAVES IN THE TABLE!
YOU'LL NEED MORE LEAVES THAN THERE'S ON A HICKORY TREE TO PLACE THAT MOB!
WHEN DO WE EAT?
I'M SITTIN' NEXT TO BUBBY!
AND I'M SITTIN' NEXT TO THE ICE CREAM!
OW! THIS IS A BIRTHDAY PARTY-NOT A "BOY SCOUT" ENCAMPMENT!
LOOK! I NEVER THOUGHT I HAD SO MANY FRIENDS BEFORE!
4-17
© 1937, King Features Syndicate, Inc. World rights reserved.
THE "ELITE" RESTAURANT? YES, I WISH TO ENGAGE ONE OF YOUR DINING-ROOMS-THE LARGEST ONE!

BETTY BOOP
-BY-
MAX FLEISCHER
Registered U S Patent Office
WHY, HUNKY DORY! DO YOU MEAN TO SAY YOU HAVEN'T BEEN IN TO ASK AUNT TILLIE FOR HER HAND?
I'M AFRAID SHE'LL GIVE ME HER FOOT INSTEAD!
BUCK UP - SHE CAN'T DO NO MORE THAN SAY 'NO'!
THAT'S IT I'M SCARED SHE MIGHT SAY 'NO' WITH GESTURES!
I FIGURE THE ONLY SAFE WAY TO PROPOSE TO TILLIE IS BY 'PHONE OR TELEGRAPH!
DON'T BE BILLY - THAT MANNER IS ENTIRELY TOO COLD!
YEAH AND I MIGHT BE COLD - KNOCKED COLD - IF I PROPOSE IN PERSON - YOU KNOW HOW ROUGH SHE IS!
YES BUST A DIAMOND IN THE ROUGH, BUT---
TOO ROUGH IF YOU ASK ME - NO I THINK I'LL PROPOSE BY PHONE OR SAY IT WITH FLOWERS!
NO NO! THAT'S OUT! WHERE'S YOUR MANHOOD. WAIT!
AND REMEMBER FAINT HEART NEVER WON FAIR LADY!
WELL SHE AIN'T FAIR IN HER REFUSALS - SHE'S MUCH TOO ROUGH!
WITH IT ALL AUNT TILLIE IS OF A VERY ROMANTIC NATURE - DO LIKE THE KNIGHTS OF OLD AND LIKE ROMEO AND--
MAYBE YOU'RE RIGHT, BETTY!
COURSE, I'M RIGHT! ALL WOMEN ARE ROMANTIC!
"THE ROMEO TECHNIQUE" AH! THAT'LL GET HER - I HOPE!
OH! SUCH A BEAUTIFUL PROPOSAL THAT OUGHT TO SOFTEN HER!
-AND HERE ON BENDED KNEES - WITH MY HEART OVER FLOWING WITH LOVE I ASK YOU, NAY, I PLEAD WITH YOU, MY HIBISCUS, FLOWER OF-
OH! POOR HUNKY!
YOO HOO! BETTY! WATER, QUICK!
©1937, King Features Syndicate, Inc. World rights reserved.
?
SOCKED HIM, ME EYE - HE JUST PROPOSED TO ME AND WHEN I SAID "YES" - HE UPS AND SWOONED!
4-24

BETTY BOOP
BY MAX FLEISCHER
Registered U S Patent Office
IT'S TIME HE WAS UP - HE'S GOT TO BE BATHED AND DRESSED FOR LIL' DAISY DUGAN'S PARTY - THIS VACUUM WILL WAKE HIM - I HOPE!
I'M SURPRISED! - DAISY DUGAN IS HIS BEST GIRL TOO - YOO-HOO! BUBBY! WAKE UP!
O-OH! AUNT TILLIE! HE'S NOT IN HIS BED - BUBBY!? WHERE ARE YOU?
NO DICE! HE KNOWS HE'S GOT TO BE BATHED AND DRESSED SO HE'S ABDICATED!
I NEVER SAW A CHILD THAT HATED TO BE BATHED LIKE BUBBY! YOU SEARCH THE CELLAR - I'LL ASK HIS CHUMS!
AND YOU HAVEN'T SEEN HIM TODAY?
NO! AND HE WAS S'POSED TO HELP US BUILD OUR CLUB HOUSE, TOO!
AW! THE BIG SISSY IS 'FRAID HE'D GET DIRTY 'CAUSE HE'S GOIN' TO HIS GIRL'S PARTY
NOPE! MISS BOOP - BUBBY AIN'T BEEN IN YET FOR A SODA OR NOTHIN'!
NOW I AM WORRIED!
NOT IN THE CELLAR EITHER? OH! THIS IS GETTING SERIOUS!
DON'T BE SILLY - WHEN IT'S TIME TO GIVE HIM HIS BATH HE'S ALWAYS MISSING LIKE THE WELL-KNOWN "LINK"!
I WOULDN'T WORRY SO IF IT WASN'T THAT HE'S TO ATTEND DAISY DUGAN'S PARTY - HIS BEST GIRL - OH! OPERATOR, GIVE ME THE POLICE STATION!
YES! HE WOULDN'T WANT TO MISS THAT AND HE'D WANT TO LOOK HIS BEST, TOO!
NO USE SEARCHING THE HOUSE - WE'VE LOOKED FROM TOP TO BOTTOM!
WELL, WE'LL GIVE IT A GOIN' OVER TO MAKE SURE!
WOW! THEY FOUND HIM!
OH! I WONDER WHERE! WE SEARCHED EVERY PLACE HE COULD POSSIBLY BE!
HERE HE IS UP HERE, MA'AM!
NO WONDER WE COULDN'T FIND HIM - WE'D NEVER THINK OF LOOKING FOR HIM THERE!
THAT WOULD BE THE LAST PLACE WE'D EVER LOOK FOR HIM!
HEY! CAN'T A FELLER TAKE A BATH ALL BY HISSELF WITHOUT YOU CALLING THE COPS?
5-8
©1937, King Features Syndicate, Inc. World rights reserved.

BETTY BOOP
-BY-
MAX FLEISCHER
Registered U S Patent Office
O-OH! AUNT TILLIE, LOOK! DON WAHN WITH HIS NEW LEADING LADY SPREAD ALL OVER THE DAILY TABLOID"!
WHAT! THE BIG TWO-TIMER, IF HE WAS MY BOY FRIEND I'D SPREAD HIM ALL OVER THE FRONT LAWN - IN PIECES!
WHY SHOULDN'T I BELIEVE IN HIM? HE SEEMED SO TRUSTING!
I TOLD YOU I WOULDN'T TRUST THAT BIRD AS FAR AS I COULD THROW A SAFE!
YES, GIVE ME ALL OF HIS PHOTOS - I'M GOING TO TEAR THEM UP!
OBOY! IF I WAS YOU I'D TEAR HIM UP - IN PERSON!
"BURNING LOVE LETTERS" IS RIGHT. HE SURE HAD A GREAT "LINE"!
YES, AND I FELL FOR IT LIKE A POOR FISH!
GET ME THE REST OF HIS FLOWERS - I DON'T WANT ANYTHING AROUND TO REMIND ME OF HIM!
I'M HOLDING OUT THE ORCHIDS - HE AIN'T DONE NOTHIN' TO ME!
I'LL GET RID OF HIS CANDY FOR YOU, SIS!
WHAT TECHNIQUE! HE EVEN USED ROMANTIC BOOKS IN HIS COURTING!
THROW THEM OUT, TOO!
WHY NOT KEEP 'EM TO THROW AT THAT BIG TWO-TIMING ROMEO?
I'D LIKE TO! OH! I HATE HIM (SNIFF) HE CAN'T DO THIS TO ME!
R-R-ING
HERE HE IS NOW - GIVE HIM THE WORKS AND CALL ME IF YOU NEED HELP!
DON'T WORRY - I'LL HANDLE HIS CASE WITH DISPATCH!
YES, DEAR, I CALLED TO EXPLAIN ABOUT ALL THAT ROMANCE STUFF IN THE PAPERS ABOUT MY NEW LEADING LADY AND MYSELF - YOU SEE, IT WAS A PUBLICITY STUNT - THE STUDIO'S ORDERS AND--
-ER- WHAT? OH! OF COURSE, DEAR, I KNEW THAT - WHY---
I KNEW YOU WOULD, DEAR! OBOY! WHAT A GIRL - NOT A JEALOUS BONE IN HER BODY - SO UNDERSTANDING - YES, SIR, YOU'RE THE MOST BROADMINDED GIRL IN THE WORLD!
THANKS, DON!
-ER- BUT WOULD YOU GIVE ME ANOTHER SET OF YOUR PHOTOS AND SEND ME SOME MORE FLOWERS 'N' BOOKS 'N'---
©1937, King Features Syndicate, Inc. World rights reserved.
5-15

BETTY BOOP
-BY-
MAX FLEISCHER
Registered U S Patent Office
WHAT'S THE IDEA? LOOKS LIKE A ROGUES' GALLERY!
DON, DICK AND HARRY EACH PROPOSED TO ME AND THEY'RE ALL VERY FINE CATCHES!
WELL, YOU CAN'T ACCEPT 'EM ALL- YOU AIN'T TRIPLETS, YOU KNOW!
THAT'S IT, BUT I CAN'T DECIDE WHICH ONE TO ACCEPT. DON HAS LOOKS, DICK HAS MONEY AND HARRY HAS POSITION!
WHY NOT PUT THEIR NAMES IN A HAT OR TRY "EENIE, MEENIE, MINEY MO," OR TRY "BINGO"?
I KNOW! I'LL CONSULT THE "FORTUNE-TELLER" DOWN THE ROAD!
PALMIST, HUH? SHE'LL JUST PALM OFF A LOT OF HOKUM ON YOU WHILE PALMIN' YOUR DOUGH!
NO! THIS "MADAME ZAZA" IS SUPPOSED TO BE GOOD!
MADAM ZAZA
H576
---AND I SEE HERE WHERE YOU WILL WED A TALL, HANDSOME, BLOND MAN--
OH! THAT'S DON!
IT WOULD BE!
WHY ANOTHER FORTUNE-TELLER?
I WANT TO BE SURE- THESE CRYSTAL-GAZERS SEE ALL, KNOW ALL, ETC.-
SWAMI TELI ALI CRYSTAL-GAZER
AH! I SEE VERY PLAINLY WHERE YOU WILL WED A MAN OF MUCH WEALTH AND---
OH! THAT'S DICK!
NOW YOU'RE ALL BALLED UP!
YES. ANOTHER FORTUNE-TELLER- I WANT TO BE SURE I ACCEPT THE RIGHT MAN!
TSK. TSK! ANY TIME I'D LET ANY-BODY PICK OUT MY HUSBAND OUT OF A CUP O' TEA
GYPSY TEA ROOM
---AH! I SEE WHERE YOU WILL WED A MAN OF HIGH POSITION-
PS-ST! THAT'S HARRY!
NOW YOU'RE BACK WHERE YOU STARTED!
AH! YOUR FORTUNE WITH YOUR WEIGHT- I'LL LET THIS DECIDE - I MUST MAKE A DECISION!
WELL, THIS IS THE MACHINE AGE - SO WHY NOT?
YOUR FORTUNE
5-22
OW! LOOK! I DREW A BLANK!
A BLANK! THAT MUST MEAN MY BOY FRIEND, HUNKY DORY, THE CHISLIN' LIL' MO--
©1937, King Features Syndicate, Inc. World rights reserved.

BETTY BOOP
BY
MAX FLEISCHER
Registered U S Patent Office
WHAT A PREDICAMENT! DON, DICK AND HARRY EACH PROPOSED TO ME AND I CAN'T DECIDE WHICH ONE TO ACCEPT!
THEY'RE ALL SUCH DARLINGS - DON HAS LOOKS, DICK HAS MONEY AND HARRY HAS POSITION - I MUST MAKE A DECISION -- I'M SO CONFUSED - I'LL HAVE TO SEEK SOME ADVICE!
OH! FIFI, YOU'VE NOTICED MY BOY FRIENDS WHEN THEY'VE CALLED, HAVEN'T YOU?
OUI, OUI, MEES BETTY, AND HOW!
NOW IF YOU WERE ME - WHICH ONE WOULD YOU MARRY?
O-OH! MEESTER DON - HE'S SO-O HANDSOME! OO-LALA! THOSE EYES - THEM LIPS.
THEY SAY IF A CHILD OR A DOG LIKES A PERSON IT'S A SURE SIGN HE'S ALL RIGHT - - HEY! COME HERE, BUBBY - I WANT YOUR ADVICE
YOU AIN'T KIDDIN' ME - YOU WANT MY CAKE!
OH! YOU CAN HAVE YOUR CAKE AND EAT IT, TOO - I JUST WANT TO KNOW WHO YOU LIKE BEST, DON, DICK OR HARRY!
DICK! HE'S A SWELL EGG - WISH YOU'D MARRY HIM SO I COULD HAVE DIMES EVERY DAY!
FINE! HERE COMES HUNKY DORY - A MAN'S ADVICE IS A GOOD THING IN A CASE OF THIS KIND!
R-R-ING!
AND YOU ADVISE ME TO ACCEPT HARRY?
YES! DON HAS LOOKS, DICK HAS MONEY, BUT HARRY HAS POSITION AND POSITION IS EVERYTHIN' IN LIFE, YOU KNOW!
NOW I'M MORE CONFUSED THAN EVER - THEY ALL LIKE A DIFFERENT ONE - I KNOW - I'LL LET AUNT TILLIE'S SELECTION DECIDE - OH! AUNT TILLIE!
I'M IN HERE ADMIRIN' Y'DARLIN' BOY FRIENDS!
WHICH ONE WOULD YOU DECIDE ON IF YOU WERE ME? NOW WITH ALL YOUR EXPERIENCE AND - - -
EXPERIENCE, ME EYE - WHY, I'VE NEVER HAD MORE'N ONE TO DECIDE ON AT ONE TIME IN MY LIFE - AH! ME! THEY'RE ALL PERFECT!
HERE'S ALL THEM BOOKS YOU ORDERED ON "NUMEROLOGY," "ASTROLOGY," ETC. TSK! TSK! LETTIN' BOOKS PICK YOUR HUSBAND!
WELL, I'D HAVE TO BE TRIPLETS TO FOLLOW YOUR DECISIONS!
©1937, King Features Syndicate, Inc. World rights reserved.
5-29

BETTY BOOP
BY
MAX FLEISCHER
Registered U S Petent Office
DON HAS LOOKS, DICK HAS MONEY AND HARRY HAS POSITION, OH, DEAR, HOW AM I TO KNOW WHICH IS THE BEST TO ACCEPT? ER- - I HAVE IT!
THAT'S WHAT I SAID - I'M GOING TO LET "BLINKY" HERE DECIDE FOR ME - YOU KNOW, A DOG'S INTUITION!
NOT A BAD IDEA - THEY SAY YOU CAN TRUST A MAN WHOM A DOG LIKES!
OH! HELLO, DON! DO YOU MIND IF LITTLE "BLINKY" SITS WITH US?
OFCOURSE NOT, BETTY, I LIKE DOGS!
HM-M! HE DOESN'T SEEM TO LIKE ME!
SO IT SEEMS AND HE'S SUCH A FRIENDLY LIL' PUP, TOO!
WOOF! WOOF!
WELL, THAT ELIMINATES DON - "BLINKY" BARKED AT HIM ALL THE TIME HE WAS HERE!
THERE MUST BE SOMETHING DIZZY ABOUT HIM THEN - WELL, YOU HAVE DICK AND HARRY LEFT!
OW! LISTEN TO HIM BARK AT DICK AND I THOUGHT HE WAS A NICE BOY, TOO!
WOOF WOOF WOOF WUF WUF
MUST BE SOMETHING WRONG WITH THEM 'CAUSE "BLINKY" IS SUCH A FRIENDLY PUP!
NOW HARRY IS THE ONLY ONE LEFT!
SLAM
WHY, THE ONLY ONE I EVER HEARD "BLINKY" BARK AT BEFORE WAS THAT NO-ACCOUNT BOY FRIEND OF MINE, HUNKY DORY!
OH! HERE'S HARRY! I WONDER IF HE'LL PASS THE TEST?
-R-R-INC-
MY WORD, BETTY! TAKE HIM AWAY, THE LIL' BOUNDER SEEMS TO DISLIKE ME!
AND HOW! I'M SORRY HARRY, BUT I GUESS YOU'LL HAVE TO LEAVE!
WOOF! WOOF!
WELL, THAT SHOWS NONE OF 'EM CAN BE TRUSTED!
THAT'S RIGHT! "BLINKY" BARKED AT EACH ONE OF THEM!
SURE, "BLINKY" BARKED AT 'EM -
?
-HE HAD HIS BONE HIDDEN UNDER THE COUCH-CUSHION THEY SAT ON!
?
6·5

BETTY BOOP
BY MAX FLEISCHER
Registered U S Patent Office
DON HAS LOOKS, DICK HAS MONEY AND HARRY POSITION - WHAT A LUCKY GIRL TO HAVE A SWELL TRIO LIKE THAT TO SELECT A HUSBAND FROM!
YES, BUT I CAN'T DECIDE WHICH ONE TO ACCEPT - I CAN'T MARRY ALL THREE, YOU KNOW!
WELL, I CAN'T HELP YOU - I NEVER HAD BUT ONE AT A TIME TO PICK FROM IN ALL MY LIFE!
I MUST ARRIVE AT A DECISION SOMEHOW, BUT HOW?
OW! HOW CAN I CONCENTRATE WITH ALL THAT RACKET?
HM-M! THAT "HOT AND COLD STUFF" SOUNDS FAMILIAR!
HA-HA YOU'RE HOT! HA-HA! COLD! COLD!
?
PS-ST! LOOK! THIS MAY BE THE ANSWER TO YOUR PROBLEM!
HOT! HA-HA COLD!
YES, SIR! THERE'S AN IDEA!
HA-HAR! COLD! COLD!
'ROUND AND 'ROUND HE GOES - WHERE HE'LL STOP NOBODY KNOWS - HA-HA!
DONKEY TAIL GAME
YOU'VE TRIED ASTROLOGY, NUMEROLOGY, PALMISTS AND EVERYTHING - WHY NOT THAT?
YES, THIS IDEA SEEMS PRETTY GOOD - HERE, BUBBY, I'LL GIVE YOU THIS DOLLAR FOR YOUR "DONKEY TAIL GAME"!
SOLD!
WE'LL TACK UP THE PHOTOS IN MY ROOM - THERE'S MORE SPACE THERE!
I'M SO EXCITED NOW THAT I AT LAST SEE A SOLUTION TO MY PROBLEM!
NOW I'LL SPIN YOU AROUND - IT'S ONE OF THE RULES OF THE GAME!
I FEEL FATE WILL GUIDE ME TO THE RIGHT ONE!
YOU'RE COLD! COLD!
DON'T PROMPT ME - WHICH-EVER ONE FATE GUIDES ME TO I WILL MARRY!
WHY ALL THE HILARITY, AUNT TILLIE? THIS IS NO LAUGHING MATTER!
SEZ YOU! HA-HA-HA - A TAIL BELONGS ON HIM, BUT LOOK!
YOU PINNED IT ON THE PHOTO OF MY BOY FRIEND, HUNKY DORY!
©1937, King Features Syndicate, Inc. World rights reserved. 6-19

BETTY BOOP
-BY-
MAX FLEISCHER
Registered U S Patent Office
WHAT A TRIO OF SUITORS! DON HAS LOOKS, DICK HAS MONEY AND HARRY HAS POSITION!
AND I CAN'T DECIDE WHICH ONE TO ACCEPT,- I'VE TRIED ASTROLOGY, NUMEROLOGY 'N'EVERYTHIN'!
COME ON, BETTY, I JUST FOUND A WAY TO SELECT THE ONE TO MARRY AND YOU'LL HAVE FUN DOING IT!
FUN, ME EYE - THIS IS A VERY SERIOUS MATTER!
SEE! TACK THEIR PHOTOS ON THE TARGET - THE ONE YOU HIT FIRST, YOU MARRY!
NOT A BAD IDEA - THERE'LL BE THE ELEMENT OF FATE IN IT!
OH! YOU WON'T GIVE IT UP, HUH?
PLEASE, BUBBY, I WANT TO SHOOT AT SOME PHOTOS OF DON, DICK AND HARRY!
PHOTOS? NO SOAP! I THOUGHT Y'WANTED TO SHOOT 'EM IN PERSON!
"THIS HAS GOT "EENIE, MEENIE, MINIE MO", OR PICKING THEIR NAMES OUT OF A HAT BEAT, HUH?
YES, IT'S A SPORTING WAY TO DECIDE THE MATTER AND I LOVE THE CUPID ANGLE TO IT, TOO!
TAKE AIM - SHOOT!
AND I FEEL FATE WILL GUIDE MY AIM TO THE RIGHT ONE!
HA-HA! WHAT'S THAT CRACK - "I SHOT AN ARROW INTO THE AIR - - -"
OOPS! MISSED AGAIN!
THEY OUGHTA BE A LAW!
PICKING MY NEW "BOWLER" FOR A TARGET
AIN'T THEY NO CLOSED SEASON FOR CITIZENS?
HM-M! YOU LOOK LIKE "CUSTER'S LAST STAND"!
HEY! WHAT D'YE THINK YOU ARE - A FEMALE "WILLIAM TELL" OR SUMPIN'?
OH! OFFICER I'M ONLY USING THIS ARCHERY TO HELP ME DECIDE ON A HUSBAND
YOU SEE, THE ONE I HIT FIRST I WILL MARRY!
WITH YOUR AIM YOU'LL BE AN OLD MAID! WAIT! I'LL CALL THE CHIEF!
NO! NOT TO SHOOT A HUSBAND! I SAID SHE WANTS TO SHOOT FOR A HUSBAND! SEND A MACHINE-GUN FOR HER TO USE!
?
?

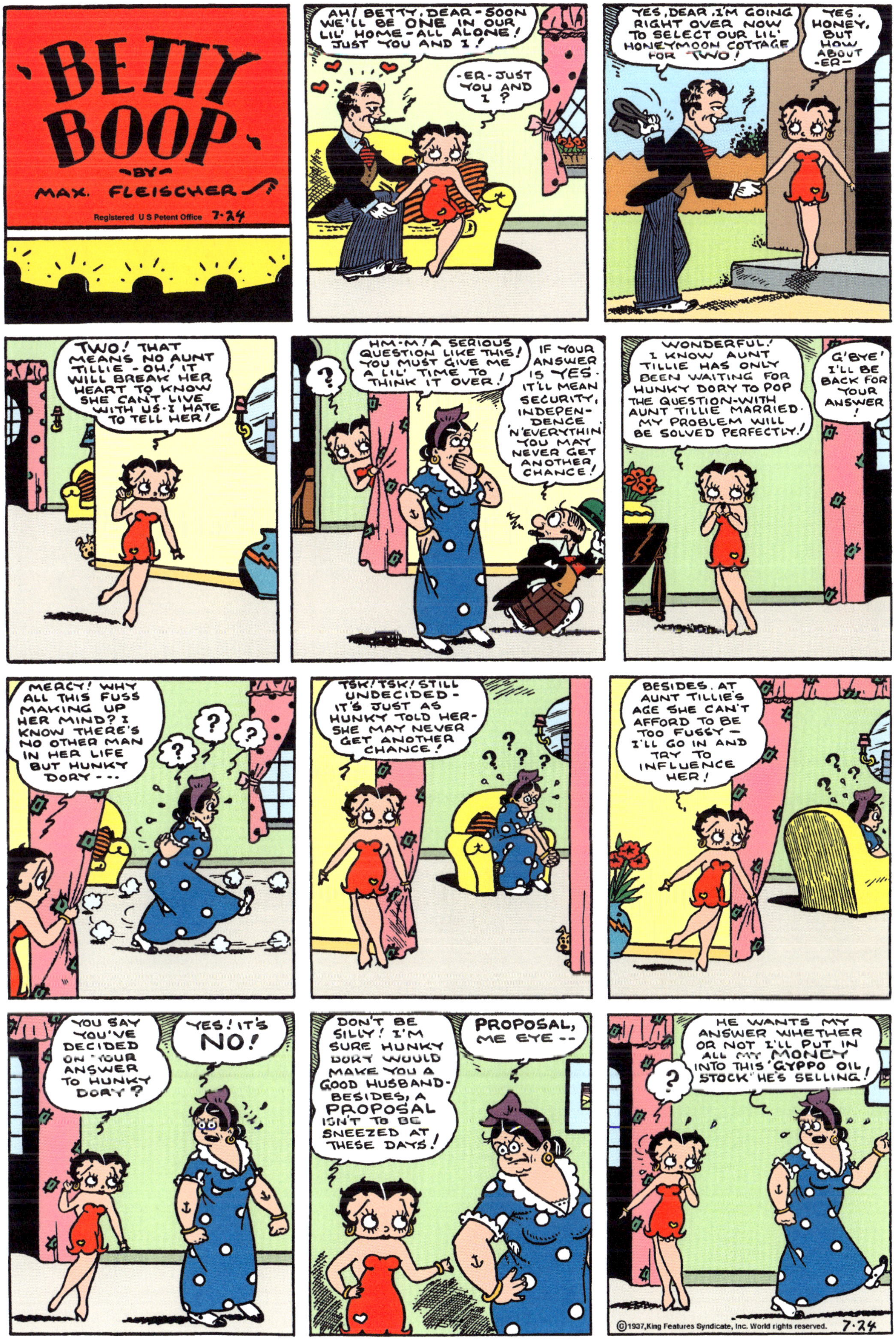
BETTY BOOP
BY MAX. FLEISCHER
Registered U S Patent Office 7-24
AH! BETTY, DEAR - SOON WE'LL BE ONE IN OUR LIL' HOME - ALL ALONE! JUST YOU AND I!
-ER- JUST YOU AND I?
YES, DEAR, I'M GOING RIGHT OVER NOW TO SELECT OUR LIL' HONEYMOON COTTAGE FOR TWO!
YES, HONEY, BUT HOW ABOUT -ER-
TWO! THAT MEANS NO AUNT TILLIE - OH! IT WILL BREAK HER HEART TO KNOW SHE CAN'T LIVE WITH US - I HATE TO TELL HER!
HM-M! A SERIOUS QUESTION LIKE THIS! YOU MUST GIVE ME A LIL' TIME TO THINK IT OVER!
IF YOUR ANSWER IS YES IT'LL MEAN SECURITY, INDEPENDENCE 'N' EVERYTHIN' YOU MAY NEVER GET ANOTHER CHANCE!
WONDERFUL! I KNOW AUNT TILLIE HAS ONLY BEEN WAITING FOR HUNKY DORY TO POP THE QUESTION - WITH AUNT TILLIE MARRIED MY PROBLEM WILL BE SOLVED PERFECTLY!
G'BYE! I'LL BE BACK FOR YOUR ANSWER!
MERCY! WHY ALL THIS FUSS MAKING UP HER MIND? I KNOW THERE'S NO OTHER MAN IN HER LIFE BUT HUNKY DORY - - -
TSK! TSK! STILL UNDECIDED - IT'S JUST AS HUNKY TOLD HER - SHE MAY NEVER GET ANOTHER CHANCE!
BESIDES, AT AUNT TILLIE'S AGE SHE CAN'T AFFORD TO BE TOO FUSSY - I'LL GO IN AND TRY TO INFLUENCE HER!
YOU SAY YOU'VE DECIDED ON YOUR ANSWER TO HUNKY DORY?
YES! IT'S NO!
DON'T BE SILLY! I'M SURE HUNKY DORY WOULD MAKE YOU A GOOD HUSBAND - BESIDES, A PROPOSAL ISN'T TO BE SNEEZED AT THESE DAYS!
PROPOSAL, ME EYE --
HE WANTS MY ANSWER WHETHER OR NOT I'LL PUT IN ALL MY MONEY INTO THIS 'GYPPO OIL STOCK' HE'S SELLING!
©1937, King Features Syndicate, Inc. World rights reserved. 7-24

BETTY BOOP
-BY-
MAX FLEISCHER
Registered U S Patent Office
7-31
HERE I AM WITH THE PLANS OF OUR HONEY-MOON COTTAGE, DEAR!
OH! TO SAY I'M ANXIOUS TO SEE THEM WOULD BE PUTTING IT MILDLY!
YEP! A COTTAGE BUILT FOR TWO - YOU'LL NOTICE THERE'S NOT EVEN A GUEST-ROOM!
-ER- WHAT! NO GUEST-ROOM?
NOPE! Y'KNOW THAT OLD CRACK, "TWO IS COMPANY, ETC." - I KNEW YOU'D OKAY THE PLANS!
-ER- YES, THEY'RE OKAY AS FAR AS THEY GO, BUT-ER-
WELL, THAT MEANS HE DOESN'T INTEND TO HAVE AUNT TILLIE LIVE WITH US AND I HAVEN'T THE HEART TO TELL HER THE BAD NEWS!
HERE'S HUNKY DORY! OH! IF HE'D ONLY PROPOSE TO AUNT TILLIE IT WOULD SOLVE THIS PROBLEM PERFECTLY!
YES, HUNKY, I WANT TO TALK TO YOU BEFORE YOU SEE AUNT TILLIE!
DON'T TELL ME SHE'S IN ONE OF HER TANTRUMS AGAIN!
COME! I HAVE SOMETHING VERY PERSONAL I FEEL I MUST CONSULT YOU ABOUT!
NOT BROKEN OFF YOUR ENGAGEMENT - I HOPE!
NO! IT'S ABOUT YOU - YOUR FUTURE HAPPINESS 'N'EVERYTHIN'!
HM-M! YOU INTEREST ME STRANGELY!
-AND THINK OF THE HAPPINESS OF HAVING SOMEONE TO SHARE YOUR TROUBLES - YOUR JOYS AND --
YES, YES, GO ON!
BESIDES, IT MEANS FUTURE HAPPINESS - THE COMFORT OF YOUR OWN LIL' HOME AND -
AH! A HOME - A FUTURE SECURE 'N'EVERYTHIN JUST FOR THE ASKIN'!
©1937, King Features Syndicate, Inc. World rights reserved.
?
I'LL STEP RIGHT OVER AND PROPOSE TO MRS. GOTJACK, THE RICH WIDOW, THIS VERY MINUTE!
7-31

BETTY BOOP
-BY-
MAX FLEISCHER
Registered U S Patent Office 8·14
YES, BETTY - HERE'S THE FINAL PLANS OF OUR HONEYMOON COTTAGE!
BUT -ER- I THOUGHT YOU WERE GOING TO ADD AN EXTRA ROOM?
NO! THAT'S OUT! AN EXTRA ROOM WOULD MAKE IT POSSIBLE FOR RELATIVES TO PARK IN ON US!
-ER- MAYBE YOU'RE RIGHT, DEAR, BUT--
YOU KNOW THAT OLD WISE-CRACK- "TWO'S COMPANY THREE'S A CROWD" WELL, WE'RE NOT GOING TO BE CROWDED!
HM-M! THAT ELIMINATES AUNT TILLIE!
MY! I HATE TO TELL AUNT TILLIE! OH! IF HUNKY DORY WOULD ONLY PROPOSE TO HER. IT WOULD SOLVE THIS PROBLEM PERFECTLY!
WELL, BETTY, I HAVE FINALLY DECIDED TO PROPOSE TO AUNT TILLIE!
OH! I'M SO GLAD THAT YOU AT LAST MUSTERED UP ENOUGH COURAGE!
GO RIGHT IN BEFORE YOU LOSE YOUR NERVE!
DON'T PUSH! I CAN GO IN UNDER MY OWN POWER - (I HOPE)
HE'S STILL IN THERE - THAT'S A GOOD SIGN AND I'M SURE AUNT TILLIE HAS ONLY BEEN WAITING FOR HUNKY TO POP THE QUESTION!
MERCY! HE'S IN THERE LONG ENOUGH - OH! I HOPE HE HASN'T LOST HIS NERVE AGAIN!
TELL ME, QUICK! DID SHE SAY NO!
NO! SHE SAID YES!
THEN WHY SO GLUM? YOU SHOULD BE HAPPY - WHEN DOES THE MARRIAGE TAKE PLACE?
THAT'S IT! THE MARRIAGE IS POSTPONED INDEFINITELY.
8·14
?
SHE SAYS SHE'LL MARRY ME JUST AS SOON AS I GET A JOB!
©1937, King Features Syndicate, Inc. World rights reserved.

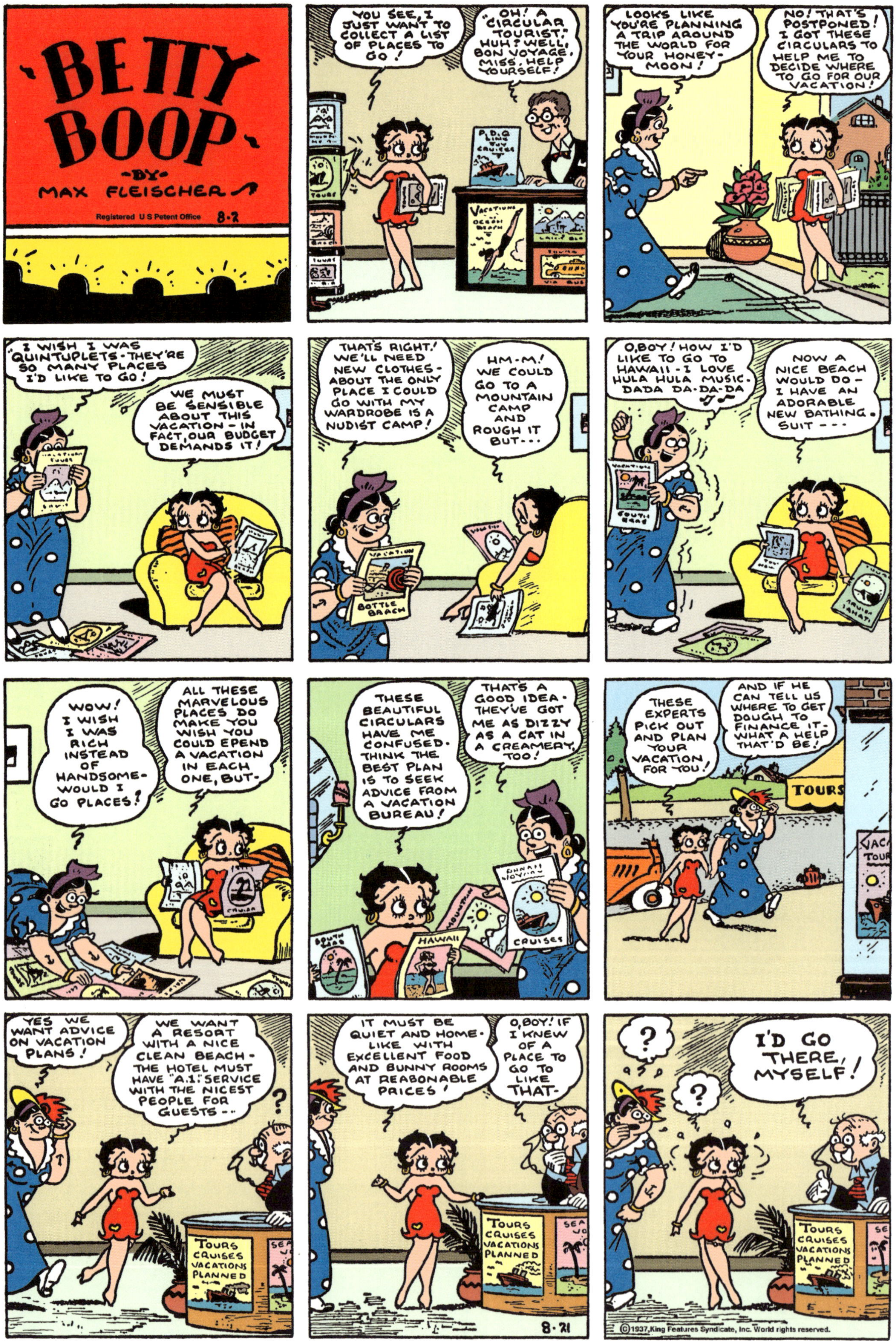
BETTY BOOP
-BY-
MAX FLEISCHER
Registered U S Patent Office
8-2
YOU SEE, I JUST WANT TO COLLECT A LIST OF PLACES TO GO!
"OH! A CIRCULAR TOURIST," HUH? WELL, BON VOYAGE, MISS. HELP YOURSELF!
LOOKS LIKE YOU'RE PLANNING A TRIP AROUND THE WORLD FOR YOUR HONEY-MOON!
NO! THAT'S POSTPONED! I GOT THESE CIRCULARS TO HELP ME TO DECIDE WHERE TO GO FOR OUR VACATION!
"I WISH I WAS QUINTUPLETS - THEY'RE SO MANY PLACES I'D LIKE TO GO!
WE MUST BE SENSIBLE ABOUT THIS VACATION - IN FACT, OUR BUDGET DEMANDS IT!
THAT'S RIGHT! WE'LL NEED NEW CLOTHES - ABOUT THE ONLY PLACE I COULD GO WITH MY WARDROBE IS A NUDIST CAMP!
HM-M! WE COULD GO TO A MOUNTAIN CAMP AND ROUGH IT BUT---
BOTTLE BEACH
O,BOY! HOW I'D LIKE TO GO TO HAWAII - I LOVE HULA HULA MUSIC. DADA DA-DA-DA
NOW A NICE BEACH WOULD DO - I HAVE AN ADORABLE NEW BATHING SUIT---
WOW! I WISH I WAS RICH INSTEAD OF HANDSOME - WOULD I GO PLACES!
ALL THESE MARVELOUS PLACES DO MAKE YOU WISH YOU COULD SPEND A VACATION IN EACH ONE, BUT-
THESE BEAUTIFUL CIRCULARS HAVE ME CONFUSED. THINK THE BEST PLAN IS TO SEEK ADVICE FROM A VACATION BUREAU!
THAT'S A GOOD IDEA. THEY'VE GOT ME AS DIZZY AS A CAT IN A CREAMERY, TOO!
HAWAII
CRUISES
THESE EXPERTS PICK OUT AND PLAN YOUR VACATION FOR YOU!
AND IF HE CAN TELL US WHERE TO GET DOUGH TO FINANCE IT, WHAT A HELP THAT'D BE!
TOURS
YES WE WANT ADVICE ON VACATION PLANS!
WE WANT A RESORT WITH A NICE CLEAN BEACH - THE HOTEL MUST HAVE "A.1." SERVICE WITH THE NICEST PEOPLE FOR GUESTS--
?
TOURS CRUISES VACATIONS PLANNED
IT MUST BE QUIET AND HOME-LIKE WITH EXCELLENT FOOD AND SUNNY ROOMS AT REASONABLE PRICES!
O,BOY! IF I KNEW OF A PLACE TO GO TO LIKE THAT-
TOURS CRUISES VACATIONS PLANNED
8-21
?
?
I'D GO THERE, MYSELF!
TOURS CRUISES VACATIONS PLANNED
©1937, King Features Syndicate, Inc. World rights reserved.

STICK AROUND BOYS! I'M ALWAYS COOKING UP SOMETHING!!
OH! HOW I HATE TO WAKE UP IN THE MORNING!
LIKE A LONG SHOT "SLEEPER" WHEN THE CHECKS ARE DOWN - AFTER YOU SEE THE MORNING PAPERS
YES, THEY'VE GOT HIM PARKED IN THE CHIEF'S OFFICE!
HE'S WEARING DARK GLASSES!

# BETTY BOOP

## THE DAILIES

July 23, 1934 – March 18, 1935

I DO WISH MY LAWYERS WOULD GIVE THEM BACK THOSE CROWN JEWELS!
DUKE POPOFF AND HIS LAWYERS JUST CALLED AGAIN ASKING FOR 'EM AND WE GAVE 'EM THE BUM'S RUSH!
FOR THE STEENTH TIME- NO! AND THAT'S FINAL!
WHAT WAS ALL THE COMMOTION? WERE THEY BACK AGAIN?
YES BUT WE TOSSED 'EM OUT THIS TIME FOR KEEPS, I MEAN!
ARE WE TO TAKE THIS AS A REFUSAL, SIR?
ALL THIS PUBLICITY HAS ME DIZZY- I WISH MY LAWYERS WOULD GIVE BACK THOSE CROWN JEWELS!
JUST SHOWS THE ADVANTAGE OF HAVING BIG LAWYERS, BETTY!
THE DUKE AND HIS STAFF? TELL THE PESTS TO SEE MY LAWYERS!
NEXT!
5 BARBERS
I JUST CAN'T ACT, THINKING OF THE DUKE AND HIS LAWYERS!
YES- BUT SUPPOSE THEY SHAVE THEM OFF?
AND AFTER SHAVING OFF THEIR WHISKERS THEY TOOK ONE LOOK AT THEMSELVES, AND CHECKED OUT
I SUPPOSE THEY FELT LIKE A BUNCH OF NUDISTS!

LADIES AND GENTLEMEN— I HAVE THE PLEASURE OF INTRODUCING
INK
—PARDON ME A MOMENT— THIS IS HER DRESS AND HER SHOES—
—AND THIS IS HER HAIR AND NOSE-ALSO HER JEWELRY AND GARTER—
7·23
—LADIES AND GENTLEMEN— MEET "BETTY BOOP"!
HELLO! EVERYBODY— I'LL BE SEEIN' YOU HERE EVERY DAY!
© 1934, King Features Syndicate, Inc., Great Britain rights reserved.

NOW BETTY- WE'RE READY FOR THE BED-ROOM SCENES!
OH! DOESN'T IT LOOK COMFY?
© 1934, King Features Syndicate, Inc. Great Britain rights reserved
WE'LL BE ALL SET IN A MINUTE, BETTY— LIGHTS AND CAMERA IN POSITION—
HO-HUM-M!
WHAT'S ALL THE DELAY ON THIS SET?
SH-H-!
SH-H-H! UNDER HER CONTRACT SHE'S NOT TO BE DISTURBED WHILE SLEEPING!
7-24

SPRAYING YOUR THROAT- FINE! HOPE YOU'RE IN GOOD VOICE, BETTY- LET'S SEE IF EVERY-THING IS OKAY FOR THE RECORDING!
-AND HOW'S THE SPARK-GAP AND EVERYTHING?
ALL IN PERFECT ORDER, CHIEF?
YEAH? AND HOW'S THE SOUND TRACK?
EVERY-THING HAS BEEN TESTED AND RE-TESTED CHIEF!
THE SOUND-RECORDING MACHINES ARE ALL SET, BETTY- SO GET READY TO DO YOUR STUFF!
7·25
BOOP!
MIKE
© 1934, King Features Syndicate, Inc. Great Britain rights reserved
WELL, THAT'S THAT- HOME, JAMES!

COME ON BETTY- WE'RE WAITING FOR YOU TO GO ON LOCATION!
HO-HUM-M! WHAT!! SO-O-O-O EARLY?
LOCATION TRAILER NO. 7
LOCATION CAR NO. 3
© 1934 King Features Syndicate, Inc. Great Britain rights reserved.
7-26
AT LAST!
SORRY TO KEEP YOU WAITING, BUT THE PACKING TOOK SO LONG!
TOODLE-O-O!! I'LL SEE YOU ON LOCATION!

?
GET INTO THIS BATHING-SUIT, BETTY - FOR THE NEXT BEACH SHOTS!
MUST I WEAR THAT?
YOU KNOW YOUR CONTRACT, BETTY?
© 1934, King Features Syndicate, Inc. Great Britain rights reserved
WELL, I WILL UNDER ONE CONDITION!
ANYTHING YOU SAY, BETTY!
7-27
--AND NO FAIR PEEKING!
OKAY! CAMERA!!

WHAT! NO "ROMEO"?
HE'S HOME SICK-BUT THE PICTURE MUST GO ON, BETTY-I'VE GOT TO DIG UP A SUBSTITUTE!
© 1934, King Features Syndicate, Inc., Great Britain rights reserved.
WOZZAT?
WHO WANTS TO TRY-OUT FOR THE "ROMEO" PART WITH BETTY?
7-28
GANGWAY! GANGWAY!
HEY! I'LL DO IT FOR NOTHIN'!
COMING, SIR!
OH! DO IT AGAIN, BOYS-IT'LL MAKE A SWELL "MOB SCENE" FOR MY NEXT PICTURE!

OH! IT'S YOU, "FEARLESS FRED"— SO IT WAS YOU I HAD THE DATE WITH-HUH?
THIS LOOKS LIKE A POPULAR PLACE, FRED!
NO! IT'S TOO CROWDED, BETTY-LET'S GO TO A PLACE WHERE WE CAN TALK!
PARISIEN
C ZY-HUH? NICE AND QUIET-NO CROWDS AND-ER-
LOOK!! THERE'S BETTY BOOP!
PARISIEN RESTA
BETTY BOOP!! WHERE?
OBOY! SHE'S RIGHT ACROSS THE STREET!
© 1934, King Features Syndicate, Inc., Great Britain rights reserved
YOO-HOO! BETTY!
LET'S ASK HER TO AUTOGRAPH THE MENUS!
WHAT DO YOU MEAN-THE NEXT TIME I'LL HAVE TO DO A "GARBO" OR WEAR A FALSE BEARD?
7-30

YES, I THINK I HAVE THE PART, OKAY!
FINE! REMEMBER THIS IS MELO-DRAMA-PUT PLENTY OF PATHOS INTO IT—
BE MINE, GAL, OR ELSE I'LL FORECLOSE THE MORTGAGE AND TURN YOU OUT INTO THE COLD, COLD WORLD—
SLAP!
HEY! WHAT'S THE IDEA?
© 1934, King Features Syndicate, Inc. Great Britain rights reserved
YOU'RE S'POSED TO BE COWED AND FRIGHTENED NOT BELLIGERENT!
WELL, HE ACTED AS THOUGH HE MEANT IT!
7-31

WE'LL BE ALL READY FOR YOUR NEXT SHOTS - I'VE JUST ORDERED THE EXTRAS FOR THE MOB SCENE!
FINE! BECAUSE I HAVE SOME RELATIVES IN TOWN TO SEE ME ACT!
YEAH? ARE THEY ON THE SET?
YES - JUST A MINUTE AND I'LL HAVE THEM IN!
© 1934, King Features Syndicate, Inc., Great Britain rights reserved.
MISTER VON SCRIPP - MEET THE FOLKS!
8·1
CANCEL THAT ORDER FOR THE MOB SCENE - I HAVE ONE!

HM-M! I WONDER WHERE I LEFT IT.
I SIMPLY MUST FIND IT - JUST CAN'T GO ON WITH THE SCENE TILL I DO!
COSTUMES SCENE IV
IT'S GOT TO BE HERE SOMEWHERE AND I HAVE NO SPARE!
© 1934, King Features Syndicate, Inc., Great Britain rights reserved.
WHAT THE SAM HILL ARE YOU LOOKING FOR - AND CAMERAS AND EVERYTHING WAITING -
8·2
AH! HERE IT IS!
HER GARTER - !!!!!

IT'S NO USE - I JUST CAN'T CRY!
PUT YOUR MIND ON IT, BETTY - THINK OF POOR LIL' NELL OUT IN THE SNOW STARVING - F-FREEZING AND -
SORRY I CAN'T CRY - IN FACT, I FEEL LIKE LAUGHING THE WAY YOU EMOTE THAT!
I'LL GET A "SOB-SISTER" TO WORK ON YOU - WE MUST FINISH THIS SCENE TODAY!
AT LAST SHE'S CRYING - OBOY! THAT'S MUSIC TO MY EARS - THE SCENE IS SAVED!
BOO HOO! SNIFF SNIFF - BOO-HOO-O
SET 4
8·3
© 1934, King Features Syndicate, Inc., Great Britain rights reserved.
SNIFF SNIFF
THERE, THERE, MISS SNIFFLES - DON'T READ ME ANY MORE IF THE STORIES AFFECT YOU LIKE THIS!
LITTLE NELL

NOW GET THIS - A SUMPTUOUS BANQUET - THE SCENE OPENS WITH BETTY MAKING A SPEECH AND --
OH-OH! THERE GOES THE LUNCH GONG!
GONG
SET VI
GANGWAY - GANGWAY
OBOY! AM I FAMISHED?
TO JOE'S
© 1934, King Features Syndicate, Inc., Great Britain rights reserved.
MAKE IT TWO WITH KRAUT - HANDSOME
COME ALONG WITH THOSE LITTLE DOGGIES - WILBUR!
COMIN' UP!
8·4

YES, CONTRACT- COME RIGHT OVER, PLEASE- THE DIRECTORS ARE WAITING FOR YOU AND--
PRESIDENT
OH! LOVELY- I'LL BE GLAD TO MISTER SPROCKETT!
IT'S AWFULLY NICE OF MISTER SPROCKETT TO INVITE ME AND THE DIRECTORS ARE SITTING IN, TOO!
ULTOMATO FILM CO
PRESIDENTS OFFICE
© 1934, King Features Syndicate, Inc., Great Britain rights reserved
YES, BETTY- WE'VE DECIDED TO HAVE YOU IN FOR A NEW CONTRACT!
CONTRACT?
8·6
OH! I THOUGHT YOU WANTED TO PLAY BRIDGE- SORRY!
CONTINUED-

NOW THAT I'VE READ YOUR NEW CONTRACT TO YOU, BETTY- ARE YOU READY TO SIGN?
NOT UNTIL MY LAWYERS OKAY IT- THEY'RE OUTSIDE- I'LL CALL THEM!
PRESIDENT
TROT 'EM IN!
YOO-HOO! COME IN, BOYS!
PRESIDENT
© 1934, King Features Syndicate, Inc., Great Britain rights reserved
8·7
MR. SPROCKETT- MEET MR. HABEAS, MR. CORPUS, MR. BAILER AND MR. BRIEF!
AHEM! SIT DOWN, MISTER SPROCKETT, WHILE WE GO OVER THIS NEW CONTRACT!
JOHNSON, JOHNSON, JONES, OLESON, COHEN AND KELLY'S LAW OFFICE?~ WELL, SEND OVER THE WHOLE STAFF- YES - I NEED 'EM ALL!
CONTINUED-

I HAVE YOUR NEW CONTRACT READY- CALL YOUR LAWYERS!
COME IN BOYS IT'S ALL SET!
HAVE YOU ANY SUGGESTIONS OR OBJECTIONS, GENTLEMEN?
YES - SHE MUST HAVE QUARTERS FOR HER SERVANTS AND CARS -
-AND A PRIVATE SWIMMING-POOL WITH ATTENDANTS!
-WITH N.R.A HOURS- WITH FOUR HOURS FOR LUNCH -
ULTOMATO FILM CO
-AND YOU MUST PROVIDE HER WITH A BUNGALOW ON THE SET-
-WITH HER NAME IN LIGHTS SIX FEET TALL!
AND SHE MUST HAVE A SIX MONTHS VACATION-
YES AND NOT ONLY THAT, BUT-
© 1934, King Features Syndicate, Inc., Great Britain rights reserved
I MUST HAVE IT TWICE A YEAR, TOO!
CONTINUED-

-AND SHE MUST HAVE ALL STAR PARTS AND-
ALL PARTS MUST BE SECONDARY TO HERS-
AND FEATURE PLAYERS IN THE OTHER PARTS--
AGREED! NOW LET ME CONTINUE--
© 1934 King Features Syndicate Inc Great Britain rights reserved
WHEREAS, THE PARTY OF FIRST PART HEREBY AGREES, GUARANTEES, AVERS, AFFIRMS, THAT BETTY BOOP THE PARTY OF THE SECOND PART--
I OBJECT!
I OBJECT! I OBJECT!
I OBJECT TO THAT LAST PARAGRAPH!
OH! YEAH?
AW! DON'T BE MEANIES-
8·9
-LET HIM HAVE A PARTY IN THE FIRST PART IF HE WANTS TO!
CONTINUED-

GENTLEMEN, AS BETTY'S REPRESENTATIVES I HAND YOU HER CONTRACT FOR EXAMINATION!
LOOK IT OVER WELL, BOYS!
? ?
ULTUMATO FILM CO CONTRACT
8-10
I OBJECT TO PARAGRAPH NUMBER SIX-
PARAGRAPH TWELVE MUST BE ELIMINATED AND--
-AND STRIKE OUT PARAGRAPH NINE-
CROSS OUT THAT WHOLE PARAGRAPH-
© 1934, King Features Syndicate, Inc., Great Britain rights reserved.
THAT'S WHAT I SAID- WE INSIST THAT YOU STRIKE OUT THAT LAST PARAGRAPH!
NOW THAT ALL THE OBJECTIONS 'N'EVERYTHIN' ARE SETTLED- I'M READY TO SIGN!
SIGN ?
THERE'S NOTHING LEFT TO SIGN!
CONTINUED

WELL- AT LAST YOUR NEW CONTRACT IS READY FOR YOUR "JOHN HANCOCK," BETTY!
THERE'S THE PEN AND INK, BETTY- NOW AFFIX YOUR MONICKER, AND EVERYTHING'S KAYO!
OH! WE MUST HAVE A FLASHLIGHT OF ME SIGNING- IT'LL BE GOOD PUBLICITY!
O-O-O! I'M SO NERVOUS!
ALL SET!
8-11
© 1934, King Features Syndicate, Inc., Great Britain rights reserved.
FLASH!
BOOM
OH! I FORGOT TO TELL YOU- ANY SUDDEN NOISE MAKES ME JUMPY!
OW! YOU WOULD!
CONTINUED-

OH! THERE'S BETTY BOOP- YOO-HOO!
WON'T YOU GIVE US YOUR AUTOGRAPH, BETTY?
© 1934, King Features Syndicate, Inc., Great Britain rights reserved
I SAW HER FIRST!
HURRY- BEFORE SHE RUNS OUT OF INK!
AUTOGRAPH MINE TWICE- MISS BOOP. ONE'S FOR MY KID BROTHER!
DON'T FORGET ME, MISS BOOP!
I'M NEXT!
DOES IT FEEL BETTER, MISS BOOP?
NOPE! I GUESS IT'S NO USE, CELESTE!
WELL, BETTY- NOW THAT YOUR LAWYERS ARE HERE ARE YOU READY TO SIGN?
8-13.
SORRY- I CAN'T SIGN- I'VE GOT WRITER'S CRAMP!
CONTINUED-

WELL, BETTY, HAVE YOUR LAWYERS FINISHED DRAWING UP YOUR NEW CONTRACT YET?
I THINK SO- I'LL CALL THEM!
COME IN, BOYS!
COMING, MISS BOOP!
© 1934, King Features Syndicate, Inc., Great Britain rights reserved.
WELL, GENTLEMEN I'D LIKE TO READ YOUR VERSION OF MISS BOOP'S NEW CONTRACT!
OKAY! TROT IN THE CONTRACT- HEMINGWAY!
8-14
CONTINUED-

WELL, I'M ALL READY TO SIGN, MISTER SPROCKETT!
NOT UNTIL I READ THIS CONTRACT YOUR LAWYERS DREW UP, CLEAR THROUGH FIRST!
© 1934 King Features Syndicate, Inc., Great Britain rights reserved
YOU'LL FIND EVERYTHING IN PROPER FORM-RIGHT DOWN TO THE LAST PARAGRAPH, SIR!
OH! YEAH?
8-15
WELL, HERE'S AN OVER-SIGHT ON PAGE 412 - PART FOUR!
WHAT!!
IMPOSSIBLE!
INCREDIBLE!
SPEAK, SIR, WHAT IS IT?
YOU LEFT OUT A PERIOD!
PHEW!
O-OH! WHAT A SHOCK!
A-AH!
CONTINUED

YES, BETTY - YOUR LAWYERS CONDENSED THE CONTRACT - NOW SIGN RIGHT THERE AND ---
AT LAST! WHAT A RELIEF TO HAVE IT FINALLY SIGNED!
© 1934 King Features Syndicate, Inc., Great Britain rights reserved
HEY! BRING OVER THE WIND-MACHINE-I'M TAKING SOME SHOTS 'SIDE OF THE ADMINISTRATION BUILDING!
8-16
WOT THA-
OH! LOOK-THEY'RE GOING RIGHT INTO THE LAKE, TOO!
CONTINUED

I WANT YOU TO READ OVER THAT NEW CONTRACT I DREW UP FOR YOU, BETTY!
--WHEREAS, THE PARTY OF THE FIRST PART HEREBY AGREES, AVERS, AFFIRMS, GUARANTEES AND SAYS-
BETTY BOOP CONTRACT
MORE WORRY!
SORRY, CHIEF, TO BUTT IN, BUT WE MUST DIG UP A GOOD COMEDY QUICK-ONE WITH REAL LAUGHS!
8-17
© 1934, King Features Syndicate, Inc., Great Britain rights reserved.
YOU'RE TELLING ME - BUT WHERE - OH WHERE CAN WE FIND ONE WITH REAL LAUGHS?
YES, WHERE!!
WHY DON'T YOU PRODUCE ONE OF YOUR OWN CONTRACTS?
THAT OUGHT TO GET PLENTY OF LAUGHS!
CONTINUED

YOGI AHMEN? YES, I'D LIKE YOUR ADVICE ON A VERY IMPORTANT MATTER!
I WANT TO KNOW IF IT IS A GOOD DAY FOR ME TO SIGN MY NEW CONTRACT!
WAIT TILL "ALI AHMEN" CONSULTS THE CRYSTAL!
YOU SAY YOU SEE AN OFFICE FILLED WITH LAWYERS-YES, YES, GO ON!
AND THEY HAVE A CONTRACT BEFORE THEM!
-AND THE BALL SAYS NOT TO SIGN TODAY, HUH?
TO BE DOUBLY SURE-I WILL ALSO READ YOUR HOROSCOPE, MISS BOOP!
8-18
© 1934, King Features Syndicate, Inc., Great Britain rights reserved
WHAT! WITH THE CONTRACT 'N' EVERYTHIN' READY AND YOU REFUSE TO SIGN?
MY HOROSCOPE SAYS THE STARS ARE WRONG AND NOT TO SIGN UNTIL THURSDAY WEEK!
CONTINUED

THIS NEW CONTRACT IS SURE AN AWFUL PUZZLE - HM-M!?? I CAN'T MAKE HEAD OR TAIL OF IT!
I'LL ASK NICK - HE'S SUPPOSED TO BE THE SMARTEST GUY AROUND THE LOT!
GREEKO
STUDIO CAFE
CAFE
8-20
© 1934, King Features Syndicate Inc., Great Britain rights reserved
NOPE, NICKY - I CAN'T READ ANY SENSE IN THIS NEW CONTRACT - SEE WHAT YOU CAN MAKE OUT OF IT!
I'LL DO MY BEST, BETTY!
BY GOLLY, BETTY - IT'S ALL GREEK TO ME!
OH! YEAH?
THEN EXPLAIN IT TO ME, PLEASE!
CONTINUED

WELL HAVE YOU THOUGHT OVER CLAUSE 63 IN BETTY'S NEW CONTRACT?
THAT'S A VERY COMPLICATED CLAUSE - WILL YOU EXCUSE US A MOMENT WHILE WE TALK IT OVER WITH BETTY?
IT'S UP TO OUR CLIENT - WE'LL HAVE TO GET HER OPINION!
ARTICLE 63 AFFECTS CLAUSE 86 WHICH MAKES IT A QUESTION OF LAW!
BUT WE MUST PUT IN A NEW CLAUSE TO COVER THE LOOP-HOLE IN PARAGRAPH 759 AND - - -
8-21
© 1934, King Features Syndicate, Inc., Great Britain rights reserved
ARE YOU ALL SET NOW?
WE AGREED THAT CLAUSE 63 HAS NO BEARING ON THIS CONTRACT!
WE THINK ARTICLE 537 CAN BE MADE MORE PLAUSIBLE, ACCORDING TO THE LAWS OF THIS COMMONWEALTH!
WHAT DO YOU THINK, BETTY?
WHO, ME? I THINK I'LL CHANGE MY LIPSTICK - IT'S TOO DARK!
CONTINUED

THEY LOOK REAL SPIFFY - I MUST WEAR THEM IN MY NEXT PICTURE!
WE'RE AGREED ON THE FEATURES, BUT IF THEY WANT HER TO APPEAR IN SHORT PICTURES -
THAT'S OUT!
ABSOLUTELY - POSITIVELY!!
BETTY MUST HAVE GOOD FEATURES!
WELL, IT'S UP TO US TO SEE THAT SHE GETS GOOD FEATURES!
WHAT'S WRONG WITH MY FEATURES?
THERE, NOW THEY CAN'T GET AROUND THAT CONTRACT - IT'S BULLET PROOF!
FINE! NOW YOU'LL BE IN EVERY FEATURE, BUT THEY CAN'T PUT YOU IN SHORTS!
DON'T BE SILLY -
8-22
© 1934, King Features Syndicate, Inc., Great Britain rights reserved
WHY, I LOOK CUTE IN SHORTS!
CONTINUED

THAT'LL BE ALL, BETTY - I WON'T NEED ANY MORE SITTINGS!
AH! THERE YOU ARE, BETTY - LET ME READ THE NEW CLAUSE IN YOUR CONTRACT!
- - AND WHEREAS, THE PARTY OF THE FIRST PART AGREES, AVERS, AFFIRMS AND GUARANTEES - ETC - -
- AND WHEREBY THE PARTY OF THE SECOND PART SHALL RECEIVE, ACQUIRE, TO HAVE AND TO HOLD - ETC. - ETC. - - -
© 1934, King Features Syndicate, Inc., Great Britain rights reserved
8-23
WHAT DO YOU THINK OF THAT NEW DUMMY OF ME, MR. SPROCKETT?
CONTINUED

GLUG-GLUB-- YES, SIR-I THINK I'M IN VERY GOOD VOICE!
FINE! STEP OVER TO THE SOUND STAGE-I HAVE EVERYTHING ALL READY FOR THE SCENE!
BOOP! BOOP!
MIKE
OKAY! BETTY-CAMERA!
STOP! CUT!!
© 1934, King Features Syndicate, Inc., Great Britain rights reserved
8-24
THAT'S WHAT WE SAID-UNDER HER NEW CONTRACT NOW BEING WRITTEN SHE CAN ONLY SAY ONE BOOP!
?
CONTINUED-

"THE ULTOMATO FILM CO." WILL NOT STAND FOR ANY MORE DILLY-DALLYIN-BETTY MUST SIGN THE CONTRACT TODAY-OR-
OH! SHE'LL SIGN RIGHT NOW!
-AND YOU WANT ME TO COME? SURE, I CAN MAKE IT-MY CAR'S OUTSIDE-I'LL CATCH THE NEXT 'PLANE!
OH! BETTY!!
YOU ALMOST MISSED THE 'PLANE, MISS BOOP-WE'RE HOPPING OFF RIGHT AWAY!
HEY, BETTY-WAIT!!
EAGLE AIRLINE NO. 3506
© 1934, King Features Syndicate, Inc., Great Britain rights reserved
8-25
BUT, I CAN'T REACH IT!
CONTINUED-

WELL IS EVERYTHING ALL SET FOR THE SIGNING?
EVERYTHING-RIGHT DOWN TO THE SMALLEST DETAIL, SUH!
WHAT! NO PEN?
MIGOSH AIN'T ANY OF YOU GOT A FOUNTAIN-PEN?
IT MUST BE IN MY OTHER SUIT!
OW! WE GOTTA GET A PEN SOMEWHERE, QUICK!
FOUNTAIN-PEN? YASSUH-I'SE GOT NUTHIN ELSE BUT!
SAVED!
OBOY! WHAT A RELIEF!
OH! GOODY!
QUICK BETTY-SIGN!
BUT IT WON'T WRITE-IT'S EMPTY!
CONTINUED-
8-27

I JUST CAN'T GET INTO THE MOOD OF SIGNING WITHOUT A MIKE AND CAMERA CLICKING!
OKAY! IT'LL BE GOOD PUBLICITY, TOO!
MAKE IT TWO "MIKES" AND THREE CAMERAS!
PS-ST! SAY A FEW WORDS-BETTY!
-ER-IT'S BEEN A COLOSSAL-I MIGHT SAY STUPENDOUS STRAIN-MY DEAR PUBLIC-ER-
© 1934, King Features Syndicate, Inc., Great Britain rights reserved
LA-DEE-DA-BOOP-BOOP-A-DOOP-
RING-AROUND-A-ROSIE
BOYS, BOYS-REMEMBER, MY CONTRACT FORBIDS ANY SILLY CAPERS!
WOW! AT LAST MY TROUBLES ARE OVER!
8-28
WHAT'S THAT, MISTER BRIEF?
I SAID, SIR-AFTER PERUSING THIS CONTRACT AS YOUR LAWYER-I'M ADVISING YOU THEY'VE JUST BEGUN!
CONTINUED-

-AND BETTY MUST ALSO LIVE UP TO CLAUSE #705 - NO CANDY, PASTRY, ETC - SHE MUST KEEP HER WEIGHT UNDER 100 LBS.-
WE WILL GUARANTEE THAT, SUH!
NOW THAT BETTY IS SIGNED UP AT LAST - WE SHOULD CELEBRATE IT IN A FITTING MANNER - HOW ABOUT A NICE DINNER?
A CAPITAL IDEA, SUH - WHAT D'YE SAY, BETTY?
OH! GOODY - I'M STARVED!
AH! A NICE PLANKED STEAK - POTATO SOUFFLE AND FIXINGS - YUM-M-M -
OBOY! I'LL HAVE THAT JELLIED CAPON WITH TRUFFLES AND - - -
ASSORTED HORS-D'ŒUVRES - BROILED LAKE TROUT - ROAST GUINEA HEN - ROMAINE, AVOCADO SALAD - THAT'S ME!
I'LL ORDER FOR BETTY!
?
YES, BETTY - TEA AND TOAST IS A BANQUET TO YOU FROM NOW ON!
8-29
CONTINUED -
© 1934, King Features Syndicate, Inc. Great Britain rights reserved

BUT, BETTY - YOU'VE GOT TO CALL YOUR LAWYERS OVER - IT LOOKS LIKE THEY'VE GOT ME IN A BRACE WITH THIS CONTRACT!
WELL, YOU ASKED FOR IT - BUT I'LL CALL THEM.
HELLO! HELLO!
-AND NOT ONLY THAT, GENTLEMEN - BUT YOU MUST MODIFY SOME OF THESE CLAUSES AND -
NO DICE - THE CONTRACT MUST STAND AS IS, SIR!
BUT LISTEN - I FIND THESE CLAUSES COVER EVERY MINUTE OF HER TIME - IT'LL BE IMPOSSIBLE TO MAKE A PICTURE -
HOW COME? HOW COME NO PICTURE?
-THERE'S NO PROVISION, MADE FOR TIME FOR HER TO ACT!
8-30
CONTINUED -
© 1934, King Features Syndicate, Inc., Great Britain rights reserved

-AND NOT ONLY THAT - BUT WE'RE HERE TO SEE THAT YOU DON'T VIOLATE ANY OF THE CLAUSES IN BETTY'S NEW CONTRACT!
OH, YEAH? BUT WE AIN'T FILMIN' THE CONTRACT - I DON'T DIRECT COMEDIES!
?
I SEE THE SCRIPT CALLS FOR ME TO RIDE A HORSE IN THIS NEXT SHOT!
YES - YOU SEE YOU MAKE YOUR ESCAPE ON OLD FAITHFUL DOBBIN - BUT THE VILLAIN STILL PURSUES AN'
OOPS!
HEY! YOU CAN'T MAKE BETTY DO THOSE STUNTS - IT'S NOT IN THE CONTRACT!
I WISH YOU HAD TOLD THE HORSE!
8-31
CONTINUED -
© 1934, King Features Syndicate, Inc., Great Britain rights reserved

I HAVE THE PART DOWN ALL RIGHT!
FINE! AND I'M GLAD YOUR GANG OF LAWYERS ARE NOT AROUND TO BUTT IN - THEY CRAMP MY STYLE!
I DON'T WANT ANY HITCH IN THIS RESCUE SCENE - IT'S THE MOST IMPORTANT SHOT OF THE PICTURE - NOW YOU'RE TO STAND AT THIS WINDOW AN' - -
OKAY, BETTY - JUMP! CAMERA!
STOP! BETTY CAN'T DO THAT - IT'S NOT IN THE CONTRACT!
COSTUMES SCENE XI SET 6
9-1
CONTINUED -
© 1934, King Features Syndicate, Inc., Great Britain rights reserved

QUICK, BETTY - BEFORE YOUR LAWYERS GET WISE - WE'RE GOING OUT ON LOCATION!
I THOUGHT THE SWIMMING POOL SHOT WAS TO BE MADE AT THE STUDIO?
WHY GO AWAY OUT HERE TO SHOOT THE SCENE?
I'M TAKING NO CHANCES - BUT I'VE OUT-SMARTED YOUR LAWYERS - THEY WON'T BE ABLE TO FIND US THIS TIME!
© 1934, King Features Syndicate, Inc., Great Britain rights reserved.
YES, SUH - LOOKS LIKE LAURA HAS HIT THE TRAIL AT LAST!
SNIFF SNIFF SNIFF
9-3
ALL READY FOR THE DIVE BETTY? OKAY - CAMERA!
STOP! WE OBJECT! IT'S NOT IN THE CONTRACT!

YOUR LAWYERS OUT-SMARTED US WITH THAT BLOODHOUND - BUT I'VE GOT 'EM STOPPED TODAY - SO GET READY!
MY COSTUME HAS JUST ARRIVED!
© 1934, King Features Syndicate, Inc.
I KNOW THEY'D OBJECT TO THIS BRIEF BATHING-SUIT, TOO!
DON'T WORRY I'VE GOT ALL THE GATES AND EVERYTHING GUARDED - NO CHANCE FOR 'EM TO BUTT IN!
SCENE III SET 6
NOW DIVE PRETTY, BETTY - ARE YOU ALL SET? OKAY - CAMERA!
HOLD EVERYTHING - DESIST! IT'S NOT IN THE CONTRACT!
CONTINUED

-AND PUT GUARDS AT EVERY GATE - ALSO SEARCH EVERY PROP BEFORE THE SCENE!
YES, SUH - YES, SUH!
YOUR LAWYERS AIN'T GOT A CHANCE TO BUTT IN - NOW YOU'RE AN ANIMAL-TRAINER AN' - -
I KNOW THEY'D OBJECT TO THAT!
9-5
YOU'RE TELLING ME - SEE, THIS IS A SIMPLE SHOT - THE TIGERS ARE WELL-TRAINED - IT'S ONLY GOING TO BE A LITTLE PLAYFUL COMEDY SCENE - -
-ER Y'SURE THE TIGERS KNOW THAT?
OKAY! MEN - LET OUT THE TIGERS AND STAND BY!
Y-YES, SUH!
CIRCUS
DESIST!! IT'S NOT IN THE CONTRACT!
© 1934, King Features Syndicate, Inc., Great Britain rights reserved.
CONTINUED

I THOUGHT YOU WERE SHOOTING IT AT THE STUDIO?
NO! I'M AFRAID YOUR LAWYERS WOULD OBJECT TO THE STUNT!
I'M TAKING NO CHANCES THAT'S WHY I RENTED THIS CIRCUS SET OUT ON THE DESERT!
© 1934, King Features Syndicate, Inc., Great Britain rights reserved.
9-6
SHOOT! WHEN READY, VON SCRIPP!
EVERYBODY READY? QUIET! CAMERA!
STOP! YOU CAN'T MAKE BETTY DO THAT STUNT - IT'S NOT IN THE CONTRACT!
FILM CAN NO. 3
FILM CAN NO. 5
FILM CAN NO. 4
FILM CAN NO. 2
CONTINUED

YES- SELECT FOUR FAT EXTRAS- I WANT 'EM FOR COMIC ROMAN SOLDIERS!
THERE'S NO CHANCE OF YOUR LAWYERS OBJECTING TO THIS CHARIOT RACE SHOT- I MEAN!
I'M AFRAID THEY WILL!
DON'T WORRY- I'VE GOT GUARDS ALL AROUND THE SET!
OH-OH! THIS COSTUME WOULD NEVER PASS THEM!
9-7
WHOA! NOW IS THAT NICE? WHOA!
EXTRAS! ROMAN GUARDS! INTO YOUR PLACES- READY, BETTY? CAMERA!
© 1934, King Features Syndicate, Inc. Great Britain rights reserved
STOP! WE OBJECT TO THIS STUNT— IT'S NOT IN THE CONTRACT!
CONTINUED-

OBOY! AFTER WE DO THIS LAST SHOT THE PICTURE IS FINISHED!
BUT S'POSE MY LAWYERS OBJECT TO IT!
THAT'LL BE JUST TOO BAD—FOR YOUR LAWYERS! I HAVE A QUARTET OF BOUNCERS ON THE JOB IF THEY SHOULD CRASH IN!
?
© 1934, King Features Syndicate, Inc. Great Britain rights reserved
CUT THAT STUNT— IT'S NOT IN THE CONTRACT!
OH, YEAH? NEITHER IS THIS STUNT- OKAY, MEN- PUT ON THE HEAT!
ALLAY OOP!
EXIT
?
9-8
CONTINUED-

NOW, MISS BOOP- WOULD YOU TELL ME YOUR PLANS FOR NEW FEATURES?
YES, MISS BOOP WILL STAR IN A BIG COSTUME PICTURE NEXT-FOLLOWED BY A HIGH-CLASS COMEDY!
TELL ME, MISS BOOP- ARE YOU IN LOVE?
NO! MISS BOOP IS STILL WHOLE HEART AND FANCY FREE- SHE'S WEDDED TO HER ART!
NOW, MISS BOOP, WOULD YOU TELL ME YOUR LIKES AND DISLIKES, HOBBIES, ETC.?
MISS BOOP ABHORS CLAM FRITTERS, BUT LOVES CHILDREN- HER PET HOBBY IS PLAIN AND FANCY SEWING!
9-10
THANKS, MISS BOOP, FOR THE INFORMATION!
OH, DON'T MENTION IT— I'M ONLY TOO GLAD TO TELL YOU!
© 1934, King Features Syndicate, Inc., Great Britain rights reserved

HAVE YOU GOT ALL THE "PROPS" ON— TELEPHONE 'N' EVERYTHIN'?
YES, SIR,- ALL SET, SIR!
?
FILM CAN
FILM CAN
© 1934, King Features Syndicate, Inc. Great Britain rights reserved
YES- I HAVE MY LINES FOR THIS NEXT SHOT DOWN OKAY!
FINE! 'CAUSE I DON'T WANT ANY HITCH IN THIS SCENE!
?
OKAY, BETTY! QUIET- CAMERA!
HEY! WHY DON'T YOU SAY YOUR LINES? WE'RE WASTING FILM- YOU'RE S'POSED TO TALK TO YOUR SWEETHEART AND---
?
BUT I CAN'T GET THE OPERATOR!
9-11

OBOY! AT LAST THE PICTURE IS FINISHED-ALL BUT THE FADE-OUT!
IT HAS BEEN A TERRIBLE STRAIN!
© 1934, King Features Syndicate, Inc. Great Britain rights reserved.
YOU'RE TELLING ME-NOW GET INTO YOUR COSTUME FOR THE FADE-OUT KISS WITH VAN SCARSDALE!
KISS FADE-OUT? NOT WITH HIM-NEVER!
YOU'LL JUST HAVE TO USE A DOUBLE-THAT'S ALL!
WHAT! WITH ALL THE MONEY INVOLVED-YOU WON'T DO THE KISS FADE-OUT WITH VAN SCARSDALE-WHY NOT!!! -WHY NOT--
BECAUSE I'M MAD AT HIM!
9-12

NOW THE SCRIPT CALLS FOR YOU TO PUSH THE VILLAIN OFF THE CLIFF IN THIS NEXT SCENE!
NOT REALLY?
FILM CAN
YOU MUST PUT PLENTY OF ACTION INTO THIS SCENE-WE WANT A GOOD, SNAPPY CLIMAX!
WHAT A DELIGHTFUL VIEW!
?
HEY! STOP!! NOT HIM-IT'S THE ONE ON THE LEFT--HEY--
WELL, HE LOOKED LIKE THE "DUMMY" TO ME!
HELP!
© 1934, King Features Syndicate, Inc. Great Britain rights reserved
9-13

AW! PLEASE DANCE FOR US, BETTY?
I'LL FURNISH THE MUSIC, BETTY-GET HOT!
OKAY! I'LL DO SOME OF THE DANCES I'M REHEARSING FOR MY NEW PICTURE!
HOW D'YE LIKE THIS ROUTINE I'M DOING IN THE BALL-ROOM SCENE?
OBOY! CAN SHE DANCE-OR CAN SHE DANCE?
GREAT, BETTY-THAT'S A REAL HOT NUMBER!
WOW! SHE'S THE LIFE OF THE PARTY!
HERE'S ANOTHER I DO IN THE CAFE SCENE!
WHAT PEP! NOW JUST ONE MORE, BETTY-BEFORE WE LEAVE!
© 1934, King Features Syndicate, Inc. Great Britain rights reserved.
AND THEN
WHAT!! EVERYTHING READY FOR THE DANCE SHOTS AND YOU SAY YOU CAN'T DO 'EM TODAY?
HO-HUM! SORRY-BUT I'M SO TIRED I JUST COULDN'T DANCE A STEP!
DANCE SCENE
9-14

LOOK! YOU'RE OVER-WEIGHT AND YOUR CONTRACT SAYS YOU CAN'T GO OVER 100 LBS: -YOU MUST GET SOME OF THAT AVOIRDUPOIS OFF!
DON'T GET FRESH!
PHEW! AM I REDUCING OR AM I REDUCING?
WHOA! I'LL LOSE WEIGHT ALL RIGHT, BUT THIS NAG WILL LOSE ME, TOO!
HEY! BETTY-Y' TRYIN' TO BREAK THE ENDURANCE RECORD?
OBOY! THAT EXERCISE STUFF SURE GIVES YOU SOME APPETITE--ER-STEAK AND---
RESTAURANT
SPECIAL STEAK
9-15
OW! YOU GAINED FIVE POUNDS!
D---N!!

WELL, BETTY-DID YOU FOLLOW DOCTOR WAITES REDUCING DIET THAT I GAVE YOU?
I'LL SAY I DID-EVEN TO EATING THE SPINACH!
YEAH? WELL SCALES DON'T LIE-WHY, YOU'RE HEAVIER THAN BEFORE!
? ? ?
ARE YOU SURE THAT YOU ATE NOTHING BUT THE FOOD IN THE DIET?
NOTHING--ER-
THAT IS-EXCEPTING MY ORDINARY MEALS!
© 1934, King Features Syndicate, Inc., Great Britain rights reserved.

NOW WOULDN'T THAT GET YOU?
WHAT!! NO REDUCTION!?
AND YOU SAY YOU FOLLOWED THE REDUCING EXERCISES-ALSO THAT STRICT DIET?
RIGHT DOWN TO THE LAST PIECE OF DRY TOAST!
IT DOESN'T SEEM POSSIBLE WITH THAT STRICT DIET AND THOSE EXERCISES AND NOT LOSE EVEN ONE POUND!
I KNOW IT!
I GUESS I'M ONE OF THOSE POOR LOSERS YOU HEAR ABOUT!
© 1934, King Features Syndicate, Inc., Great Britain rights reserved

THAT'S THE SCRIPT OF YOUR NEW PICTURE-"DINNER FOR TWO". WE PAID PLENTY TO GET IT FOR YOU TOO!
?
IT FITS YOU TO PERFECTION-WE'RE STARTING PRODUCTION RIGHT AWAY!
OH! THIS RESTAURANT SCENE WILL HAVE TO BE CUT OUT!
DON'T BE SILLY-WHY THE RESTAURANT SCENE IS THE MOST IMPORTANT PART OF THE PICTURE!
SORRY, BUT I'D BE A SURE FLOP IN THAT SCENE!
? ? ?
REMEMBER I'M ON A STRICT DIET!
DINNER FOR TWO
© 1934, King Features Syndicate, Inc. Great Britain rights reserved

STILL OVER-WEIGHT AND AFTER ALL MY DIETING!
HM-M! WELL, WE'LL TRY THE REDUCING SYSTEM BOXERS USE-GET INTO A RUNNING-SUIT!
HEY! NOT SO FAST-REMEMBER, I'M NO "BONTHRON"!
I KNOW THIS IS DRASTIC STUFF-BUT YOUR CASE CALLS FOR IT!
SHE HASN'T COMPLAINED SINCE THE START-I'LL HAVE TO ADMIT SHE CAN TAKE IT-I'LL SPEED UP A BIT ON THIS LAST LAP!
OBOY! I'LL BET THIS RUN HAS GOT HER DOWN TO WEIGHT-POOR KID. I'LL TAKE HER IN AT THIS NEXT TURN!
© 1934, King Features Syndicate, Inc. Great Britain rights reserved

WHY, I'M EVEN LOSING SLEEP OVER THIS WEIGHT THING!
OH! YEAH? SO ARE WE AND WE'RE LOSING PLENTY BY YOUR PICTURE BEING HELD UP - COME ON, I'VE GOT THE ANSWER!
FIRST, MISS BOOP - THE MASSEUSES WILL TAKE YOU IN HAND - THEN I WILL PUT YOU THROUGH A SERIES OF REDUCING EXERCISES AND —
THE STEAM CABINET IS READY, MISS BOOP!
NIGHT-
DAWN-
NEXT DAY-
CONGRATULATIONS! SO YOU TOOK OFF SIX POUNDS IN ONE DAY?
YES, BUT- YOU'LL HAVE TO POSTPONE THE PICTURE AGAIN!
BETWEEN THE DIET AND REDUCING EXERCISES - I'M TOO WEAK TO ACT!
© 1934, King Features Syndicate, Inc. Great Britain rights reserved
9 21

HOORAY! YOU'RE DOWN TO 100 LBS. AT LAST!
BUT WHAT A STRAIN THAT STRICT DIET IS - PHEW!
I KNOW - BUT YOU MUST KEEP IT UP - IN THE MEANTIME - SHAKE! YOU DID NOBLE!
THANKS! I THINK I DESERVE A FEW CHEERS!
WE MUST CELEBRATE THE OCCASION IN A FITTING MANNER - WHAT WOULD YOU SUGGEST?
HM-M LET ME SEE -
WHY NOT GIVE ME A DINNER?
© 1934, King Features Syndicate, Inc., Great Britain rights reserved
9 22

MY LAWYERS INSIST ON PASSING ON ALL STORIES - YOU KNOW THEY'RE FOR THIS CLEAN UP THE MOVIES THING STRONG?
WHO AIN'T? BUT THOSE BIRDS ARE BEGINNING TO GET IN MY HAIR!
WELL, LET 'EM PASS ON THESE STORIES - WE PAID THOUSANDS FOR THESE CLASSICS - THEY'RE YOUR NEXT FEATURES!
WHAT!! YOU REFUSE TO OKAY ANY OF THOSE CLASSICS?
ABSOLUTELY!
EMPHATICALLY!
RIGHTO!
WE DO, SUH!
LISTEN - IS THERE ANY STORY YOU MUGGS WILL OKAY FOR BETTY?
YES, SUH - I'LL SAY THERE IS!
AHEM! WE WROTE IT, OURSELVES!
LITTLE MISS MUFFET

UNDERSTAND, BETTY - WE'RE IN FULL ACCORD WITH THE MOVIE CLEAN UP CAMPAIGN AND -
I KNOW - BUT MY LAWYERS INSIST ON PASSING ON EVERYTHING TO MAKE SURE!
THEY WOULD - WELL THERE'S THE SCENES N DIALOGUE OF YOUR NEXT PICTURE AND IT COSTS US PLENTY - SHOW IT TO 'EM!
YOO HOO! OKAY, BOYS!
YOU MAY USE THAT OFFICE ON THE LEFT SIRS!
THANK YOU SUH!
BONG BONG
TWO HOURS LATER
THAT'S WHAT WE SAID — WE FIND NOTHING BUT THE "THEME SONG" PASSABLE!
BETTY BOOP BE MINE
O.K.

WHERE ARE YOU SHOOTING MY NEXT PICTURE-"SALLY OF THE SLUMS"?
OVER ON SET SIX -THEY'VE BEEN WORKING ON IT FOR A WEEK- BUT IT'S ALL READY TO SHOOT TODAY!
OH! WHAT A MESS- WHERE'S THE PROP-ROOM, BOY?
IN THE NEXT BUILDING MISS BOOP!
OW! WHAT'S THE IDEA OF SPOILING THIS COSTLY SLUM SET?
WHY, HAVEN'T YOU HEARD ABOUT THE "CLEAN-UP THE MOVIES" CAMPAIGN?
WE MUST DO OUR PART!
-AND WE INSIST ON PASSING ON ALL COSTUMES THAT BETTY IS TO WEAR!
OKE BY ME - WE'RE HEARTILY IN FAVOR OF THE "MOVIE CLEAN-UP" CAMPAIGN AND ONLY TOO GLAD TO CO-OPERATE
HM-M-M! ALL OKAY BUT THIS BATHING-SUIT - CUT TOO LOW IN THE FRONT- TOO RISQUE. SUH!
OH. WE CAN CHANGE THAT!
HOW'S THAT, GENTLEMEN?
THAT'S BETTER-YESSUH! IT HAS OUR STAMP OF APPROVAL, SUH!
READY FOR THE DIVE, BETTY - QUIET,- CAMERA!!
YOU KNOW, MY LAWYERS ARE WITH THE "CLEAN-UP THE MOVIES" CAMPAIGN 100%?
SO AM I- LISTEN-THERE'S NOTHING IN THIS DIALOGUE THAT THE STRICTEST CENSORSHIP WOULDN'T PASS!
D--N!!
STOP! CUT!!
NO, SUH-- YOU CAN'T MAKE BETTY USE THAT KIND OF LANGUAGE- WE OBJECT, SUH!
SKIP IT- THAT EXCLAMATION IS NOT IN THE SCRIPT-
I JUST TRIPPED OVER THIS WIRE AND FORGOT MYSELF!
WHAT'S THE IDEA OF GOING AWAY OUT ON THE DESERT TO SHOOT THE SCENE?
JUST TO GET AWAY FROM YOUR LAWYERS AND THEIR STRICT CENSORSHIP!
REMEMBER- MY CONTRACT GIVES THEM THE RIGHT TO PASS ON EVERYTHING?
LISTEN, BETTY-WE'RE FOR THIS "MOVIE CLEAN-UP" 100%, BUT THOSE BIRDS CRAMP MY STYLE- THERE'S NO ROOM FOR 'EM, ANYHOW!
SORRY, GENTLEMEN. BUT, AS YOU CAN SEE, THERE'S NO ROOM FOR YOU!
SKIP IT- DON'T WORRY, SUH! WE HAVE OUR OWN CAR!
STEP ON IT, BOYS!
CAN'T SHAKE 'EM-THEY MUST HAVE FOUR MOTORS, TOO!

WHAT! NO MOB SCENE?
NOPE! IT'S TOO EXPENSIVE - THE PRODUCER ORDERED ME TO ECONOMIZE ON EVERYTHING!
CARRIE, CALL ALL THESE NUMBERS AND TELL THEM TO MEET ME ON SET "SIX" THIS AFTERNOON!
OBOY! LOOKS LIKE THE "WHO'S WHO" DIRECTORY!
© 1934, King Features Syndicate, Inc. Great Britain rights reserved.
HEY! IS THIS A CONVENTION? WHAT'S ALL THAT CROWD ON MISS BOOP'S SET?
THEY'RE BOY FRIENDS OF MISS BOOPS - SHE INVITED 'EM!
SET NO. 6 -QUIET-
YOU SEE - I FIGURED WE COULD USE THEM FOR THE MOB SCENE AND SAVE PAYING EXTRAS!
ARE YOU A GENIUS - OR ARE YOU A GENIUS? OBOY!
10-1

WELL, I SURE SAVED YOU PLENTY BY HAVING MY BOY FRIENDS ACT AS A MOB SCENE!
I'LL SAY - NOW IF YOU COULD ONLY HAVE THEM FOR THE RIOT SCENE IT WOULD SAVE PLENTY MORE!
© 1934, King Features Syndicate, Inc. Great Britain rights reserved.
OBOY! IF WE COULD ONLY THINK OF SOME WAY TO GET 'EM ALL FIGHTING AND--
THAT'S AN IDEA - I'LL USE MY GARTER!
HEY, BOYS! THE ONE WHO RETURNS MY GARTER WILL BE MY ESCORT TO THE PREMIER OF THE PICTURE!
I'VE GOT IT!
IT'S ALL MINE!
10-2
CAMERA!!! WOW! THIS REALISTIC RIOT SHOT WILL MAKE THE PICTURE!
OW! WAMP BAM SOCK

WHY, WE MUST HAVE REAL FLOWERS FOR THE FLOWER SHOW SHOT!
SORRY! BUT YOU KNOW THE PRODUCER'S ORDERS - CUT COSTS ON EVERYTHING?
© 1934, King Features Syndicate, Inc. Great Britain rights reserved.
YES, SAM - POST THOSE RIGHT AWAY - THEY'RE NOTES TO MY BOY FRIENDS THAT I'M LEAVING FOR LOCATION TOMORROW!
I GET CHA - MISS BOOP!
NEXT DAY
FLOWERS FOR MISS BOOP!
BRING THEM RIGHT THIS WAY!
10-3
C'MON, BETTY - THE FLOWER SHOW SHOT IS ALL READY TO SHOOT - THANKS TO YOU!

BUDGET, ME EYE - THESE MANSION INTERIOR AND EXTERIOR SHOTS ARE TOO IMPORTANT TO CUT!
I KNOW - BUT THE SET WOULD COST TOO MUCH TO BUILD -
-AND THE BOSS INSISTS THAT I ECONOMIZE - NOW IF WE COULD ONLY RENT A MANSION CHEAP OR BORROW ONE -
HM-M! THAT REMINDS ME - I HAVE A LUNCHEON DATE AT JACK DARBY'S HOME!
© 1934, King Features Syndicate, Inc. Great Britain rights reserved.
10-4
YES - THAT'S HIS MANSION THERE!
WOW! I HOPE YOU'RE RIGHT, BETTY - IT'S A PERFECT SETTING!
CUT! NOW WE'LL SHOOT THE EXTERIOR SCENES!

WELL, YOU KNOW, BETTY- WE'RE ON A STRICT BUDGET AND MUST CUT COSTS EVERYWHERE
BUT HOW ARE YOU GOING TO HAVE A DOG SHOW SHOT WITHOUT DOGS?
© 1934, King Features Syndicate, Inc., Great Britain rights reserved
WE'LL JUST HAVE TO CUT OUT THE SCENE - BUYING A LOT OF BLOODED DOGS IS TOO EXPENSIVE!
BUT IT'S AN IMPORTANT SCENE!
10-5
YOU'RE TELLING ME - BUT SHOW DOGS COST PLENTY AND OUR BUDGET WON'T STAND IT!
WAIT! I'LL CALL SCHUYLER VAN GILT-HE HAS A KENNEL--
READY WITH THE RIBBONS-BETTY-OKAY! CAMERA!

WHY, THE YACHTING SCENES ARE THE MOST IMPORTANT OF ALL!
DON'T I KNOW IT? BUT THE PRODUCER SAYS WE MUST CUT COSTS TO THE BONE!
BUT THE SCRIPT CALLS FOR A YACHT AND-
WELL, WE CAN'T AFFORD IT-YOU'LL HAVE TO CHANGE IT TO A ROW BOAT!
WAIT! HOLD EVERYTHING!
THE YACHTING SCENES ARE SAVED - REGGIE VAN KUSH JUST TOLD ME WE COULD USE HIS YACHT!
BETTY, YOU'RE A LIFE SAVER! HEY! GET THE SOUND CREW AND CAMERAS READY!
10-6
ALL SET, BETTY? QUIET-- CAMERA!
© 1934, King Features Syndicate, Inc., Great Britain rights reserved.

YEAH! I'M ASKING YOUR LAWYERS UP TO DISCUSS YOUR NEW PART, BETTY!
I'M NOT SURE I WANT TO PLAY THAT PART!
OH! BUT YOU MUST, BETTY- IT WOULD BE A VIOLATION OF YOUR CONTRACT TO REFUSE!
I'M NOT REFUSING - I'M JUST UNDECIDED!
© 1934 King Features Syndicate Inc Great Britain rights reserved
WELL, HERE ARE YOUR LAWYERS - WHY DON'T YOU ASK THEIR ADVICE ON THE MATTER?
OH! I INTEND TO -
10-8
JUST AS SOON AS I DECIDE WHAT I AM GOING TO DO!

WELL, BETTY-HAVE YOU READ YOUR NEW PART-"THE GIRL IN GREEN"?
YES, BUT I DON'T THINK I'LL DO IT!
GIRL IN GREEN
WHAT! AFTER ALL THE MONEY WE PAID FOR IT-WHY, IT'S A VIOLATION OF YOUR CONTRACT!
SORRY- YOU'LL HAVE TO TAKE THAT UP WITH MY LAWYERS!
© 1934, King Features Syndicate, Inc., Great Britain rights reserved
BUT, BETTY- HAVE YOU ANY SANE REASON WHY YOU DON'T WISH TO PLAY "THE GIRL IN GREEN"?
I'LL SAY I HAVE -
10-9
I LOOK TERRIBLE IN GREEN!

A "BANANA SPLIT" SMOTHERED WITH A DOUBLE PORTION OF WHIPPED CREAM!
YES, MISS BOOP!
HEY! BETTY IS IN YE STUDIO SHOPPE WITH A BANANA SPLIT!
WHAT! AND SHE ON A DIET-CALL HER LAWYERS, QUICK!
YOU CAN'T HAVE FATTENING FOODS OR DRINKS, MY DEAR, IT'S A VIOLATION OF YOUR CONTRACT!
BESIDES YOU KNOW ORANGE JUICE IS WONDERFUL FOR ONE'S FIGURE!
WELL, HOW ABOUT YOUR-SELVES?
© 1934, King Features Syndicate, Inc., Great Britain rights reserved.
10-10

EVERYTHING IS ALL SET FOR YOUR RECORDING-HOPE YOU'RE IN GOOD VOICE, BETTY?
AH-CHOO-O-
OW! CUT!! GET A DOCTOR AND AN AMBULANCE-QUICK!
CLANG
CLANG
CLANG
WEE-E-E-E
HOSPITAL
HM-M! HER PULSE IS NORMAL-STICK OUT YOUR TONGUE!
OPEN YOUR MOUTH MISS BOOP AND SAY, AH!
GET THE WHOLE STAFF HERE-SPARE NO EXPENSE THE PICTURE MUST GO ON!
CONTINUED
© 1934, King Features Syndicate, Inc., Great Britain rights reserved.
10-15

HOPE THOSE SPECIALISTS CURED YOUR VOICE-STRAIN, BETTY, 'CAUSE EVERY-THING IS READY FOR YOUR RECORDING!
BOOP! BOOP!
OW! SHE CAN ONLY WHISPER-HEY! GET ALL THOSE SPECIALISTS HERE, QUICK!
YES, SIR-WE'VE TRIED EVERY KNOWN CURE FOR VOICE-STRAIN ON HER-NOW TRY AGAIN, MISS BOOP!
BOOP! BOOP!
'S NO USE-SHE CAN'T SPEAK ABOVE A WHISPER-OH! WHAT CAN WE DO?
EE-E-E-EEK! O-O-O! A MOUSE!!
VON SCRIPT DIRECTOR
CONTINUED
© 1934, King Features Syndicate, Inc., Great Britain rights reserved.
10-16

YEP! SOUND TRACK 'N EVERYTHIN' IS READY FOR BETTY!
HOPE THAT MOUSE SCARE YESTERDAY BROUGHT BACK HER VOICE PERMANENTLY!
OW! STILL WHISPERING-AND THE RECORDING THREE DAYS LATE ALREADY!
WHSS-S-S S-S-S-S
ON OUT TO THE FOOTBALL GAME-MAYBE YOU NEED A LIL' RECREATION-WE'VE TRIED EVERY-THING ELSE!
YEE-OW!! A TOUCH-DOWN!
?
CONTINUED
© 1934, King Features Syndicate, Inc., Great Britain rights reserved.
10-17

WELL-TAKING YOU TO THE FOOTBALL GAME SURE BROUGHT YOUR VOICE BACK-NOW WE CAN GO ON WITH THE RECORDING-EVERYTHING'S READY!
ALL SET, BETTY-QUIET! CAMERA!!
WHSS-S-S S-S-S-S
OW!'S NO USE SHE'S DOWN TO A WHISPER AGAIN-CUT!! CALL THE SPECIALISTS!
WHSS-S-S -S-S-S-S-
YOO-HOO! HELLO, SALLY!!
© 1934, King Features Syndicate, Inc., Great Britain rights reserved. 10-18
CONTINUED-

YES, SIR-EVERYTHING'S HO-KEE-DOKE, BETTY'S VOICE IS NORMAL AGAIN!
LET'S HOPE YOU'RE RIGHT THIS TIME-IT'S BEGINNING TO WEAR ME DOWN!
WHSS-S- -S-S-S-S S-S-S
OW! SHE'S STILL WHISPERING!!
WE CAN'T UNDERSTAND IT-NO, SIR!
WE'VE TRIED EVERY CURE FOR VOICE STRAIN AND--
THINK! AIN'T THERE ANYTHING ELSE YOU CAN DO?
PS-ST! YOU'RE WANTED ON THE 'PHONE, MISS BOOP!
WHAT! YOU SAY MY GOWN WON'T BE FINISHED FOR THE "PREMIER" BUT LISTEN-
© 1934, King Features Syndicate, Inc., Great Britain rights reserved.
10-19
CONTINUED

YES, SIR-WE PRONOUNCE MISS BOOP'S VOICE STRAIN COMPLETELY CURED!
HOO-RAY! CONGRATULATIONS-AT LAST WE CAN FINISH THE RECORDING!
YES, BETTY-WE MUST CELEBRATE THE OCCASION IN A FITTING MANNER-I'LL INVITE YOUR LAWYERS, THE SPECIALISTS AND--
10-20
LADIES AND GENTLEMAN-WE WILL NOW HEAR A FEW WORDS FROM OUR GUEST OF HONOR--
© 1934, King Features Syndicate, Inc., Great Britain rights reserved.
LADIES AND GENLTLEMAN-WHIS-S-S-S-S-S-S-S-S-S-S-S-S-S
OW! SHE'S WHISPERING AGAIN!
CONTINUED-

WHSS-S S-S-S-S S-S-S- S-S
OW! STILL WHISPERING-CALL IN THE SPECIALISTS AGAIN!
YES, SIR-WE ARE CONFIDENT THAT WE HAVE SOLVED MISS BOOP'S LOSS-OF-VOICE CASE AT LAST BUT FOR ONE THING!
OH! THERE WOULD BE A CATCH IN IT!
--AND WE DISCOVERED HER VOICE WAS OKAY UNTIL SHE STEPPED BEFORE THE "MIKE"-JUST A CASE OF "MIKE FRIGHT"-NOW WE MUST FIND A WAY TO OVER-COME THAT!
© 1934, King Features Syndicate, Inc., Great Britain rights reserved.
OKAY-BUT NOT SO LOUD, BETTY!
AND SHE KNOCKS ME FOR A LOOP-WITH HER BOOP-BOOP-A-DOOP--
10-22

YOU'VE GOT TO CRY IN THIS NEXT SCENE. BETTY - SO I'VE HIRED MAESTRO PAYSTRO TO PLAY SOME SAD MUSIC TO PUT YOU IN THE MOOD!
?
WELL I'LL BE — HEY! BETTY - WAKE UP!! THAT SAD MUSIC IS TO HELP YOU CRY NOT SLEEP!
I KNOW - HO-HUM-M-
BUT YOU SEE, SAD MUSIC ALWAYS AFFECTS ME THAT WAY!
10-23
CONTINUED

BUT I FEEL TOO HAPPY TO CRY!
BUT YOU'VE GOT TO FOR THIS NEXT SHOT - NOW THIS SAD STORY OUGHTA HELP YOU CRY!
MIKE
LITTLE NELL
?
"POOR LIL' NELL - ZERO WITHOUT AND NO FIRE WITHIN - WITH BUT AN OLD COTTON SHAWL FOR PROTECTION AGAINST THE WINTRY BLASTS - NO FOOD - NO -
WHAT'S THE IDEA OF LAUGHING INSTEAD OF CRYING OVER THIS HEART-RENDING STORY?
HA HA HA HA HA HA HA HA HA HA HA
IT'S YOU I'M LAUGHING AT - GOSH! YOU'D MAKE A GREAT COMEDIAN!
10-24
© 1934, King Features Syndicate, Inc.
Great Britain rights reserved.
CONTINUED

YES SIR - BOSS! I'VE HIRED TILLY TORCH, "THE GIRL WITH A TEAR IN HER VOICE," TO HELP MAKE BETTY CRY!
GOOD! THAT GAL COULD MAKE YANKEE DOODLE SOUND SAD!
PRESIDENT
"SHE WAS HAPPY TILL SHE MET YOU AND THE FAULT WAS ALL YOUR OWN -"
"SHE WAS ONLY A BIRD IN A GILDED CAGE AND -"
SNIFF SNIFF
BOO HOO-O
BLUB BLUB
?
ER - PARDON ME - BUT DO YOU KNOW ANY HOT NUMBERS?
PLOP!
© 1934, King Features Syndicate, Inc.
Great Britain rights reserved.
10-25
CONTINUED

YOU'VE GOT TO DOPE OUT SOME WAY TO MAKE BETTY CRY - THE SCENE IS LATE AND -
WE'VE TRIED ABOUT EVERYTHING BUT IT'S NO DICE - ER - WAIT! OBOY, WHAT'S THAT?
BOO-HOO - SNIFF SNIFF
WHO WOULDN'T CRY? BOO-HOO! I JUST NOTICED I RIPPED A BIG HOLE IN MY NEW GOWN LAST NIGHT!
AT LAST - PS-ST! ORDER A FLOCK OF GOWNS - QUICK!!
© 1934, King Features Syndicate, Inc., Great Britain rights reserved.
? ? ?
MIKE
NOW RIP UP THAT LASTEST PARIS CREATION - THAT OUGHT TO PUT HER INTO HYSTERICS!
RIP RIP!
10-26
OW! $1,000 WORTH OF GOWNS AND NOT A TEAR - HOW COME?
I SHOULD CRY OVER SOMEONE ELSE'S GOWNS - DON'T BE SILLY!
CONTINUED

WELL YOU'VE JUST GOT TO FINISH THAT PICTURE TODAY OR ELSE-
WE'VE TRIED ABOUT EVERY WAY TO MAKE BETTY CRY-MAYBE THESE SAD STORIES WILL DO THE TRICK!
PRESIDINT
'S NO USE-NOTHING WILL MAKE HER CRY-YOU'LL HAVE TO RE-WRITE THE SCRIPT!
OH!
MIKE
HEY! WHO LET THAT DIRTY LITTLE MUTT ON THIS SET? LOOK OUT BETTY-ER-
O-OH! YOU DEAR, LIL' HELPLESS THING-
SNIFF
SNIFF
BOO-HOO! SNIFF-SNIFF-YOU POOR, LIL' NEGLECTED DARLING BOO-HOO-
WOW! EVERYTHING'S HO-KEE-DOKE-SOUND CREW, GET READY FOR THE CRYING SCENE, QUICK!
10-27

HURRY, BETTY-WE'RE LEAVING FOR LOCATION TO SHOOT SOME WESTERN SCENES!
JUST PACK THINGS THAT ARE ABSOLUTELY NECESSARY-WE'RE GOING TO ROUGH IT-LIVE IN TENTS-CLOSE TO NATURE-
OH! I LIKE THAT IDEA OF ROUGHING IT-SOUNDS THRILLING!
THREE HOURS AND NOT READY YET-HM-M-M-SOMETHING FLOOIE ABOUT THIS!
BUT THEY'RE JUST THINGS THAT I ABSOLUTELY NEED!
YOU HEARD ME NEVER MIND BRINGING THE ROADSTER-SEND A MOVING VAN INSTEAD!
10-29
CONTINUED-

YES, WE'RE ALL UNPACKED-NOW WHERE'S THE SHOWER?
THE SHOWER? LISTEN, BETTY WE'RE OUT ON LOCATION-YOU'LL HAVE TO DO YOUR BATHING IN THE CREEK!
THE WILDS OR NOT-I MUST HAVE MY SHOWER-BRING THAT BARREL ALONG, PROPS. ALSO GET ME A VEGETABLE COLANDER AND A PIECE OF PIPE!
I GET YUH, MISS BETTY!
WHAT'S THE IDEA OF THE BUCKET BRIGADE-WHERE'S THE FIRE?
NO FIRE, BOSS-THE WATER IS FOR BETTY!
10-30
CONTINUED-

ANYTHING ELSE MISS BOOP?
YES-AFTER MY BATH-GET THINGS READY FOR A HAIR WAVE, FACIAL AND MANICURE!
WILL THAT BE ALL, MISS BOOP?
WELL YOU MIGHT TINT MY TOE NAILS. TOO-A GRASS GREEN TO MATCH THE HILLS!
HAVE MY TOWN CAR READY AT FOUR, HIGGINS-I'M GOING FOR A RIDE OUT THAT NEW STATE HIGHWAY!
YES, MISS!
GOOD AFTERNOON, BETTY-HOW ARE YOU ENJOYING YOURSELF?
OH! I DON'T THINK THIS ROUGHING-IT IS WHAT IT'S CRACKED UP TO BE!
10-31
CONTINUED-

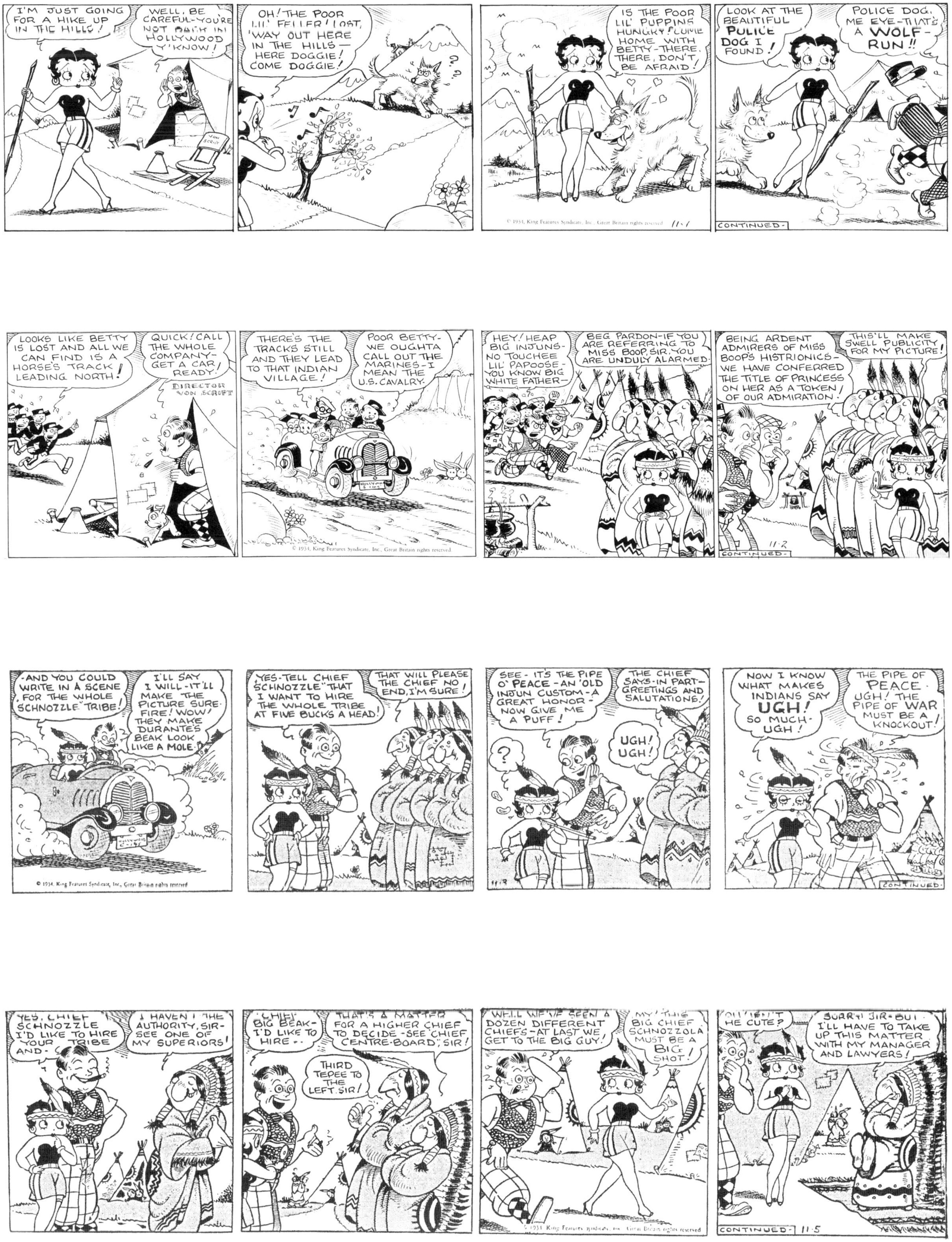
I'M JUST GOING FOR A HIKE UP IN THE HILLS!
WELL, BE CAREFUL-YOU'RE NOT BACK IN HOLLYWOOD Y'KNOW!
OH! THE POOR LIL' FELLER! LOST, 'WAY OUT HERE IN THE HILLS— HERE DOGGIE! COME DOGGIE!
IS THE POOR LIL' PUPPINS HUNGRY? COME HOME WITH BETTY-THERE, THERE, DON'T BE AFRAID!
© 1934, King Features Syndicate, Inc., Great Britain rights reserved 11-1
LOOK AT THE BEAUTIFUL POLICE DOG I FOUND!
POLICE DOG, ME EYE-THAT'S A WOLF-RUN!!
CONTINUED-
LOOKS LIKE BETTY IS LOST AND ALL WE CAN FIND IS A HORSE'S TRACK LEADING NORTH!
QUICK! CALL THE WHOLE COMPANY-GET A CAR READY!
DIRECTOR VON SCRIFT
THERE'S THE TRACKS STILL AND THEY LEAD TO THAT INDIAN VILLAGE!
POOR BETTY-WE OUGHTA CALL OUT THE MARINES-I MEAN THE U.S. CAVALRY.
© 1934, King Features Syndicate, Inc., Great Britain rights reserved
HEY! HEAP BIG INJUNS-NO TOUCHEE LIL' PAPOOSE-YOU KNOW BIG WHITE FATHER—
BEG PARDON-IF YOU ARE REFERRING TO MISS BOOP, SIR, YOU ARE UNDULY ALARMED.
BEING ARDENT ADMIRERS OF MISS BOOP'S HISTRIONICS-WE HAVE CONFERRED THE TITLE OF PRINCESS ON HER AS A TOKEN OF OUR ADMIRATION!
THIS'LL MAKE SWELL PUBLICITY FOR MY PICTURE!
11-2
CONTINUED-
-AND YOU COULD WRITE IN A SCENE FOR THE WHOLE "SCHNOZZLE" TRIBE!
I'LL SAY I WILL-IT'LL MAKE THE PICTURE SURE FIRE! WOW! THEY MAKE DURANTE'S BEAK LOOK LIKE A MOLE.
© 1934, King Features Syndicate, Inc., Great Britain rights reserved
YES-TELL CHIEF "SCHNOZZLE" THAT I WANT TO HIRE THE WHOLE TRIBE AT FIVE BUCKS A HEAD!
THAT WILL PLEASE THE CHIEF NO END, I'M SURE!
11-3
SEE- IT'S THE PIPE O' PEACE-AN' OLD INJUN CUSTOM-A GREAT HONOR-NOW GIVE ME A PUFF!
THE CHIEF SAYS-IN PART-GREETINGS AND SALUTATIONS!
UGH! UGH!
NOW I KNOW WHAT MAKES INDIANS SAY UGH! SO MUCH-UGH!
THE PIPE OF PEACE-UGH! THE PIPE OF WAR MUST BE A KNOCKOUT!
CONTINUED-
YES, CHIEF SCHNOZZLE I'D LIKE TO HIRE YOUR TRIBE AND-
I HAVEN'T THE AUTHORITY, SIR-SEE ONE OF MY SUPERIORS!
CHIEF BIG BEAK-I'D LIKE TO HIRE--
THAT'S A MATTER FOR A HIGHER CHIEF TO DECIDE-SEE CHIEF "CENTRE-BOARD," SIR!
THIRD TEPEE TO THE LEFT, SIR!
WELL WE'VE SEEN A DOZEN DIFFERENT CHIEFS-AT LAST WE GET TO THE BIG GUY!
MY! THIS BIG CHIEF SCHNOZZOLA MUST BE A BIG SHOT!
© 1934, King Features Syndicate, Inc., Great Britain rights reserved
OH! ISN'T HE CUTE?
SORRY, SIR-BUT I'LL HAVE TO TAKE UP THIS MATTER WITH MY MANAGER AND LAWYERS!
CONTINUED- 11-5

OW! THE WHOLE "SCHNOZZLE TRIBE" ARE AFTER BETTY- CALL EVERYBODY- QUICK!!
MAYBE THEY'RE ON THE WAR-PATH!
HALT! STOP! WAIT!
O-OH! THEY'RE GAINING ON ME!
© 1934, King Features Syndicate, Inc., Great Britain rights reserved
UP AND AT 'EM, MEN!
ALL TOGETHER- CHARGE!!
JUST WANT UM AUTOGRAPH- MISS BETTY!
11-6
CONTINUED-

THEY MAY OBJECT!
COME ON- WE'LL TALK EM INTO IT- AFTER ALL, INDIANS ARE A SIMPLE PRIMITIVE FOLK!
AND WE WANT TO USE YOUR TRIBE FOR A "SNAKE DANCE" SHOT!
WE'LL HAVE TO GO IN- TO CONFERENCE ON THAT, SIR!
11-7
HM-M! HUDDLE STUFF- FORMER COLLEGE FOOT- BALL PLAYERS- HUH?
© 1934, King Features Syndicate, Inc., Great Britain rights reserved
SORRY, SIR- BUT WE'VE DECIDED THAT YOU'LL HAVE TO USE DOUBLES FOR THAT SNAKE DANCE!
CONTINUED-

I MUST LEARN TO SHOOT FOR A SCENE IN MY PICTURE!
I'LL GIVE YOU ANOTHER LESSON TOMORROW- IN THE INTERIM- MISS BOOP, PRACTISE!
OH-OH! I MISSED THE TARGET AGAIN!
© 1934, King Features Syndicate, Inc., Great Britain rights reserved
HEY!!
WHY AIN'T THAT SET I ORDERED BUILT? WHAT'S ALL THE DELAY?
NO. 5
11-8
BETTY IS TARGET PRACTISING, CHIEF!
OW!
CONTINUED-

I MUST STAND GOOD- THEY MADE ME A PRINCESS!
Y'CAN'T TELL- INJUNS NEVER SHOW THEIR FEELINGS -C'MON, WE'LL GO OVER THE SCRIPT AGAIN!
WONDER WHAT'S UP? HERE COMES THE WHOLE "SCHNOZZLE TRIBE"!
LOOKS LIKE A PARADE- HOPE THEY'RE NOT ON THE WAR-PATH!
WHAT D'YE MEAN- INDIANS NEVER SHOW THEIR FEELINGS?
BETTY BOOP
© 1934, King Features Syndicate, Inc., Great Britain rights reserved.
11-10
CONTINUED-

THIS NEXT SCENE SHOWING ME WITH THE WHOLE "SCHNOZZLE TRIBE" WILL BE GOOD!
I'M MAKIN' IT THE BIG SHOT OF THE PICTURE - SO TELL THE CHIEF TO HAVE HIS TRIBE DOLL UP IN THEIR BEST!
Y'SEE, CHIEF - IT'S A VERY IMPORTANT SCENE SO ASK YOUR TRIBE TO COME IN THEIR BEST SUNDAY OUTFITS!
THEY WILL REPORT ATTIRED IN THEIR FINEST RAIMENT, MISS BOOP!
WELL, I'LL BE ~ WHAT'S THIS - AN EASTER PARADE?
© 1934, King Features Syndicate, Inc., Great Britain rights reserved. 11-12

HOW D'YE LIKE THAT NEXT SCENE? GOOD HUH?
YES, BUT HAVE THE CHIEF GO OVER IT TO MAKE SURE EVERYTHING IS OKAY!
FILM CAN
© 1934, King Features Syndicate, Inc. Great Britain rights reserved
AND SEE IF THE DIALOGUE AND COSTUMES ARE CORRECT, CHIEF!
YES HAVE UM LOOKSEE - SEE IF UM CATCH UM ERROR - SAVVY?
DOES BIG CHIEF SEE UM ANY HEAP BIG MISTAKES?
YES, INDEED, SIR!
THERE'S A GLARING GRAMMATICAL ERROR IN THE THIRD PARAGRAPH!
11-13

AND I'M TO RIDE IN THIS "INDIAN RAID" SCENE, HUH?
YES - IT'LL BE A GOOD ACTION SHOT - I HAVE CAMERAS PLACED ALL ALONG THE TRAIL!
OKAY BETTY - NOW "CHIEF SCHNOZZLE" WILL LEAD - ALL YOU HAVE TO DO IS FOLLOW ALONG!
ALL SET, MISS BETTY? LET'S GO!
© 1934, King Features Syndicate, Inc., Great Britain rights reserved
SLOW UP, BETTY - WE'RE STOPPING HERE FOR A PICNIC LUNCH!
11-14
WHY DON'T YOU SIT DOWN, BETTY AND BE COMFORTABLE?
-ER-I FEEL MORE COMFORTABLE STANDING, THANKS!

NOW PROPS - PILE THEM OVER THERE AND BURN THEM!
BETTY BOOP
THOSE OLD MAGAZINES AND PAPERS HAVE BEEN CLUTTERING UP MY TENT LONG ENOUGH!
THEY'LL MAKE A GOOD FIRE, MISS BETTY!
UGH! LOOKUM, SMOKE MUST TELL UM BIG CHIEF!
UGH!
11-15
BUT WHAT'S THE GAG - ON THE WAR PATH OR SOMETHIN'?
WE SAW THE SMOKE SIGNAL OF DISTRESS AND THOUGHT BETTY WAS IN DANGER!
© 1934 King Features Syndicate, Inc. Great Britain rights reserved

THIS NEXT SCENE IS TOUGH TO DOPE OUT— HAND ME THAT OTHER BOX OF CIGARS, BETTY PLEASE!
MY! YOU SURE SMOKE PLENTY WHEN YOU'RE STUCK!
I'LL WALK OVER TO THE INDIAN VILLAGE WHILE YOU'RE WRESTLING WITH THAT CONTINUITY!
© 1934, King Features Syndicate, Inc., Great Britain rights reserved.
UGH! LOOK- MISS BETTY, SMOKE SIGNAL OF HELP COMIN' FROM YOUR CAMP!
UGH!
SMOKE SIGNAL?
OH! THAT'S JUST THE DIRECTOR IN DISTRESS- HAVE YOU GOT ANY IDEAS?
11-16

LET'S GO OVER TO THE INDIAN VILLAGE AND BUY SOME RARE OLD INDIAN THINGS!
MEMENTOES OF OUR TRIP HUH? OKAY BETTY!
PS-ST! LOOK AT THIS MASTERPIECE OF INDIAN WEAVING!
OH! ISN'T THIS VASE A RARE SPECIMEN OF INDIAN ART?
RARE OLD INDIAN POTTERY
IT'S A SHAME TO TAKE ADVANTAGE OF THESE SIMPLE PEOPLE, BETTY, BUT--
AND THINK OF THE TIME IT TAKES 'EM TO WROUGHT 'EM
© 1934, King Features Syndicate, Inc., Great Britain rights reserved. 11-17
MADE IN JAPAN!!!
MADE IN HOBOKEN, N.J.

AND I WANT THE BRAVES TO SING SOME OLD INDIAN CEREMONIAL SONGS- TELL CHIEF SCHNOZZLE!
I SEE- INCANTATIONS TO THE RAIN GOD AND GREAT SPIRIT. HUH? OKAY!
© 1934 King Features Syndicate Inc. Great Britain rights reserved.
THEY'LL SING 'EM? GREAT! IT'LL MAKE THE PICTURE!
BUT THEY INSIST ON SINGING THEM IN THEIR OWN WAY- HERE THEY COME FOR AN AUDITION!
11-19
OW! THEY'RE CROONERS!
BUB-BUB-BUB-A-BUB-A-BOO- LOVE THY NEIGHBOR ----- --BUB-A--- BUB-BUB-BUB-A-BUB--

SEE! WE MUST HAVE A "SNAKE DANCE" IN THIS NEXT SHOT- USE YOUR INFLUENCE, BETTY!
WELL, I'LL TRY TO GET 'EM TO DO IT!
© 1934, King Features Syndicate, Inc. Great Britain rights reserved.
YOU SEE, CHIEF SCHNOZZLE, THIS IS A BIG SCENE AND IT CALLS FOR A REAL INDIAN "SNAKE DANCE"--
I'LL TAKE THE MATTER UP WITH MY COUNCIL, MISS BOOP!
WHAT D'YE MEAN- WE'LL HAVE TO CHANGE THE SCRIPT?
SORRY, VON- BUT THE SNAKE DANCE IS OUT--
THE ONLY DANCES THEY KNOW ARE THE CARIOCA AND RUMBA!!
11-20

A REAL INDIAN PONY RACE WOULD MAKE A SWELL ACTION SHOT
YOU'RE TELLIN' ME - WHY, IT WILL MAKE THE PICTURE BETTY!
IT'S TO BE A REAL INDIAN SPORTING SHOT, CHIEF!
YEAH? IT'S TO SHOW THE INBRED, SUPERB HORSEMANSHIP OF THE VANISHING INDIAN!
PONY RACE?
WHAT! NO HORSES?
MAKE IT AN AUTOMOBILE RACE, SUH - AN' WE'LL BE ONLY TOO GLAD TO ACCOMMODATE YOU!
PARKING 25¢
© 1934, King Features Syndicate, Inc., Great Britain rights reserved
11-21

REDMAN MAKE LOVE IN A FAR DIFFERENT WAY THAN US WHITES!
I KNOW - THEY RUB NOSES LIKE ESKIMOS OR SUMPIN' - BUT WE MUST HAVE AN INDIAN LOVER FOR THIS SHOT - I DON'T WANT TO USE A DOUBLE!
I'M AFRAID YOU'LL HAVE TO - INDIANS ARE FUNNY THAT WAY!
STILL THERE MIGHT BE ONE AMONG 'EM MODERN ENOUGH NOT TO HAVE SCRUPLES ABOUT KISSING -
HEY! IS THERE ANY BRAVE IN THE TRIBE WHO'D BE WILLING TO PLAY OPPOSITE BETTY IN THIS LOVE SCENE?
UGH! ME EYE - I SAID LOVE SCENE NOT MOB SCENE!
UGH! UGH! UGH! UGH! UGH! UGH! UGH! UGH UGH! UGH!
11-22

YES, SUH - MISS BETTY IS QUITE ADEPT IN MANIPULATING A CANOE, SUH!
FINE! GET READY, BETTY - THIS IS AN IMPORTANT SHOT!
REGISTER SERIOUSNESS AND FEAR, BETTY! OKAY - CAMERA! NOW SHOOT THE RAPIDS!
WHAT THA - - CUT!!
COME ON, BETTY - WE'LL DO THAT OVER AGAIN IT'LL MAKE A GREAT COMEDY SHOT!
© 1934, King Features Syndicate, Inc., Great Britain rights reserved
11-23

YES, BETTY - WE'RE GOING TO RE-TAKE THAT CANOE SHOT!
YEAH? WELL, I'M GOING TO MAKE SURE THAT I DON'T DUMP OUT THIS TIME!
NO, IT ISN'T A JIG-SAW PUZZLE - JUST FOLLOW THOSE PLANS AS IS!
HM-M! I GET THE IDEA, MISS BOOP!
PLANS
OKAY, BETTY! WE'RE WAITING - PADDLE AROUND THAT BEND AND STEER INTO THE RAPIDS - - -
WELL, I'LL BE ~~ SAY! HOW COME THE OUT-RIGGING? THIS AINT NO HAWAIIAN SURF SHOT!
NO, AND IT'S NOT GOING TO BE NO "DUCKING" STUNT, EITHER!
© 1934, King Features Syndicate, Inc., Great Britain rights reserved
11-24

?
COME ON, BETTY - WE HAVE AN APPOINTMENT WITH BIG CHIEF SCHNOZZLE!
Y'SEE, WE'VE GOT TO GET HIS CONSENT FOR ONE OF HIS BRAVES TO PLAY OPPOSITE YOU IN THAT LOVE SCENE!
© 1934, King Features Syndicate, Inc., Great Britain rights reserved.
HOPE WE DON'T HAVE TO SMOKE A "PIPE OF PEACE," UGH!
UGH, IS RIGHT - BUT IT'S AN OLD INDIAN CUSTOM - SO I GUESS WE'LL HAVE TO!
11-26
WHAT! NO PIPE OF PEACE, CHIEF?
PIPE OF PEACE? OH, THAT'S PASSE' - LIKE THE TOMAHAWK AND BOW 'N' ARROW!
CLICK
CONTINUED -

STUDIO NO.3
LOOK! THE WHOLE SCHNOZZLE TRIBE'S COMING FOR THE JOB OF PLAYING OPPOSITE TO BETTY IN THE LOVE SCENE!
WHAT! SELECT ONE OUT OF THAT GANG - THERE'S OVER A HUNDRED REASONS WHY I WON'T!
I'LL SEE IF I CAN REASON WITH THEM!
© 1934, King Features Syndicate, Inc., Great Britain rights reserved.
-AND YOU SEE, WE ONLY NEED ONE FOR THE PART!
THAT'S ME!
I'M HEEM!
DOT'S I'M!
NO! ME!
GUESS YOU'D BETTER PLAY SAFE AND CHANGE IT TO A MOB SCENE!
11-27
CONTINUED -

BUT HOW ABOUT THE INDIAN TO PLAY OPPOSITE YOU IN THE LOVE SCENE?
THEY'RE GOING TO DECIDE WHO GETS THE PART IN THEIR OWN WAY!
© 1934, King Features Syndicate, Inc., Great Britain rights reserved.
HOW ARE THEY DECIDING IT - WITH A PONY RACE, RUNNING RACE, BOW 'N' ARROW CONTEST OR BUMPIN'?
I DON'T KNOW - I LEFT THAT UP TO THEM - THE WINNER GETS THE JOB!
WHAT'S THAT - A RIOT - OR ARE THEY ON THE WAR-PATH?
GUESS THAT'S THE WAY THEY DECIDE WHO'S WINNER!
POW
YEE-OW
WOW
EE-YOO-
SLAM
BAM
SOCK
ME? I'M THE WINNER!
11-28

OH! A CHILD PART - AN INDIAN "SHIRLEY TEMPLE," HUH?
THAT'S THE IDEA - I WANT YOU TO GO TO THE VILLAGE AND PICK OUT THE CUTEST, IN THE TRIBE
FILM CAN
1934, King Features Syndicate, Inc., Great Britain rights reserved.
YES, CHIEF SCHNOZZLE - I WANT TO SELECT THE CUTEST KIDDIE OF YOUR TRIBE FOR A PART IN THE NEXT SCENE!
YOU MAY PICK ANY ONE YOU WISH, MISS BOOP!
BUT I SAID ONE - WHY THE WHOLE JUVENILE POPULATION?
YOU'LL HAVE TO CHANGE THE SCRIPT TO AN INDIAN BABY SHOW -
-THEY'RE ALL SO CUTE I JUST COULDN'T SELECT THE CUTEST!
11-29
CONTINUED -

BETTY BOOP

By MAX FLEISCHER

BETTY BOOP

By MAX FLEISCHER

BETTY BOOB

By MAX FLEISCHER

BETTY BOOB

By MAX FLEISCHER

BETTY BOOB

By MAX FLEISCHER

BETTY BOOB

By MAX FLEISCHER

BETTY BOOB

By MAX FLEISCHER

BETTY BOOP

By MAX FLEISCHER

BETTY BOOB

By MAX FLEISCHER

BETTY BOOB

By MAX FLEISCHER

BETTY BOOB

By MAX FLEISCHER

BETTY BOOP

By MAX FLEISCHER

BETTY BOOP

By MAX FLEISCHER

BETTY BOOB

By MAX FLEISCHER

BETTY BOOB

By MAX FLEISCHER

BETTY BOOP

By MAX FLEISCHER

BETTY BOOB

By MAX FLEISCHER

BETTY BOOB

By MAX FLEISCHER

BETTY BOOB

By MAX FLEISCHER

BETTY BOOP

By MAX FLEISCHER

BETTY BOOP

By MAX FLEISCHER

BETTY BOOP By MAX FLEISCHER

BETTY BOOP By MAX FLEISCHER

BETTY BOOP By MAX FLEISCHER

BETTY BOOP By MAX FLEISCHER

BETTY BOOP

By MAX FLEISCHER

BETTY BOOP

By MAX FLEISCHER

BETTY BOOP

By MAX FLEISCHER

BETTY BOOP

By MAX FLEISCHER

BETTY BOOP

By MAX FLEISCHER

BETTY BOOP By MAX FLEISCHER

BETTY BOOP By MAX FLEISCHER

BETTY BOOP By MAX FLEISCHER

BETTY BOOP By MAX FLEISCHER

BETTY BOOP

By MAX FLEISCHER

BETTY BOOP

By MAX FLEISCHER

BETTY BOOP

By MAX FLEISCHER

BETTY BOOP

By MAX FLEISCHER

BILLY, LET ME SIT THERE AND YOU CAN SIT IN MY LAP WHILE I GIVE YOU ANOTHER LESSON IN MANNERS!
OKAY, SIS!
-AND ANOTHER THING, BILLY, IF YOU'RE SITTING DOWN AND SOME **OLDER PERSON** ENTERS THE ROOM-YOU SHOULD OFFER THAT PERSON YOUR SEAT!
OH! THAT'S EASY TO REMEMBER!
© 1935, King Features Syndicate, Inc., Great Britain rights r
GREETINGS AND SALUTATIONS, BETTY!
OH! HELLO, VAN I DIDN'T HEAR YOU COME IN!
?
TAKE MAH SEAT, SUH!
?
3-18

BOOP-BOOP-A-DOOP!

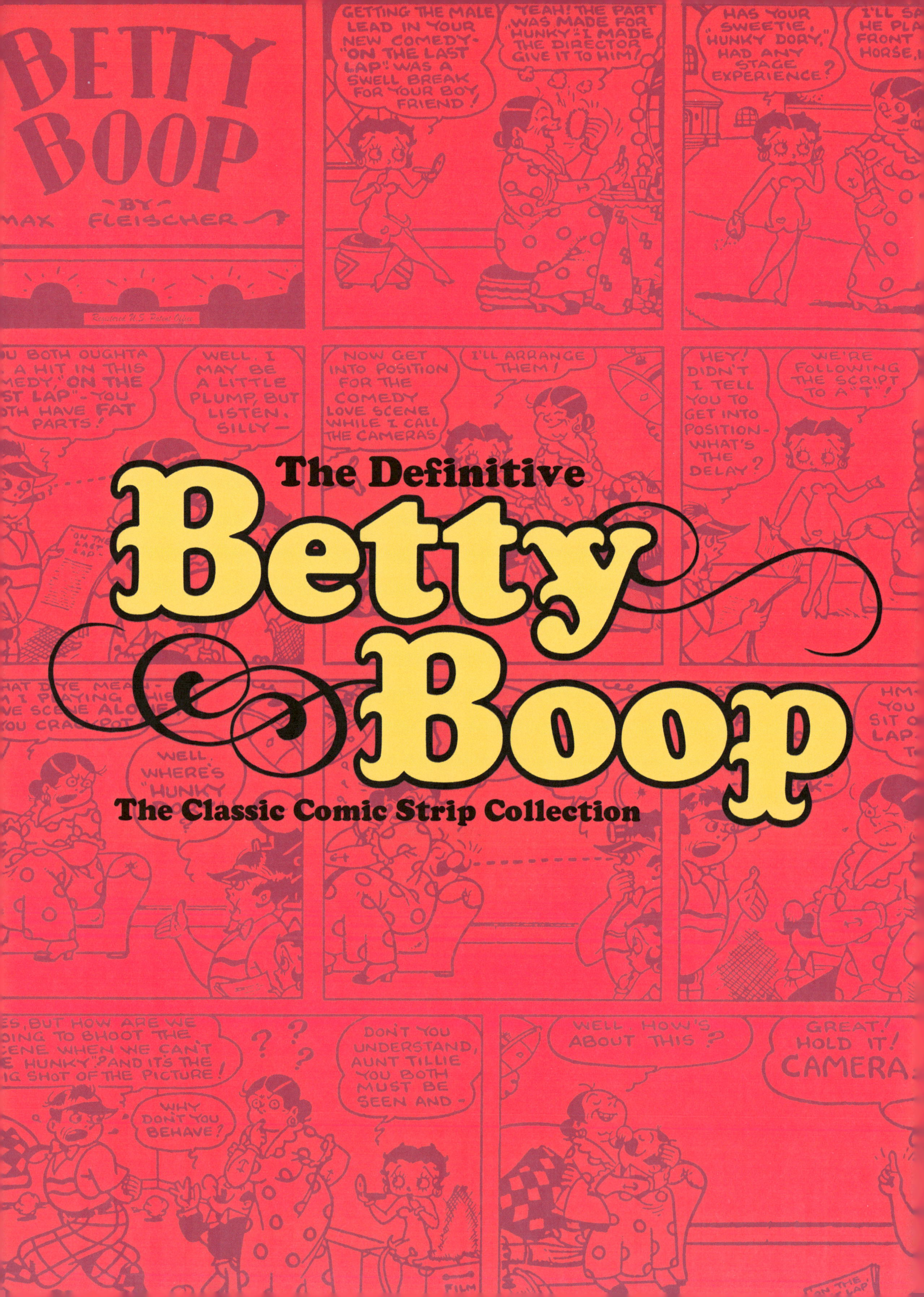


The Definitive

# Betty Boop

The Classic Comic Strip Collection

EXHIBITORS
YES THEY'VE GOT HIM PARKED IN THE CHIEF'S OFFICE!